The Enterprise Engineering Series

Enterprise Engineering is an emerging discipline for coping with the challenges (agility, adaptability, etc.) and the opportunities (new markets, new technologies, etc.) faced by contemporary enterprises, including commercial, nonprofit and governmental institutions. It is based on the paradigm that such enterprises are purposefully designed systems, and thus they can be redesigned in a systematic and controlled way. Such enterprise engineering projects typically involve architecture, design, and implementation aspects.

The Enterprise Engineering series thus explores a design-oriented approach that combines the information systems sciences and organization sciences into a new field characterized by rigorous theories and effective practices. Books in this series should critically engage the enterprise engineering paradigm, by providing sound evidence that either underpins it or that challenges its current version. To this end, two branches are distinguished: Foundations, containing theoretical elaborations and their practical applications, and Explorations, covering various approaches and experiences in the field of enterprise engineering. With this unique combination of theory and practice, the books in this series are aimed at both academic students and advanced professionals.

Jan L. G. Dietz · Hans B. F. Mulder

Enterprise Governance and Management

Setting a Route for an Enterprise and Keeping It on the Route

Springer

Jan L. G. Dietz
Delft University of Technology
Delft, The Netherlands

Hans B. F. Mulder
Antwerp Management School
University of Antwerp
Antwerp, Belgium

ISSN 1867-8920 ISSN 1867-8939 (electronic)
The Enterprise Engineering Series
ISBN 978-3-032-24317-1 ISBN 978-3-032-24318-8 (eBook)
https://doi.org/10.1007/978-3-032-24318-8

This Springer imprint is published by the registered company Springer Nature Switzerland AG
The registered company address is: Gewerbestrasse 11, 6330 Cham, Switzerland

Preface

So much of what we call management consists of making it difficult for people to work

—Peter Drucker

Through the publication of this book, the 'trilogy' Enterprise Ontology–Enterprise Design–Enterprise Governance and Management is completed. The work is finished. The three parts fit together, because they are built on a solid theoretical basis. Each part has its own core theory: the PSI theory (or EE organisational operation theory) for Enterprise Ontology, the BETA theory (or EE design theory) for Enterprise Design, and the SIGMA theory (or EE governance and management theory) for Enterprise Governance and Management.

As one will discover, these core theories are connected: both the BETA theory and the SIGMA theory are ultimately built on the PSI theory, the theory that 'prescribes' how organisations operate, whether one likes it or not. At the basis lies the complete transaction pattern, which includes now (that is with the second edition of Enterprise Ontology) the revocation of all basic steps, thus the request, the promise, the decline, the declare, the accept, and the reject. It is fully complete now.

Regarding the SIGMA theory as the core theory for Enterprise Governance and Management, we like to stress here that it is classified as an ideological theory, thus a theory that can only be predicated as significant to its applicants. It is not truthful (like the ontological theories), nor rigorous and relevant (like the technological ones). One has to believe in it or not. Fortunately, a growing number of people do, as we will show in the book part Applications.

Voorburg, The Netherlands
The Hague, The Netherlands
January 2026

Jan L. G. Dietz
Hans B. F. Mulder

Acknowledgements

We know that many people support our efforts to write this book, which is the finishing touch of Enterprise Engineering. We will not mention them by name. But there is one person who deserves to be put in the limelight. It is Silke van Rooij, who wrote both Chaps. 10 and 11.

Summary of the Book

The book is divided into three parts: *Introduction*, *Theories*, and *Applications*.

The Introduction consists of three chapters. Chapter 1 contains an introduction to *Enterprise Engineering* (EE). It is headed by this quote from Henry Petroski; *Science is about knowing; engineering is about doing*, and this quote by Henry Mintzberg: *Organisations are communities of human beings, not collections of human resources*.

EE is presented as an emerging discipline that takes an engineering perspective on enterprises. It aims to address the problems in organisations that cannot be solved by the traditional organisational sciences. Organisational changes are conceived as situations of (re)design and (re)implementation. The conceptual pillars of Enterprise Engineering are the notions of Enterprise Ontology, Enterprise Architecture, and Enterprise Governance. By applying them, three goals are respectively attained: intellectual manageability, organisational concinnity, and social devotion.

Chapter 2 introduces the notion of *management*. Henry Mintzberg offers a useful analysis of managerial work, resulting among others into ten roles of a manager. Next, Enterprise Management appears to be closely intertwined with Enterprise Governance. Fortunately, the two can be distinguished on the basis of Enterprise Ontology. As long as the essential model of an enterprise stays intact, a change is the result of a managerial action. Changing the model requires for governmental action. Unfortunately, modern educational institutes that teach management and governance promote the idea of 'professional manager', as if the kind of enterprise this professional manager is steering or controlling is immaterial. This is a hoax.

Chapter 3 introduces the notion of *governance*. It states that enterprise governance is about inciting and accomplishing enterprise change. In contrast, enterprise management belongs to enterprise operations. A distinction is made between the traditional way of governing enterprises and the human-centric way. The traditional way is founded in the Taylorian distinction between bosses and workers; only bosses are considered to be able to reflect on the work to be done, workers are just alienated from it. The human-centric way involves all employees, with a special role for the natural leaders in the enterprise. Leaders have followers, based on mutual trust.

Part II consists of five chapters. They are summarised below.

Chapter 4 offers an overview of the theories in Enterprise Engineering. The foundations of the discipline of Enterprise Engineering (EE), as envisioned by the Ciao Network, consist of the CIAO Paradigm and a number of theories. After the discussion of the paradigm, which has its origins in the communication-centric view on information systems engineering that emerged around 2000, the role of the EE theories and their relationships with the EE methods and the practice of EE is explained. After having been arranged in a suitable classification scheme, each of the theories is briefly discussed.

In Chap. 5, the KAPPA theory is presented. The EE assignment theory (or KAPPA theory) is a theory about the assignment of actor roles to individual employees. It is based on the competences that are needed to fill the actor roles. The basic notions, both on the demand side and on the supply side of the labour market, are formally defined. The needed competence of an actor role is connected to the authority and the responsibility that role fillers are assumed to exert, as elaborated in the PSI theory (Performing in Social Interaction).

Chapter 6 contains an extended summary of the GAMMA or EE delegation theory. According to the PSI theory, delegation is the transfer of authority, and the corresponding responsibility, by some actor to another employee. In most cases, delegation regards only a subset of the steps in the complete transaction pattern. In current practice, and contrary to the PSI theory, delegation is considered to be the transfer of authority to ICT artefacts. The negation of the most important role of human beings in enterprises and in society as a whole leads to poignant cases.

In Chap. 7, the CHI or EE transaction cost theory is presented. The transaction cost theory is an important economic theory, developed in the twentieth century by several economic researchers, like Coase, Dahlman, North, and Commons, and especially by Williamson. This economic theory is the basis for the EE transaction cost theory. The EE transaction is the central notion. Tracking all steps in the complete transaction pattern, the knowledge needed to perform responsibly the request act as well as the final accept/reject act appears to be the most crucial for the decision to outsource the executor role of a transaction kind.

Chapter 8 contains an extended summary of the core theory of this book: the SIGMA or EE Governance and Management theory. It is a theory about the core notions of this book: governance and management. In current literature, a clear distinction between governance and management is not always made. These notions can, however, be distinguished and properly defined in EE on the basis of the essential model of an enterprise: when the model is changed, it is called governance, when the model is not affected, it is called management. A useful metaphor for understanding the distinction is the sailing of a ship. Setting the route is a governance act, keeping the ship on a set route, is a matter of management.

Part III consists of four chapters. They are summarised below.

In Chap. 9, the DEMO methodology (Design and Engineering Methodology for Organisations) is presented. It comprises a Way of Thinking (WoT), a Way of Modelling (WoM), and a Way of Working (WoW). The WoT consists of a number of theories. The WoM consists of an integrated whole of four aspect or sub models: the Cooperation Model (CM), the Action Model (AM), the Process Model (PM), and the Fact Model (FM). The CM of a Scope of Interest (SoI) is the ontological model of its construction, thus of the identified transactor roles and the coordination structures among them: the interaction structure, the interimpediment structure, and the interstriction structure. The AM of an SoI is the ontological model of its operation. For every actor role in the focus (of the SoI), it provides the rules that guide the role fillers in doing their work. The guidelines for responding to coordination events are called action rules, the ones for performing production acts are called work instructions. The PM of an SoI is the ontological model of the state space and the transition space of its coordination world. It contains the existence laws and occurrence laws for all transaction kinds in the SoI. The FM of an SoI is the ontological model of the state space and the transition space of its production world. It contains the existence laws and occurrence laws for all identified entity types, value types, property types, attribute types, and event types. For producing essential models of enterprises, the WoW of DEMO offers the OER method (Organisational Essence Revealing). It consists of a number of steps in which the four DEMO models are produced, preferably in a spiral way. For (re)developing organisations as well as for developing enterprise information systems, DEMO offers the DAO method. The name is an acronym of Designing under Architecture from Ontology. Lastly, for devising and establishing governance and management, DEMO offers the HOS method. The name is an acronym of Human-centric Operating and Steering.

Chapter 10 offers the first practical exercise, the British Post Office. The British Post Office Horizon scandal is commonly qualified as a major miscarriage of justice in recent British history. The case reconstruction defines the scope of interest and reconstructs the progression of the failure across organisational and legal contexts. The Enterprise Engineering perspective uses DEMO to establish the essential model of the British Post Office. This model serves as the reference for distinguishing changes in organisational essence from changes in its realisation during the period under study. The analysis indicates a categorical confusion of fact types: system-recorded and system-derived representations (informational and documental) were treated as if they were original production facts. As a consequence, the coordination acts required for timely revocation and correction within the involved transaction instances became practically unavailable, and the correction of the relevant representations was systematically delayed.

Chapter 11 offers the second and third exercise, Semco and Netflix. This chapter analyses the two contrasting cases. The case material is interpreted through complementary interpretive anchors (Deming, Drucker, and Covey) that sharpen attention to aim-guided learning, responsible autonomy, and the normative conditions for truthful transparency. Across both cases, the chapter identifies a decisive governance variable: alignment between commitment authority, responsibility attribution, and inspectable information in the coordination layer. The chapter concludes with design implications for governing knowledge-intensive and digitally mediated enterprises while preserving responsible autonomy.

Lastly, Chap. 12 provides short contributions in the STARR format (Situation, Task, Approach, Result, Reflection).

Contents

Part I
Introduction

Part I contains the three introductory chapters to the main contents in the Parts II (Theories) and III (AApplications). Chapter 1 offers an introduction to the field of Enterprise Engineering, in which a design-oriented view is taken towards organisations. In Chap. 2 the reader is introduced to Enterprise Management. Chapter 3 offers an introduction to the related notion of Enterprise Governance, the main objective of this book.

Chapter 1
Introduction to Enterprise Engineering

Science is about knowing; engineering is about doing
(Henry Petroski)
Organisations are communities of human beings, not collections of human resources
(Henry Mintzberg)

Abstract Enterprise Engineering is an emerging discipline that takes an engineering perspective on enterprises. It aims to address the problems that cannot be solved by the traditional organisational sciences. Organisational changes are conceived as situations of (re)design and (re)implementation. The conceptual pillars of Enterprise Engineering are the notions of Enterprise Ontology, Enterprise Architecture, and Enterprise Governance. By applying them, three goals are respectively attained: intellectual manageability, organisational concinnity, and social dedication.

1.1 Introductory Remarks

In perfect agreement with Petroski's quote above, the discipline of Enterprise Engineering (EE) is about doing. The general goal of EE is to make better enterprises, or to make enterprises better, in every meaning of the word. By "enterprise" we refer to all kinds of organised human activities (like companies, agencies, institutions, supply chains, etc., but also the organisation of a birthday party). Indeed, science alone doesn't solve the problems humanity faces, engineering is needed to develop and implement effective solutions [1]. At the same time, doing without a proper understanding of what one is doing, may be worse than doing nothing. That is why every serious engineering discipline is rooted in a solid theoretical foundation.

The societal need of a discipline of EE is urgent because modern societies are increasingly complex networks of an increasing number of enterprises, with increasingly complex interrelationships. Moreover, the traditional organisational and management sciences fail to provide effective help [2]. Deming [3] offers a

J. L.G. Dietz and H. B. F. Mulder, *Enterprise Governance and Management*, The Enterprise Engineering Series, https://doi.org/10.1007/978-3-032-24318-8_1

convincing account, which can be paraphrased as follows: *almost all (94%) manifestations of inadequate enterprise performance are the inevitable result of how enterprises are organised*. The purport of this finding is that only in 6% of all instances of operational failure, one can correctly blame workers. In all other cases, the cause is a design (or an implementation) error of the organisation.

Over the years insights have been developed about how to (1) enhance the effectiveness and efficiency of enterprises, (2) ensure quality, service and customer orientation, and (3) avoid core reasons for strategic failure. One would expect that a century after Taylor published the principles of scientific management, his influence would have diminished. However, as Doz and Thanheiser observed recently: "Despite the 'modernisation' of corporate structures and systems, the mindset of managers appears to be remarkably similar to the Taylorist model developed at the beginning of the century" [4]. Thus, principles that follow from "a machine-like concept of the organisation still dominate managerial practice". Others argue that "Corporations continue to operate according to a logic invented at the time of their origin, a century ago" [5].

The continuation of the Taylorist model can additionally be demonstrated by observing the increase in the number of management functions. For example, in the country where Taylor expressed his views, managers accounted for less than 1% of the labour force in 1900. Thirty years later this figure was already 7.5%, increasing to 10.5% by 1970. By 1990, the figure was approaching 14% [6]. We will elaborate the subject of management and managers in Chap. 2.

The needed paradigm shift is provided by the emerging discipline of EE. It is a theory-based approach to the (re)development of enterprises in an all-encompassing way. A sound and rigid theoretical foundation is crucial. As Deming states: "Experience alone, without theory, teaches management nothing about what to do to improve quality and competitive position, nor how to do it" [3]. In view of our previous discussion, and the tenacity of Taylor's principles, little learning seems to have taken place. We posit that an explanatory theory is required to give experience meaning, and in doing so to provide the basis for appropriately understanding enterprises.

1.2 The Discipline of Enterprise Engineering

In 2013, a paper titled "The discipline of Enterprise Engineering" was published [7]. The main authors are Jan Dietz and Jan Hoogervorst, but there are many co-authors. They are the key members of the Ciao! Network. We list them in alphabetic order, including their academic affiliation at that time: Antonia Albani (University of St. Gallen, Switzerland), David Aveiro (University of Madeira, Portugal), Eduard Babkin (Higher School of Economics at Nizhny Novgorod, Russia), Joseph Barjis (Delft University of Technology, The Netherlands), Artur Caetano (University of Lisbon—IST,[1] Portugal), Philip Huysmans (University of Antwerp, Belgium),

[1] IST stands for Instituto Superior Tecnico.

Junichi Iijima (Tokyo Tech, Japan), Steven van Kervel (Delft University of Technology), Hans Mulder (University of Antwerp—AMS[2]), Martin Op 't Land (University of Antwerp—AMS), Henderik Proper (Radboud University Nijmegen, The Netherlands), Jorge Sanz (IBM Research, San José, California, USA), Linda Terlouw (Delft University of Technology), José Tribolet (University of Lisbon—IST), Jan Verelst (University of Antwerp), and Robert Winter (University of St. Gallen). The academic affiliations of the main authors are respectively Delft University of Technology, and University of Antwerp—AMS. In this founding article, three general goals are identified for EE: intellectual manageability, organisational concinnity, and social dedication.[3]

Intellectual manageability is about getting and keeping insight into and overview over complexity. People who have to govern or run enterprises, or to devise and implement substantial changes, need first of all a proper understanding of what they are doing. Current practice shows that this basic premise is often not met. Obviously, enterprise phenomena that are not properly understood, cannot be addressed adequately. Consequently, the necessary changes cannot be determined, and if they can, they cannot be brought about effectively. In addition, current development approaches, for enterprises as a whole and for ICT[4] applications in particular, are cursed with combinatorial impacts of changes. So, in addition, appropriate ideas of enterprise evolvability are needed for making changes expeditious and manageable. Intellectual manageability is an indispensable quality: if you don't understand fully and deeply what you are doing, you better not do it.

The goal of intellectual manageability is achieved by applying the notion of Enterprise Ontology, as discussed in [8]. It is based on the CIAO paradigm (cf. Chap. 4) which states that communication is the prime concept in understanding organisations, where communication is defined as the sharing of thoughts between human beings. This paradigm is the foundation of the pivotal PSI theory (cf. [8] Chap. 8). The DEMO methodology (cf. Chap. 9), specifically the OER method, is the practical way to build so-called ontological models of organisations.

Organisational concinnity is about designing, engineering, and implementing an enterprise in such a way that the resulting operational organisation is a coherent and consistent whole. In order to perform optimally and to implement changes successfully, enterprises must operate as a unified and integrated whole, taking into account all relevant aspects. Many approaches to enterprise development, for example TOGAF, are ill-suited and suffer from theoretical and methodological weakness and incompleteness [9]. It is evidently not sufficient to consider Enterprise Design domains like processes, the information needs of the processes, the software applications providing the information, and their underlying infrastructure. A viable theory and methodology for EE must be able to address all relevant aspects, even those

2 AMS stands for Antwerp Management School.

3 In earlier publications, the expression "social devotion" was used. Because of its religious connotation, it is replaced from now on by "social dedication".

4 ICT stands for Information and Communication Technology. It supports the work of people by providing them with facts, and the communication between them.

that cannot be foreseen presently, in a properly integrated way. It is quite obvious that organisational concinnity must be designed; it does not emerge in a natural way [10, 11].

The goal of organisational concinnity is achieved by applying Enterprise Design as discussed in [12]. Because it is rooted in Enterprise Ontology, Enterprise Design is able to produce an understanding of the new organisation that is graspable by the human mind and analysable for its effectiveness and efficiency. Enterprise Design also includes Enterprise Architecture, defined as the principles or generic requirements that hold for a design.

Social dedication is about recognising that the operation of an enterprise's organisation is brought about, not by its managers, but by its operational employees. In [2, 7], the importance of employee involvement and participation has been argued in order to achieve enterprise productivity, product and service quality, customer orientation, learning and innovation (and subsequent enterprise change), as well as to cope with enterprise dynamics, complexity, and uncertainty leading to emerging enterprise developments. Contrary to Taylor's mechanistic view on organisations [13], EE takes a human-centric view. It considers human beings to be the 'pearls' of every enterprise. Therefore, all employees should be fully empowered and competent for the tasks they have to perform. They must be endorsed with transparent authority and have access to all information needed to perform their tasks in a responsible way. Next, managers must not only be skilled in managerial work of the kind that Deming refers to [3], they must first of all be thoroughly knowledgeable in the subject field of the enterprise they are managing. The goal of social dedication is particularly achieved by applying the notion of Enterprise Governance, as presented extensively in [2, 14]. It is the core subject of this book. Specifically Chaps. 2 and 8 elaborate the notion of Enterprise Governance, as understood within the field of EE.

The three general goals of EE are often equated, more or less, to respectively Enterprise Ontology (EO) [8], Enterprise Design (ED) [12], and Enterprise Governance and Management (EGM). Applying Enterprise Ontology does indeed make enterprises intellectually manageable, by offering the notion of an essential model, but it has also a fundamental other effect: it offers a human-centric view on enterprises. Only people constitute organisations, supported (where appropriate) by artefacts, notably ICT artefacts. Enterprise Design is primarily concerned with (re)designing an enterprise such that its organisation is a coherent and consistent network of collaborating actors. As for Enterprise Governance and Management, the subject of the current book, it will become clear that we consider human beings in every enterprise, all over the world, to be the pearls of the enterprise they are employed by.

In the founding article of EE, the crucial role of the PSI theory (cf. [8] Chap. 8), is discussed. It is the core of the notion of *essential model*, as well as of the human-centric view on enterprises. In [8] Chap. 8, the basis of its cruciality is disclosed: its being communication-centric, as opposed to information-centric (like most existing approaches to organisational engineering and ICT systems engineering are).

Communication-centric means that communication is the primary notion, defined as the sharing of thoughts between human beings [15]. The secondary notion of information is defined as the means of communicating. *Information-centric* entails that information is the primary notion, although mostly ill-defined. Consequently, communication is defined as the exchanging of information. However, as in the history of many engineering disciplines, better alternatives have come off worst [16]: the communication-centric view has not succeeded yet in surpassing the information-centric view on a large scale.

1.3 The Difference Between Lifeworld and System World

As said, the core theory in EE is the PSI theory (Performance in Social Interaction). It is based on Habermas' theory of communicative action [17]. Although not explicitly stated, the PSI theory makes a distinction between the lifeworld of an enterprise and its system world. The latter is about the products that are brought about. They are brought about in social interaction, as a consequence of entering into and complying with commitments by social individuals. This is the lifeworld of the enterprise. The process of entering into and complying with commitments evolves in the context of social norms and values, thus of culture. The distinction made in EE differs however from the distinction between lifeworld and system that Habermas makes in [18].

According to Finlayson [19], Habermas acknowledges in this book the contributions of the system to social life, but he also points out the inherent dangers with system integration: "Systems of money and power steer agents towards ends that are not related to understanding or consensus, which is a core issue in the theory of communicative action". Two consequences follow. First, the full meaning or significance of our economic and administrative actions may, and often does, escape our notice. Systems institute and reinforce patterns of action in which agents conceal their aims and do not reflect on the ends of action. They thus have a kind of in-built opacity, in contrast to the lifeworld (the home of communicative action), in which the meanings of deeds and words and the ends of action tend to be open to view, and are intelligible. Next, the ultimate aims of actors in systems (unlike the actors in the lifeworld) are not really up to them. They can choose the means but not the ultimate ends of their actions. Consequently, one can say that the lifeworld is generally conducive to autonomy, understood as the pursuit of self-chosen ends, in a way the system is not. This difference makes itself felt to agents in the following way. Lifeworld agents coordinate their actions through validity claims. The constraints on their actions that are generated by this process are self-imposed and internal in as much as they arise from the reciprocal recognition of validity claims. By contrast, systems of money and power impose external constraints on action that are in no way up to the agents. The system thus takes on the appearance of what Habermas calls a 'block of quasi-natural reality', an independent reality with an autonomous internal logic that escapes human control, and for which human beings cannot and need not take responsibility.

References

1. Petroski, H. (2010). *The essential engineer: Why science alone will not solve our global problems* (1st edn., Vol. x, p. 274). Alfred A. Knopf.
2. Hoogervorst, J. A. P. (2017). *Foundations of enterprise governance and enterprise engineering* (p. 574). Springer International Publishing.
3. Deming, W. E. (1986). *Out of the crisis: Quality, productivity and competitive position* (Vol. xiii, p. 507). Cambridge University Press.
4. Doz, Y., & Thanheiser, H. (1993). Regaining competitiveness: A process of organizational renewal. In J. Hendry, G. Johnson, & J. Newton (Eds.), *Strategic thinking: Leadership and the management of change*. Wiley.
5. Zuboff, S., & Maxmin, J. (2004). *The support economy: Why corporations are failing individuals and the next episode of capitalism* (Vol. xvii, p. 458). Penguin Books.
6. Osterman, P. (1996). *Broken ladders: Managerial careers in the new economy* (p. 259). Oxford University Press.
7. Dietz, J. L., Hoogervorst, J. A. P., Albani, A., Aveiro, D., Babkin, E., Barjis, J., Caetano, A., Huysmans, P., Iijima, J., van Kervel, S., & Mulder, H. (2013). The discipline of enterprise engineering. *International Journal of Organisational Design and Engineering, 3*(1), 86–114.
8. Dietz, J. L. G., & Mulder, J. B. F. (2024). *Enterprise ontology: A human-centric approach to understanding the essence of organisation* (2nd edn.). Enterprise Engineering. Springer Nature.
9. Dietz, J. L. G., & Hoogervorst, J. A. P. (2012). A critical investigation of TOGAF. In *Advances in enterprise engineering*. LNBIP Series. Springer.
10. Keller, S., & Price, C. (2011). *Beyond performance: How great organizations build ultimate competitive advantage* (Vol. xx, p. 280). Wiley
11. Leinwand, P., & Mainardi, C. (2011). *The essential advantage: How to win with a capabilities-driven strategy* (Vol. xii, p. 227). Harvard Business Review Press.
12. Dietz, J. L. G., & Mulder, H. B. F. (2025). *Enterprise design fundamentals: Settling an enterprise business and devising the enterprise organisation.* (Vol. 1, p. 357). The Enterprise Engineering Series. Springer Nature.
13. Taylor, F. W. (1911). *The principles of scientific management* (Vol. 2, pp. 7–77). Harper & Brothers.
14. Hoogervorst, J. A. P. (2009). *Enterprise governance and enterprise engineering* (1 Band). The Enterprise Engineering Series. Springer.
15. Reijswoud, V. E. V., Mulder, H. B. F., & Dietz, J. L. G. (1999). Communicative action-based business process and information systems modelling with DEMO. *Information Systems Journal, 9*, 117–138.
16. Hamer, M. (2017, September 6). How crooks stalled the rise of electric cars for 100 years. *New Scientist*.
17. Habermas, J. (1984). *The theory of communicative action*. Beacon Press.
18. Habermas, J. (1990). *Moral consciousness and communicative action* (Vol. xiii, p. 225). Studies in contemporary German social thought. MIT Press.
19. Finlayson, J. G. (2005). *Habermas: A very short introduction. Very short introductions* (p. 156). Oxford University Press.

Chapter 2
Introduction to Enterprise Management

Management is, above all, a practice where art, science, and craft meet
(Henry Mintzberg)
So much of what we call management consists of making it difficult for people to work
(Peter Drucker)

Abstract Henry Mintzberg offers a useful analysis of managerial work, resulting among others into ten roles of a manager. Next, Enterprise Management appears to be closely intertwined with Enterprise Governance. Fortunately, the two can be distinguished on the basis of Enterprise Ontology. As long as the essential model of an enterprise stays intact, a change is the result of a managerial action. Changing the model requires for governmental action. Unfortunately, modern educational institutes that teach management and governance promote the idea of 'professional manager', as if the kind of enterprise this professional manager is steering or controlling is immaterial. This is a hoax.

2.1 Introduction

The two 'management guru's' quoted above seem to disagree about the importance of management in enterprises. However, both statements are true. The quote by Peter Drucker fits in the modern criticism on managers, which we summarise as follows. The increasing population of managers largely consists of people who believe that management is a profession like other professions. As the renowned quality and productivity leader Deming observed: "Students in schools of business in America are taught that there is a profession of management; that they are ready to step into top jobs. That is a cruel hoax" [1]. This 'hoax' resulted in the widely observable management crisis. An article in the Standardization News (1983) stated that "Practical all our major corporations were started by technical men—inventors, mechanics, engineers, and chemists, who had a sincere interest in the quality of products. Now,

J. L.G. Dietz and H. B. F. Mulder, *Enterprise Governance and Management*, The Enterprise Engineering Series, https://doi.org/10.1007/978-3-032-24318-8_2

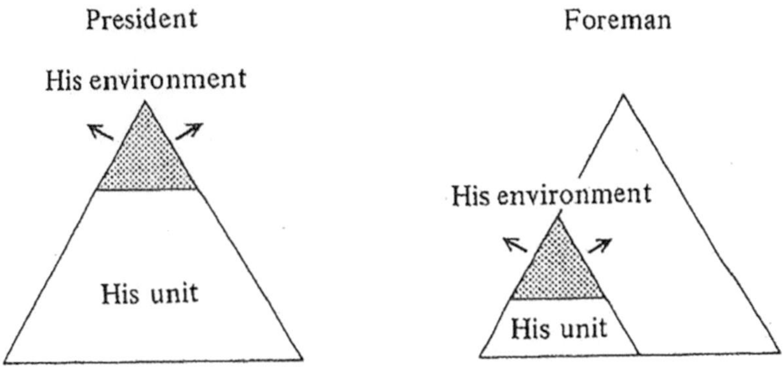

Fig. 2.1 Manager between unit and environment

these companies are largely run by men interested in profit, not product. Their pride is the P&L[1] statement or stock report" [1].

Why do organisations need managers? This is the most relevant question, to which we will try to provide a clear answer. Regardless of the outcome, one cannot deny that over time, there have been people in enterprises that have somehow directed the work of other people and that have been held responsible for how these people have done their work. As indicated in Chap. 1, the number of managers keeps increasing [2].

Henry Mintzberg, who has devoted the largest part of his life to understand the phenomenon of management, has elucidated that there may be many managers in an enterprise and that every manager has her/his own organisational unit and her/his own environment, as exhibited by Fig. 2.1. The figure is taken from Ref. [3], published in 1973. At that time, women were apparently not supposed to be managers.

Mintzberg states the next basic reasons why enterprises[2] need managers:

1. The prime purpose of the manager is to ensure that her/his enterprise serves its basic purpose—the efficient production of specific goods and services.
2. The manager designs and maintains stability of the enterprise's operations.
3. The manager takes charge of the enterprise's strategy-making system, and therein adapts the enterprise in a controlled way to its changing environment.
4. The manager ensures that the enterprise serves the ends of those persons who control it.
5. The manager serves as the key informational link between the enterprise and its environment.
6. As formal authority, the manager is responsible for the operating of the enterprise's status system.

[1] P&L stands for Profit and Loss.

[2] Although Mintzberg consistently speaks of organisations, we prefer the term "enterprise" because of our clear distinction between organisation and business (cf. [3] Chap. 7).

In modern society, products and services are consumed on a huge scale. They are conceived and brought about by experts and professionals. Examples are products and services in the field of communication, navigation, health care, medicine, transportation, and food preparation, but also products and services in culture, such as literature, music, entertainment, film, and art are appropriate examples. In all cases, the conception, production, and maintenance of the products and services involve experts and professionals. From now on, we will use the word "product" to refer to both products and services, taking thus the constructional view on enterprises (cf. [4] Chap. 7).

2.2 The Ten Roles of a Manager

In [3], Henry Mintzberg calls a manager everyone who is responsible for the operation of a unit in an enterprise. A manager thus can be a foreman or the president, as illustrated by Fig. 2.1. In all cases, a manager has subordinates. Based on extensive research, including in-depth interviews with top managers, Mintzberg distinguishes between ten roles that a manager fills. These roles are summarised in Table 2.1.

Mintzberg has put the ten roles in three groups. The first three roles he calls *interpersonal* and the next three *informational*. The last four are the *decisional* roles.

Because a manager is formally in charge of an organisational unit (cf. Figure 2.1), managers have a special position of status in an enterprise. This special position leads almost naturally to the three interpersonal roles. The most simple one is the role of *figurehead*. A manager represents her/his enterprise in all matters of formality. He/she is a symbol, obliged to perform a number of duties, ranging from trivial ones to inspirational actions. In her/his *leader* role, the manager defines the atmosphere in which the enterprise will work. This role is clearly among the most significant ones. In virtually everything a manager does, her/his actions are screened by the subordinates searching for leadership clues. The key purpose of the leader role is to effect an integration between individual needs and enterprise goals. Next, it is in the leader role that managerial power most clearly manifests itself. The *liaison* role of a manager deals with the significant web of relationships that the manager maintains with numerous individuals outside the unit that he/she heads, thus also outside the enterprise. This role gives the manager exposure in the outside world.

The second group of roles is about receiving and sending information, where the manager acts as a nerve centre. In the *monitor* role, the manager informs himself/herself about the enterprise as well as about its environment. The first information flow, regarding the internal operations, is mostly formalised, the second one (external events, analyses, ideas, and trends) will largely be informal. In the *disseminator* role, the manager transmits (monitored) information to the people in her/his enterprise. Next to factual information, the manager also disseminates values (like personal preferences) and pressures from external sources, like government, labour unions and trade organisations. In the role of *spokesperson*, the manager shares information with other people, both inside and outside the enterprise. The manager keeps specifically

Table 2.1 Summary of the ten management roles

Role	Description	Activities
Figurehead	Symbolic head, obliged to perform a number of routine duties of a legal or social nature	Ceremony, status requests, solicitations
Leader	Responsible for the motivation and activation of subordinates; responsible for staffing, training, and associated duties	Virtually all managerial activities involving subordinates
Liaison	Maintain self-developed network of outside contacts and informers who provide favours and information	Acknowledgements of mail, external work, activities involving outsiders
Monitor	Seeks and receives information to develop thorough understanding of enterprise and environment; being the nerve centre of the enterprise	Handling all mail and contacts concerned with receiving information
Disseminator	Transmits information to members of the enterprise, both factual and information that needs interpretation and integration	Forwarding mail into enterprise, verbal contacts with subordinates
Spokesperson	Transmits information to outsiders on plans, policies, actions, results, etc.	Board meetings, handling mail and contacts
Entrepreneur	Searches opportunities and initiates improvement projects to bring about change	Strategy and review sessions involving design of changes
Disturbance handler	Responsible for corrective action when enterprise faces important unexpected disturbances	Strategy and review sessions involving disturbances
Resource allocator	Responsible for the allocation of resources (money, time, material, manpower, etc.)	Scheduling and programming of subordinates' work
Negotiator	Responsible for representing the enterprise at major negotiations	Negotiation

two groups informed. The first is the enterprise's key influencers, the second one is the public, like the customers and the press.

The group of decisional roles comprises being entrepreneur, disturbance handler, resource allocator, and negotiator. In the *entrepreneur* role the manager acts as initiator and designer of much of the controlled change in the enterprise. By controlled we mean that the manager makes changes of her/his own free will, like exploiting opportunities and solving non-pressing problems. Having discovered an opportunity, the manager may decide that it is necessary for the enterprise to take action. In practice, such a decision emerges as a series of smaller decisions and other activities, sequenced over a period of time. Sometimes a manager delegates the responsibility of an improvement project to a subordinate, but also then, the manager wants to keep supervision over the project. Where the entrepreneur role focuses on voluntary action by the manager, the *disturbance handler* role deals with involuntary situations and change that is, at least partly, beyond the manager's control. Disturbances just occur, corrections are the necessary responses by the manager.

Resource allocation is the heart of the enterprise's strategy-making system. For it is in the making of choices involving significant resources that strategies are determined. Among these resources are money, time, equipment, and manpower. Resource allocation has basically three components: scheduling of time, programming of work, and authorising actions. A manager's final role is that of participant in *negotiation* activity. From time to time, an enterprise finds itself in major, non-routine negotiations with other enterprises or individuals. It is usually the manager who leads the contingent from her/his enterprise.

In closing the discussion, it is important to stress again the power that the manager of an enterprise has over the making of its strategy. This power is expressed by her/his ability to initiate and supervise improvement projects, by her/his handling of significant organisational disturbances, by her/his control over the allocation of resources, and by her/his supervision of all major negotiations.

2.3 The Distinction Between Management and Governance

In his book [3], Mintzberg doesn't make a distinction between management and governance. Actually, many researchers and practitioners, especially in North America, do not make this distinction. In EE, however, we do. The metaphor of the ship may be useful to clarify the distinction that is made in EE: governance is about setting the course or route, management is about keeping the ship on a set route. In terms of the essential model of an enterprise (cf. [4] Chap. 12), Enterprise Management never incurs changes to the model, only Enterprise Governance can do so. It means that the instruments of managers are those that change the implementation of the essential model, as discussed in [5], notably in Chaps. 9 and 10.

Let us have a new look at the ten roles of Mintzberg, with this distinction in mind. Clearly, the roles of *entrepreneur* and *disturbance handler* are governance roles, because they will generally lead to changes in the essential model of the enterprise. Whether only 'managers' can fill these roles is something we address in the SIGMA theory in Chap. 8. On the other hand, *leader*, *monitor*, *disseminator*, and *resource allocator* are clearly management roles, because they commonly do not affect the essential model. The monitoring of the operational processes, and the dissemination of information gathered in this way, are nowadays mostly delegated to ICT systems. Although at first sight, resource allocation looks like a governance role, on closer look, it becomes clear that it does not change the essential model. The roles of *figurehead*, *liaison*, *spokesperson*, and *negotiator* are less clear, because they do not directly affect the enterprise. Both governors and managers may fill them.

In a later paper, titled "Rebuilding Companies as Communities" [6], Mintzberg states that the development of managers reaches further than the individual: it regards organisations and society. "Beneath the current economic crisis", Mintzberg says, "lies another crisis of greater proportions: the depreciation in companies of community—people's sense of belonging to and caring for something larger than themselves". He also warns for the tendency that managers take control over the entire enterprise without a legitimate basis.

2.4 The Management Industry

Modern management training programs, often referred to as "business schools," appear to teach no knowledge concerning the conception, realisation, and maintenance of products (the outcomes of business processes) in any professional field. It makes leadership, which society and organisations so desperately need, impossible. The obvious consequence is to speak of "professional incompetence". This is not, however, how the educational institutions themselves see it. They have coined the concealing term 'generic management'. Some of their websites refer to it as "the profession of management". This 'profession' rests on the belief that "management as a practice is not intricately involved with any particular form of labor or state of affairs, but is a claim to coordinate the doing of all things" [7], p. 100. Generic management exercised by the 'professional manager', is however completely disconnected from the kind of activities to which it relates.

It makes little sense to ask lawyers to resolve an operational failure in a communications network or accountants to devise a strategy for energy systems. Conversely, engineers are of little use when dealing with legal complexities. In short, only experts and professionals are capable of adequate sense making within the aforementioned circular process. They should therefore be in charge to lead and steer an enterprise.

Thorough knowledge and expertise concerning the managed activities is not considered necessary because managing is methodically the same everywhere, involving such things as planning, budgeting, controlling, and evaluating. "The disastrous concept of the wonderfully mobile professional manager—the person trained in a classroom who by definition could manage any kind of business (or indeed non-business) without knowing anything about it—has arrived" [8], p. 43. As said before, Edward Deming, the founder of quality thinking, expressed his concern about the 'professional manager' and considered that idea a cruel hoax [1], p. 130. Despite this concern, the massive spread of the 'professional manager' proceeds steadily: "Yet generic leadership concepts, which often mean nothing without context, have been normalised across all kinds of professions and enterprises and distract from the core business." [8], p. 82. Thus, a management position in a chain of eyewear stores can easily be exchanged for a position in an educational institution, a hospital, or a fire department. With the increase in belief in the 'professional manager' the respect for experts is declined.

Since the teaching of knowledge and skills in a professional field is lacking, the question then pops up what the training is for. The question is all the more relevant because "business schools are [said to be] largely irrelevant to business" [7], p. 110. It is precisely the scientific and professional attention to content that ensures important contributions to society and individual lives. The answer to the question of what education is for turns out to be rather banal: making money. In reality, the answer is however veiled; one talks of increasing shareholder value, or increasing the economic value of the enterprise. It is questionable, however, that employees will wake up in the morning by the desire to increase shareholder value.

Unfortunately, the influence of business schools is enormous. Recently, the Association to Advance Collegiate Schools of Business estimates the number of schools at 16,500. It means that each year more than half a million individuals, educated in this way, enter society. Next, the annual revenues of business schools exceed 400 billion euros [7]. This spectre is made even more poignant by the fact that the vast number of business schools worldwide has thus created and sustains a gigantic ‘management industry’ that produces “vast amounts of clashing and misleading advice” [9], p. 33. There is no question of any coherence and consistency: “just about every important topic dealt with by the management disciplines could well be regarded as controversial” [10], p. 11. The professional manager is only too happy to be swayed by this nonsense.

The consequences of the management industry are also visible through the influence of consulting and advisory firms that help shape the vast management industry. Citizens experience the influence of the management industry in many ways, partly through governments because governments have “an obsession with management consulting firms” [and] “ever larger sums from the public purse are being tipped into the pockets of management consultancies” [8] p. 30. More money is often spent on the management industry than on the issue for which the industry is hired.

2.5 Conclusions

What is said above about the current managerial practice is not flattering. However, we have to deal with it, the professional managers are all around us. In many boards of directors, there are indeed ever less people who are knowledgeable in the fields they are managing or governing. In addition, the business schools in which these people are taught that management is a profession, that they are capable to take any management position, are just here. Nevertheless, we will keep a positive and hopeful view on enterprises, because we believe that morality will eventually prevail. But there is a long way to go, a long time to exercise patience.

In Sect. 2.1 we stated that management is about keeping a set direction. For illustration we used the metaphor of the ship. Managing then comes down to controlling: operating the helm on the basis of feedback information about the direction in which the ship is actually moving. As long as management has sufficient controlling instruments to keep the ship (thus the enterprise) on route, the ship will move on in the right direction. But as soon as this is not the case, governance is needed, resulting in a change of direction and/or a change of the construction of the ship/enterprise. This will be the subject of the next chapter.

References

1. Deming, W. E. (1986). *Out of the crisis: Quality, productivity and competitive position* (Vol. xiii, p. 507). Cambridge University Press.
2. Osterman, P. (1996). *Broken ladders: Managerial careers in the new economy* (p. 259). Oxford University Press.
3. Mintzberg, H. (1973). *The nature of managerial work* (Vol. xiii, p. 298). Harper & Row
4. Dietz, J. L. G., & Mulder, J. B. F. (2024). *Enterprise ontology: A human-centric approach to understanding the essence of organisation* (2nd ed.). Enterprise Engineering. Springer Nature.
5. Dietz, J. L. G., & Mulder, J. B. F. (2025). *Enterprise design fundamentals: Settling the enterprise business and devising the enterprise organisation.* Enterprise Engineering. Springer Nature.
6. Mintzberg, H. (2015). *Rebalancing society: Radical renewal beyond left, right, and center* (1st ed., Vol. xi, pp. 151). Berrett-Koehler Publishers, Inc.
7. Parker, M. *Shut down the business school: What's wrong with management education* (1st ed., 225 pages). Online Resource.
8. Goodall, A. (2023). *Credible: The power of expert leaders* (1st US ed., Vol. xii, 255 pages). Public Affairs.
9. Pfeffer, J., & Sutton, R. I. (2006). *Hard facts, dangerous half-truths, and total nonsense: Profiting from evidence-based management* (Vol. x, p. 276). Harvard Business School Press.
10. Thomas, A. B. (2002). *Controversies in management* (2nd ed., p. 272). Routledge.

Chapter 3
Introduction to Enterprise Governance

Abstract Enterprise Governance is about inciting and accomplishing enterprise change. In contrast, Enterprise Management belongs to enterprise operations. A distinction is made between the traditional way of governing enterprises and the human-centric way. The traditional way is founded in the Taylorian distinction between bosses and workers; only bosses are considered to be able to reflect on the work to be done, workers are just alienated from it. The human-centric way involves all employees, with a special role for the natural leaders in the enterprise. Leaders have followers, based on mutual trust.

3.1 Introduction

Our understanding of *Enterprise Governanc*e is based on the fundamental research by Jan Hoogervorst reported on in various publications, notably in the books [1, 2]. Enterprise Governance is about inciting and accomplishing enterprise change. It is put in opposition to enterprise operations. Thus, Enterprise Management (cf. Chap. 2) belongs to enterprise operations. Controlling the ship, keeping it in a set direction, belongs to operations, and the role of steersman is an operational role.

Both in practice and in education (notably the business schools), governance and management are often not separated as clearly as we do here. As an example, the management board of a company primarily governs the company. On the other hand, an operational manager is first of all managing, that is keeping the enterprise on the set route. He or she is not changing the enterprise, but only using the available control instruments to let the enterprise operate as smoothly as possible. An example of such an instrument is the assignment of an actor role (cf. [3] Chap. 8) to more or to less employees, dependent on the current demand. Another example is the (intended) settlement time for initiated transactions (cf. [3] Chap. 8). This parameter may be used to speed up (or slow down) a business process. But in general, an operational manager is also the person who proposes changes to the organisation after they have been brought up by (subordinated) employees in the weekly meetings. So, he/she also plays a role in governing.

J. L.G. Dietz and H. B. F. Mulder, *Enterprise Governance and Management*, The Enterprise Engineering Series, https://doi.org/10.1007/978-3-032-24318-8_3

Governance thus comprises both inciting changes and accomplishing them. Accomplishing a change ultimately implies redesign of the construction of the enterprise (cf. [3] Chap. 7). Consequently, Enterprise Governance and Enterprise Design (cf. [4]) are closely related. The way in which the incitement of a change takes place, and whether it succeeds at all, depends on the way in which governance is installed in the enterprise's organisation. We distinguish between the traditional way, to be discussed in Sect. 3.2, and the human-centric way, discussed in Sect. 3.3.

3.2 The Traditional Way of Governing

Although it is tricky to speak of just one traditional way of governing enterprises, there is for sure a big difference between how governance is carried out in most enterprises and the human-centric way that we will discuss in Sect. 3.3. By the traditional way we mean specifically that both the incitement of changes and the execution of governance decisions are the authority and responsibility of a few employees. They are commonly the members of the management board or of the board of directors. This arrangement of governance has been around in enterprises all over the world since the days of Frederic Taylor [5] (or even earlier). Its main characteristic is the distinction between bosses and workers. Bosses decide on the work to be done. They instruct workers what they should do and how they should do it. Regarding governance, it are the bosses who take care (or don't). The workers are usually not asked about how things can be improved. At best, there are suggestion boxes in the workshop, but the procedure of dealing with these suggestions is often obscure.

In the traditional way of governing enterprises, the distinction between governance and management is blurred. As if the captain and the steersman on a ship are the same function. This should not be the case, of course, but it is often hard to separate the two functions, especially when they are exercised by the same person (the boss), which is often the case. A boss is primarily managing (the work of) the workers who are subordinates to her/him. He or she also produces change initiatives and possibly discuss them with fellow bosses. If they succeed in bringing a change initiative to the attention of the 'highest' boss, it may be realised, meaning that the current organisation is subsequently redesigned and re-implemented. If not, things stay as they are, whereas the alienation of the workers from the work increases.

More than a century after Taylor, by far most enterprises appear to be governed in the way described above, meaning that not all employees are involved in discussions about improving or otherwise changing the current situation. This is certainly also due to the arrival of the 'professional managers' (cf. Chap. 2), but partly also to the persistent Taylorian misunderstanding that workers are not capable to think, let alone to participate in 'high-brow' governance discussions. As long as there are 'blue collars' next to 'white collars', little will change.

3.3 The Human-Centric Way of Governing

Being routed in a human-centric view on organisations, Enterprise Engineering, as introduced in Chap. 1, addresses governance accordingly, contrary to the traditional way of governing, presented in Sect. 3.2. Consequently, all employees are involved in governance processes, but how does one achieve this? The answer lies in a natural phenomenon that is manifest in every organisation. It is called *leadership*. Burns defines leadership as: "inducing followers to act for certain goals that represent the values and motivation—the wants and needs, aspirations and expectations—of both leaders and followers" [6]. Leadership thus has a moral component. In other words: "leadership without mutual trust is a contradiction" [7].

The reciprocal relationship between leader and followers implies that they share attention to the knowledge and expertise on which the goals and values are based. The almost inevitable consequence is that leadership can only become manifest through experts and professionals. Research demonstrates the importance of expert leadership [7]. It is not only relevant to the top of an organisation, but at every level. As a consequence, self-organisation and leadership presuppose each other. Self-organisation is based on shared goals, aspirations, values, and norms, where leadership, if based on mutual trust, stimulates the competence of employees, leading to self-confidence and personal development. In this way, opportunities for meaningful work, as well as satisfactory organisational performance, arise [8]. This is the source of *motivation*. Contrary to the usual view, motivation is not a primary condition that must be created, but a consequence of a satisfactory organisational performance. These thoughts constitute the core of the theory of human-centric organising as discussed in [3]. It is called the employee-centric theory of organisation in [1, 2].

Mary Parker Follet has described the nature of the mutual relationship in an unparalleled way [9]: "The leader guides the group and at the same time is herself/himself guided by the group, is always part of the group. No one can truly lead except from within. The power of leadership is the power of integrating. This is the power which creates community. The skilful leader does not rely on personal force; he/she controls her/his group not by dominating but by expressing it. He/she stimulates what is best in us; he/she unifies and concentrates what we feel only gropingly and scatteringly. But he/she never gets away from the current of which we and he/she are an integral part. He/she is a leader who gives form to the inchoate energy in everyone. The person who influences me most is not the one who does great deeds, but the one who makes me feel that I can do great deeds."

Given the importance of leadership, as outlined above, it seems quite natural to assign the leaders in an enterprise a role in governance, provided they possess the required level of expertise and professionalism. As discussed in Chap. 2, experts and professionals sometimes lack the appropriate understanding and intelligence and the related knowledge and skills. For example, a sociologist is obviously a professional and expert within the field, but as the boss of a civil engineering organisation, he or she will obviously fail. "Leading does not mean managing; the difference between the two is crucial" [7]. Leaders have followers and managers have subordinates. The distinctive difference is that managers are employees to whom a management actor role is assigned. The actor role determines which employees are its subordinates. Fully opposed to managers, there are no leadership positions, designed or otherwise determined by the organisation. Some people have a talent to be leader, and some people like to be her/his follower. As said, only mutual trust can let such a relationship persist.

We will elaborate the human-centric way of governing in the so-called SIGMA theory in Chap. 8.

References

1. Hoogervorst, J. A. P. (2017). *Foundations of enterprise governance and enterprise engineering* (p. 574). Springer International Publishing.
2. Hoogervorst, J. A. P. (2018). *Practising enterprise governance and enterprise engineering* (p. 574). Springer International Publishing.
3. Dietz, J. L. G., & Mulder, J. B. F. (2024). *Enterprise ontology: A human-centric approach to understanding the essence of organisation* (2nd ed.). Enterprise Engineering. Springer Nature.
4. Dietz, J. L. G. & Mulder, J. B. F. (2025). *Enterprise design fundamentals: settling the enterprise business and devising the enterprise organisation.* Enterprise Engineering. Springer Nature.
5. Taylor, F. W. (1911). *The principles of scientific management*. Harper & Brothers.
6. Burns, J. M. (1979). *Leadership. Harper torchbooks* (Vol. ix, p. 530). Harper & Row.
7. Bennis, W. G. (2003). *On becoming a leader* (Rev. ed., p. 255). Perseus Online Resource.
8. Ciulla, J. B. (2000). *The working life: The promise and betrayal of modern work* (1st ed., Vol. xvii, p. 266). Times Books.
9. Follett, M. P., Metcalf, H. C., & Urwick, L. F. (1941). *Dynamic administration: The collected papers of Mary Parker Follett* (p. 320). Harper.

Part II
Theories

There is nothing as practical as a good theory

—Kurt Lewin

There is nothing as dangerous as a bad theory

—Sumantra Goshal

Chapter 4 provides an overview of all Enterprise Engineering theories and their position in a clarifying framework. Chapters 5–8 contain extended summaries of the theories that underlie the notion of Enterprise Governance and Management. Every chapter is divided in three parts: foundations, elaborations, and discussions.

The *foundations* part regards the theoretical basis of the theory, its core ideas, as well as the core sources of knowledge that they rely on. It is considered to be the most stable part of a theory.

In the *elaborations* part, the link to practice is established (illustrations, methods, techniques, tools, etc.). It is presumably less stable, because new elaborations may come up in the course of time from applying the theory in practice.

The *discussions* part serves mainly to compare the EE theory, and the methods that are based on it, with comparable other approaches. Therefore, it is presumably also less stable than the foundations part, as new comparisons may become relevant in the course of time.

Chapter 4
The Enterprise Engineering Theories

Whether you can observe a thing or not depends on the theory that you use. It is the theory that decides what can be observed
(Albert Einstein)

Abstract The foundations of the discipline of Enterprise Engineering (EE), as envisioned by the Ciao Network, consist of the CIAO Paradigm and a number of theories. After the discussion of the paradigm, which has its origins in the communication-centric view on information systems engineering that emerged around 2000, the role of the EE theories and their relationships with the EE methods and the practice of EE is explained. After having been arranged in a suitable classification scheme, each of the theories is briefly discussed.

4.1 Introduction

In this chapter, the reader is introduced into the theoretical foundations of the discipline of Enterprise Engineering (EE), as it is developed and practised by a group of researchers and practitioners, called the Ciao Network[1] [1]. The Italian word Ciao[2] is an acronym for Communication, Information, Action, and Organisation. They are the key concepts in the CIAO Paradigm, which constitutes the basic understanding of the operation of enterprises. It also sets our engineering perspective. Even if an enterprise has not been designed consciously, changing it can be considered as redesigning and re-implementing it. At the same time, the highest appreciation is given to the 'pearls' of every enterprise: the people. Empowered with the right authority, based on competence and exerted with responsibility, they are the cornerstones of an enterprise's organisation. Without people, there is no organisation.

---

[1] For more information, visit www.ciaonetwork.org.

[2] The Italian word "Ciao" means both "hello" and "goodbye", depending on the context. The underlying commonality is that one confirms to someone else to consider him/her as a trustworthy fellow human being.

J. L.G. Dietz and H. B. F. Mulder, *Enterprise Governance and Management*, The Enterprise Engineering Series, https://doi.org/10.1007/978-3-032-24318-8_4

Fig. 4.1 CIAO tree

In order to portray the role of theories and methods in the field of EE, the Ciao Network uses the tree metaphor, as exhibited in Fig. 4.1. The EE theories constitute the roots of the tree. They feed the trunk, which represents the EE methods, with their juices. After having been made fit for consumption by the methods, the juices ultimately reach all branches, where they cause the growth of leaves and flowers, standing for the aimed at flourishing enterprises.

As the tree grows, the need may arise to develop new methods, or to graft external ones on the trunk. There is no objection against it, on the contrary, every useful contribution is welcome. The only prerequisite is that the methods are (made) compliant with the EE theories. In addition, a need may occur to develop new theories, or to add external ones to the root structure. Again, the only prerequisite is that they are (made) compliant with the existing set of theories.

Section 4.2 contains an explanation of the CIAO Paradigm. In Sect. 4.3, an overview of the currently existing EE theories is presented, followed by a brief summary of each of them in Sect. 4.4.

4.2 The CIAO Paradigm

4.2.1 From Information-Centric to Communication-Centric

Up to about 1970, there were no information systems and there was no field of information systems engineering. The application of programmed computers in enterprises, for the sake of assisting the workers and the managers, was called EDP (Electronic Data Processing). After 1970, EDP was gradually replaced by ISE (Information Systems Engineering) or like names, referring to the field that concerns the application of ICT[3] in organisations. The primal and core notion became information, generally defined as the representation of knowledge. Communication was defined as the exchange of information. The notion of action was something rather disconnected from information and communication, as was the notion of organisation, although there was the general recognition that organisation somehow implies action, communication, and information. Let us call this point of view the *information-centric* view on information systems (engineering).

One of the consequences of the information-centric view is that developing (automated) information systems is considered as something that ICT professionals do 'to the side', after having elicited requirements from the people in the organisation, basically by interviewing these people. Once the system is built, it is 'implanted' in the organisation. A widely acknowledged drawback of this 'waiter' approach is that the delivered systems rarely meet the expectations of the users. In hindsight, the main reason for this failure is that requirements determination was ill-understood. Asking the members of an organisation what information they need, presupposes that these people have such a comprehensive understanding of their tasks, that they are able to provide complete, consistent, and coherent answers. As a counter example, embedded software engineers start with getting an appropriate understanding of the system or machine for which they are going to build supporting software. Based on this understanding they will specify the requirements for the software system to be built.

For obscure reasons, the developers of 'embedded' software for organisations, thus the information system engineers, have never recognised the necessity to acquire an appropriate understanding of the objects of interest they want to support: organisations. As a consequence of the 'waiter' approach to requirements determination, relevant requirements are often missing, and irrelevant ones are included.

In the nineties of the past century, an awareness emerged that the information-centric view was not sustainable anymore. The number and size of failures in information systems engineering kept increasing, and the proclaimed benefits of standard packages, notably ERP systems, came along with the feeling of being armoured. Based on the achievements in language philosophy, notably speech act theory [2, 3] and in (social) action theory, notably the theory of communicative

[3] ICT stands for Information and Communication Technology. It refers specially to the modern practice of applying digital electronic, optical, etc., means to process, store, and transmit data.

action [4], a community of researchers in information systems engineering, called LAP (Language/Action Perspective), proposed to make a paradigm shift [5]. By taking communication as the primal notion, the path was paved to a more appropriate and more integrated understanding of the other three key notions: information, action, and organisation. Later, the name CIAO Paradigm (CIAO stands for Communication, Information, Action, and Organisation) has been coined for this *communication-centric* view on information systems (engineering). In line with the meaning of the original Latin verb "communicare", *communication* is now defined as the sharing of thoughts between subjects (human beings), and *information* as the means for communication. People, in organisations and in society at large, have a need to communicate, generally for the sake of making known what they are doing. Because it is impossible to do this directly, e.g. by connecting brains, they have to use the vehicle of information.

4.2.2 Communicative Action

In addition to the sharing of thoughts, communication became (also) understood as a form of *action*, by virtue of the intention in every communicative act, as explained by Habermas' theory of communicative action [4]. Figure 4.2 exhibits the four constituting parts of a communicative act: the performer, the intention, the addressee, and the proposition.

The *performer* and the *addressee* are subjects, i.e. human beings, particularly in their quality of social individual, which means: being capable to engage in mutual commitments. The *proposition* is a state of affairs that is or that can be the case. An example of a proposition in the café situation is that a client has got a cup of coffee.

The *intention* is the intent of the performer (the client) towards the addressee (a waiter), with respect to the proposition. If the intention is 'request', the performer wants the addressee to make the proposition become true. In this case, the client wants the waiter to bring her a cup of coffee. Habermas [4] tells us that, in performing a communicative act, the performer raises three validity claims towards the addressee: the claim to rightness, the claim to sincerity, and the claim to truth. These claims have to be assessed by the addressee, and the result of this assessment will guide her/him in

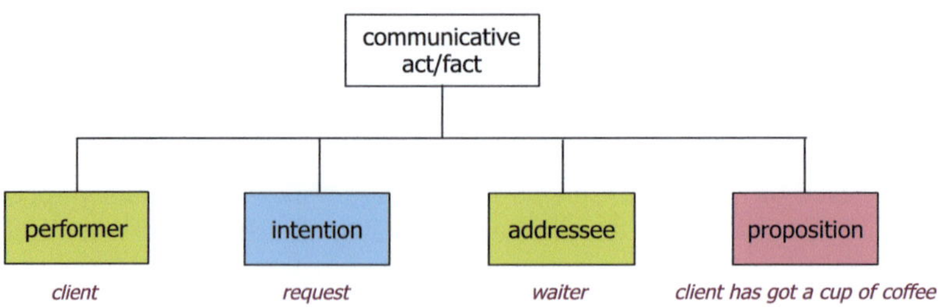

Fig. 4.2 Structure of a communicative act/fact

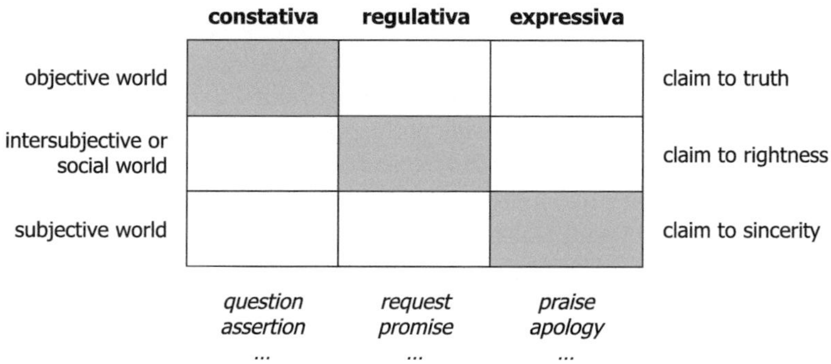

Fig. 4.3 Categories of communicative acts

the way he/she will respond. By accepting the *claim to rightness* in the above example, the waiter recognises the authority of the client to make the request. By accepting the *claim to sincerity*, the waiter expresses that he considers the client sincere in making the request. By accepting the *claim to truth*, the waiter expresses that the proposition can be made true. If all three claims are accepted, the communicative act is said to be successful. In the café example, the waiter will then respond by a promise. In case of failure, he will decline the client's request. In every communicative act, one of the validity claims is dominant. Based on this dominance, Habermas [4] distinguishes three categories of communicative acts, as well as three worlds in which these acts have effect. Figure 4.3 exhibits the distinctions. The dominance of a claim, as well as the related world, is indicated by the grey coloured rectangles.

In the category of *constativa*, the dominant claim is the claim to truth, and the world with which they are primarily concerned, is called the *objective world*. Examples of intentions in this category are question and assertion. If a railway passenger asks a railway officer for the departure time of the next train to Amsterdam, the dominant claim is the claim to truth, i.e. that the fact exists (in their shared objective world). This holds also for the answer by the officer (which would be the assertion of a fact). Facts like the departure time of trains are considered to exist in our common objective world, like the fact that the sun is shining, and the current price of a glass of beer in your favourite pub. But, the other two (non-dominant) validity claims must also be satisfied. In the train example, this means that the railway passenger respectively trusts the railway officer that he/she is authorised to provide the answer, and that this officer will provide the correct answer.

In the category of *expressiva*, the dominant claim is the claim to sincerity, and the world with which they are primarily concerned is everyone's private *subjective world*. Examples of intentions in this category are praise and apologise. If the railway passenger starts his/her conversation with the railway officer by saying "I'm sorry to disturb you, madam, but …", then the dominant claim of this phrase is the claim to sincerity. If the officer feels that the passenger is insincere, she will most likely utter a sincerity checking sentence, and she may even ignore the passenger. Facts like feeling sorry are considered to exist in everyone's subjective world. The claim to sincerity represents the most fundamental condition for human cooperation in the broadest sense of the word, which is mutual *trust*. At the same time, it is the hardest one to verify. Moreover, trust emerges from shared values and norms among people, which do change over time. In language philosophy [6] and social action theory [4] it is assumed that people constantly check and adjust their values and norms when they are communicating. In [7] we have called this second-order communication, and we have suggested that this is the lubricating oil of organisations and of society at large.

In the category of *regulativa*, the dominant claim is the claim to rightness, and the world with which they are primarily concerned, is the intersubjective or *social world*. Examples of intentions in this category are the request and the promise. If the client in the café asks the waiter for a cup of coffee, the dominant claim is the claim to rightness, i.e. the client claims that she has the authority to make the request, and that she considers the waiter to be authorised to fulfil it. This holds also for the response by the waiter. Facts like being authorised to do something are considered to exist in our common intersubjective or social world. Moreover, we have created them ourselves. Assigning each other authorities (and expecting that they will be exerted in a responsible way) is the way in which we build organisations and societies [6]. This insight has important consequences. One of them is that people are basically autonomous in deciding how to respond to (intersubjective or social) events. This is the case in every enterprise and in society at large. The fundamental autonomy implies that one may disobey rules and laws if the situation asks for it. At the same time, they must act responsibly, and they can be held accountable for their deeds. Another consequence is that all facts are basically social or intersubjective.

As will be elaborated in the PSI theory (cf. [8] Chap. 8), a fact is either a coordination fact, like having requested a cup of coffee, or a production fact, like having brought a cup of coffee, or having observed the temperature in a room. The facts that we use in our institutionalised society are always social facts.

4.2.3 Implications for Information, Action, and Organisation

Let us point out next what the consequences of the communication-centric view are for the other three concepts: information, action, and organisation, starting from the basic understanding that *communication* is the sharing of thoughts by human minds. Because human beings are not able to directly connect their minds, some vehicle for transmitting thoughts is needed, and this vehicle is information, or the sign, which is the preferred term in semiotics (cf. [8] Chap. 5). A major outcome of this study is the semiotic ladder, exhibited in Fig. 4.4. It clarifies the role of signs in the communication of human beings. *Information* then is the dyad of content and form, meaning that the two parts are distinguishable but not separable. The *content* is the thought that one wants to share, and the *form* is the agreed upon perceivable sign. The content comprises both the intention (or pragmatics) and the proposition (or semantics) of the thought, and the form comprises both the formalism (or syntax) and

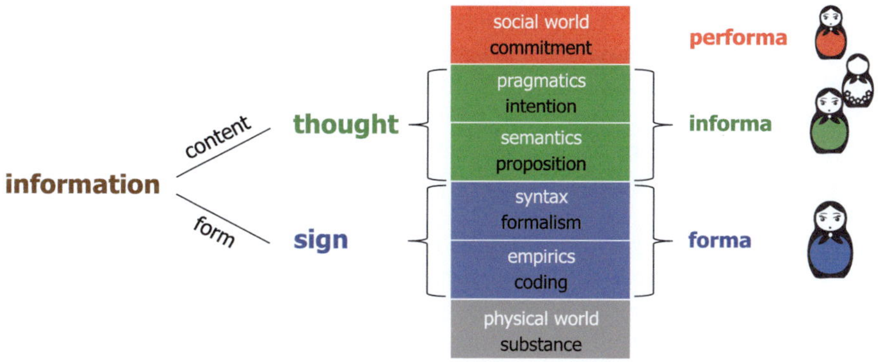

Fig. 4.4 Semiotic ladder

the coding (or empirics). Contrary to the definition in Fig. 4.4, the content of a sign is often equated with the notion of *information*, and the form with *data*. Unfortunately, precise definitions and their consistent use don't seem to have a high priority in current practice.

In the café example, the client has got the thought that she wants a cup of coffee. In order to share this thought, she expresses it in a sign that is intelligible to the waiter. The proposition is "client has got a cup of coffee" and the intention is the request. By performing the request, she enters into a commitment towards the waiter, like the waiter enters into a commitment if he performs a promise or a decline in response. The client may have expressed her thought in this English sentence: "I'd like to have a cup of coffee, please", which constitutes the form or sign part in Fig. 4.4. The applied formalism is the English grammar and the coding regards the representation of the words. The substance in which the sentence is inscribed consists of the air vibrations, produced by the client and then perceived by the waiter.

For the concept of *action*, the communication-centric view means that communicating is (also) acting, as discussed in Sect. 4.2.2. As Austin [2] puts it: people do things with words. In the PSI theory (cf. [8] Chap. 8), this is accentuated by distinguishing coordination acts and production acts, and by combining them in the concept of the (business) transaction. The new concept of *organisation* that arises from the foregoing, is a network of actors who carry out transactions in collaboration. It is a new way of looking at Mintzberg's basic idea of organisation: the need to divide labour into tasks, and the need to coordinate these tasks [9]. The idea that organisation is somehow the outcome of the social interaction of cooperating human beings, is not new. Since Max Weber [10], several sociologists have studied this relationship, like for example, Weick [11]. However, we think that none of them has made the idea as operational as the CIAO Paradigm does.

Having this new understanding of organisation, a new and more appropriate understanding of information systems emerges. Every information system can appropriately be conceived as some implementation of some part of the organisation. This view emphasises the being intrinsically intertwined of information systems and their supported organisations. It also clarifies why information system engineers should first of all study the construction and operation of the organisation before designing the information system. Basically, the information system is already there, because it is an intrinsic part of the organisation. Consequently, the functional requirements are also already there. The main task of the information system engineer is to find a new way of implementing a particular part of the organisation, in particular by applying ICT.

Although conceiving organisations as networks of actors who carry out transactions is indifferent to a particular management style or approach, it certainly matches very well with a high degree of self-management, as discussed in [12]. Making decisions at the lowest hierarchical level that is possible, implies that one grants a high degree of responsibility to the employees on that level.

4.3 Overview of the EE Theories

Paraphrasing Einstein's quote above Sect. 4.1, the EE theories are the mental glasses through which enterprise engineers observe and understand enterprises, and seek to make sense of them. In addition, the EE theories are the roots of the methods for improving enterprises, as illustrated in Fig. 4.1.

The presently identified EE theories are also listed in Fig. 4.1. The list is not exhaustive as there may appear new theories in the future. All theories are classified in Fig. 4.5, which shows an adapted version of the framework that was introduced in [1]. Four categories are distinguished: philosophical, ontological, technological, and ideological. The philosophical theories underlie all other theories. On top of that, the ontological theories underlie both the technological theories and the ideological ones. The latter two categories do not have specific interrelationships. The classification of the theories in the framework is, to some extent, disputable, because they do not always fit in exactly one category. However, the presented classification seems to do justice to their main character.

Philosophical theories concern the most fundamental ways in which people perceive and conceive the surrounding world, make sense of it, study it, etc. They are about knowledge in general, and therefore include epistemology, phenomenology, and logic. Philosophical theories are justified by their *truthfulness*. The truthfulness of a theory is established by reasoning or by judging its tenability in the face of reality.

Ontological theories are about the nature of things. They serve to explain their construction and operation, and predict the consequences of changing them, while completely abstracting from implementation. In EE, the things are organisations. Ontological theories are justified by their *soundness* and *appropriateness*. The soundness of an ontological theory is established by its being rooted in sound philosophical theories. The appropriateness of an ontological theory is established by the evaluation of its practical application, e.g. through expert judgments.

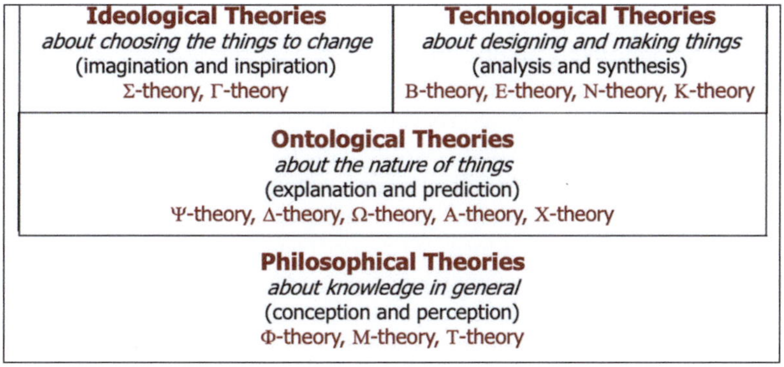

Fig. 4.5 EE theories in the EE framework of theories

Technological theories are about designing and building things, and about putting them into operation. Generally spoken, they assist in analysing and synthesising things. Technological theories are justified by their *rigour* and *relevance*. The rigour of a technological theory is established by its being rooted in sound ontological and ideological theories. The relevance of a technological theory is established by the evaluation of its practical application, e.g. through measurements and evaluative comparisons. Recall that the original meaning of the Greek word for technology is "knowing how to make".

Ideological theories are not about things themselves, but about the context in which one decides on whether to make or change them. In EE, they serve to feed the imagination of people and to assist them in inspiring other people to adopt new, better ideas for running enterprises. Ideological theories cannot a priori be predicated as truthful or as sound and appropriate, nor as rigorous and relevant, even if they are rooted in rigorous and relevant other theories. One can only speak of their societal *significance*. The significance of an ideological theory boils down to the usefulness that is assigned to it by its supporters.

The summaries of the EE theories in Sect. 4.4 are presented in an order that seems to be most logical. In Fig. 4.1, the book is mentioned where the theory is explained fully; EO stands for Enterprise Ontology [8], ED for Enterprise Design [13], and EGM for Enterprise Governance and Management, which is the current book.

4.4 Summaries of the EE Theories

4.4.1 The FI Theory

The FI theory or EE information theory (FI stands for *Factual Information*), clarifies how people acquire factual knowledge. Semiotics provides us with the *semiotic triangle* [14], which clarifies the dyadic character of information: it is the inseparable combination of *content* (the communicated thought) and *form* (the sign that signifies the thought). In addition, semiotics provides us with the *semiotic ladder* [15], in which a distinction is made between the semantics and the pragmatics of thoughts, thereby clarifying that a thought consists of a *proposition* and an *intention.*

The core of the FI theory is the *semiotic mill*, refined into the *ontological mill*, which is a generic framework for understanding perception and conception, exhibited in Fig. 4.6. A *fact* becomes existent in the mind when a perceived concrete thing conforms to (the prescription of form of) a *type*. Therefore, a fact is an *instantiation* of a type. In logical terms, it is a predication of a conceptual object, with the type as the predicate. The conceptual object represents a concrete object that is considered to be the *identity* of a concrete thing. The first is a member of a conceptual class, and the second is a member of a concrete class. Type and class are dyadic notions: a class is the *extension* of a type; conversely, a type is the *intension* of a class.

Because the form of the thing with object 701 conforms to the type human, the conceptual fact is created in the mind that the thing is a human. In addition, factual knowledge can be acquired through communication.

Types can be *declared*, as original new types, but they can also be *derived* from existing types. Three ways of deriving are discussed: specialisation, generalisation, and aggregation. An example of *specialisation* is the definition of the type student as a specialisation of person: a student is a person for which there is an admission

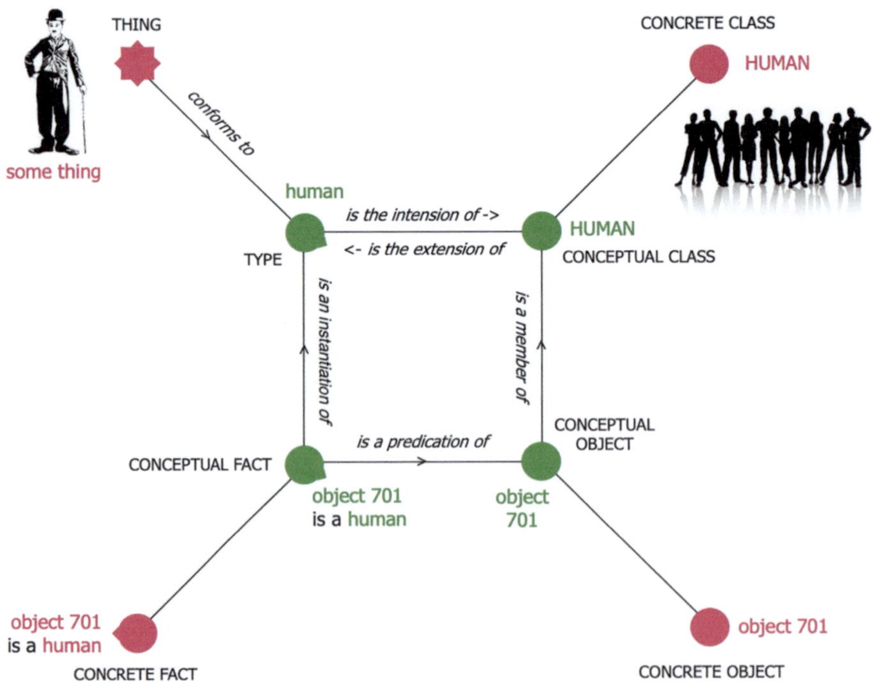

Fig. 4.6 Ontological mill

in which the person is the admitted person. An example of *generalisation* is the (extensional) definition of the type vehicle: the class VEHICLE is the set-theoretic union of the classes CAR, BIKE, SCOOTER, etc. An aggregation of a number of types is (extensionally) defined as the Cartesian product of their classes. An example of *aggregation* is the definition of the price of an article as an attribute of the Cartesian product of article kind (e.g. apple), supplier (e.g. GreenShop), and day (e.g. today).

4.4.2 The MU Theory

The MU theory or EE model theory (MU stands for *Model Universe*), is a theory of models and modelling in general, and of conceptual modelling in particular. It adopts Apostel's definition of *model* [16]: any subject using a system A to obtain knowledge of a system B, is using A as a model of B. This definition conveys the basic understanding of the concept of model as a role concept. The *model triangle*, which is based on the semiotic triangle (cf. Section 4.4.1), clarifies how complexes (systems and aggregates) of three major sorts (concrete, conceptual, and symbolic) can be viewed as models of each other. It is exhibited in Fig. 4.7.

By adding two levels of abstraction (the schema level and the meta level) on top of the conceptual complex or instance level, the *General Conceptual Modelling Framework* (GCMF) emerges. It clarifies the notions of *conceptual complex*, *conceptual schema*, and *meta schema*, for any universe of discourse or system's world. It

Fig. 4.7 Model triangle

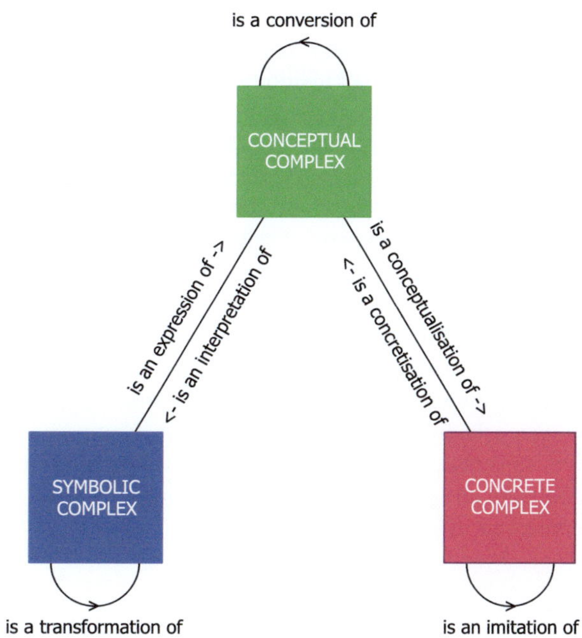

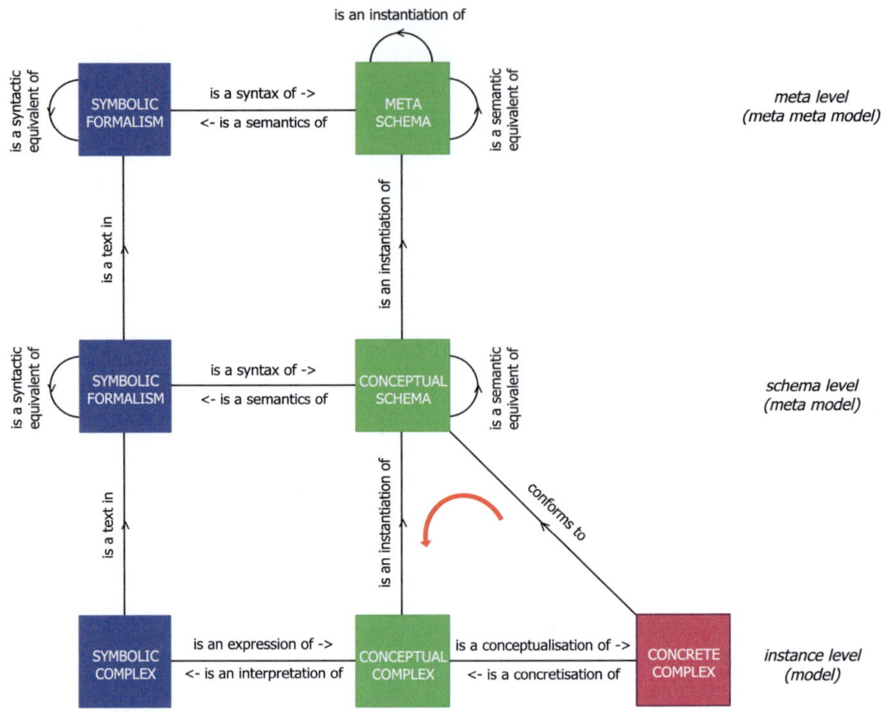

Fig. 4.8 General conceptual modelling framework

also makes clear that these notions are logical constructs, and that consequently any expression of them (in a suitable language) is directly transformable to first-order logic. The GCMF is exhibited in Fig. 4.8.

Because the form of the concrete complex conforms to the prescription of form that the conceptual schema represents, the corresponding conceptual complex is created in the mind. For communicating this ‘thought’, it is expressed in the symbolic formalism of the conceptual schema, yielding the symbolic complex.

In order to specify conceptual complexes, conceptual schemas and meta schemas, the *General Ontology Specification Language* (GOSL) is presented and discussed. The syntax of the language consists of graphical and textual symbols and constructs, as well as a textual part. The latter is an English-like formal language, which means that it is directly transformable to first order logic, like the graphical part. The split between the two is a rather pragmatic one. Compared to common graphical languages for conceptual modelling, GOSL might be called minimal: it covers only the basic concepts and constructs. More complicated logical formulas can mostly better be expressed in formal textual sentences.

4.4.3 The TAO Theory

EE is an engineering approach to tackling problems in enterprises. By nature, engineers seek to understand the *construction* and *operation* of systems (where operation is defined as the manifestation of the construction in the course of time), in addition to their *functions* and *behaviours* (where a behaviour is defined as the manifestation of a function in the course of time). The TAO theory (Teleology–Affordances–Ontology) clarifies the distinction between function and construction. One of the clarifications is that the construction of a system is an inherent property of the system, whereas all of its functions are relationships between the system and stakeholders. Consequently, functions are not properties of systems. The TAO theory builds on Gibson's Theory of Affordances [17]. As Fig. 4.9 illustrates, *affordances* emerge from the perception by subjects (with needs or purposes) of concrete objects (with properties). As an example, if you walk in the woods and feel the need to sit, you may perceive that a tree trunk offers you the sit-on-ability affordance.

Next to using the affordances that existing things offer, people also create things, with particular affordances in mind. These things are commonly called *artefacts,* and their intended affordances are *functions.* For example, chairs have the function to be sit-on-able. In addition, one can assign (new) functions to things. For example, one can assign the function of parking lot to a square, for particular days of the week.

Consequently, a strict distinction is made between the construction and the function perspective on things. In the *construction perspective*, one studies a thing in an

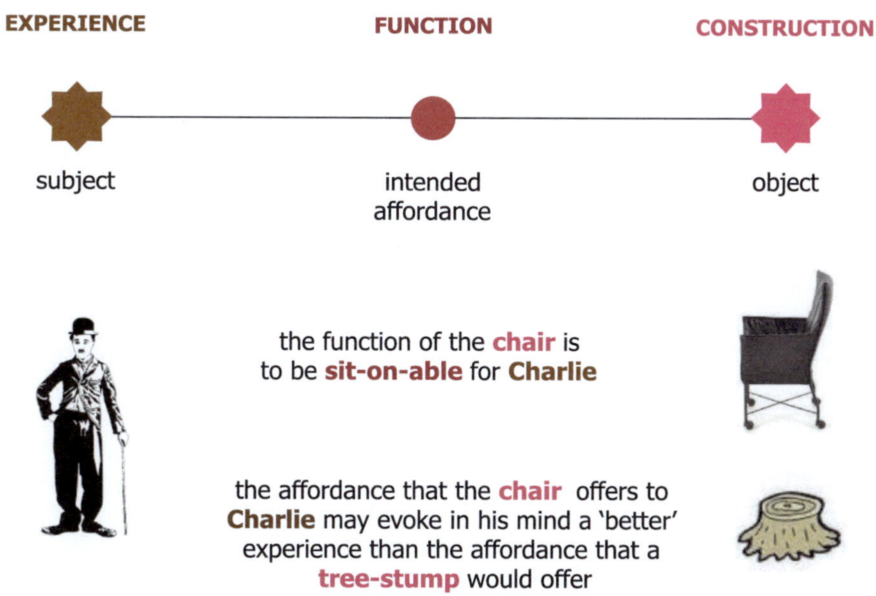

Fig. 4.9 Illustration of the TAO theory

objective way, i.e. independent of the affordances it may offer. In the *function perspective*, one studies the affordances that a thing may offer to subjects, while disregarding its construction. So, function (or affordance) is not a property of a thing, but a relationship between the thing and a stakeholder. For example, to people who know to drive, cars do offer relevant functions. This does probably not (directly) hold for the members of an isolated tribe in the jungle of Brazil. When using the affordances that things can offer, subjects may have different *experiences*. For example, you may *value* the sit-on-ability of a chair higher than that offered by a tree trunk. Experiences are subjective impressions. However, they may be shared among stakeholders.

Corresponding with the function-construction distinction, two sorts of conceptual models (cf. Section 4.4.2) are distinguished: constructional models and functional models. A *constructional model* is a representation of the construction of concrete things, like cars. A *functional model* is a representation of the possible affordances or functions that a concrete thing may offer to someone. Next, the constructional decomposition and functional decomposition of enterprises are discussed. To distinguish between them, the term "organisation" is used when referring to the construction perspective on enterprises, and the term "business" when referring to the function perspective. A decomposition of an enterprise's organisation is a *constructional decomposition*, and a decomposition of its business is a *functional decomposition*.

4.4.4 The PSI Theory

The PSI theory or EE organisational operation theory (PSI stands for *Performing in Social Interaction*) serves to study the operation of organisations. The word "organisation" indicates that it takes the construction perspective on enterprises. Organisations are systems in the category of social systems (cf. Section 4.4.3), which means that the system elements are social individuals, called actors. The operating principle is that actors enter into and comply with commitments towards each other.

An *actor* is defined as a subject (human being) in an actor role. The *actor role* determines the authority that the actor may exercise and the responsibility to do so. Commitments are raised in coordination acts, which are communicative acts in Habermas' category of regulativa (cf. Figures 4.2 and 4.3). The result of performing a coordination act is the creation of the corresponding coordination fact. For example, performing a request act concerning some product results in the fact that the product is requested.

Coordination acts/facts are the atomic building blocks of organisational (but commonly called: business) processes. They always occur in particular patterns of interaction between subjects who play either the *initiator* role or the *executor* role in the transaction. These patterns are instances of one generic pattern, called the (business) *transaction*. The basic coordination acts in every transaction are the request (by the initiator), the promise (by the executor), the declare (by the executor), and the accept (by the initiator). The complete transaction pattern comprises in addition the decline (instead of promise), reject (instead of accept), and a revocation pattern for each of the basic steps. Every transaction (instance) is of a particular *transaction kind*. A transaction kind concerns one specific *product kind* and has one specific actor role as its executor role. The combination of a transaction kind and its executor role is called a *transactor role*. It is the (molecular) building block of organisations.

Based on the semiotic ladder (cf. Section 4.4.1), three human abilities are distinguished in performing coordination acts: *forma*, *informa*, and *performa* (cf. Figure 4.4). This distinction gives rise to three levels of correspondence in the communication between subjects: the forma level (notational correspondence), the informa level (cognitive correspondence), and the performa level (social correspondence), as shown in Fig. 4.10. To be successful, all three conditions of correspondence must be satisfied, i.e. the communication must be free of distortion. Below the forma level is the medium level, where forms are inscribed in physical substances and transported between subjects. Although evenly conditional for successful communication, the 'inner self' upper level, where a person's wisdom and love reside, the basis for his/her decisions, is considered outside the field of EE. He/she is basically autonomous in deciding how to respond to coordination events. At the same time, actors can always be held accountable, by other actors, for the acts that they decide to perform.

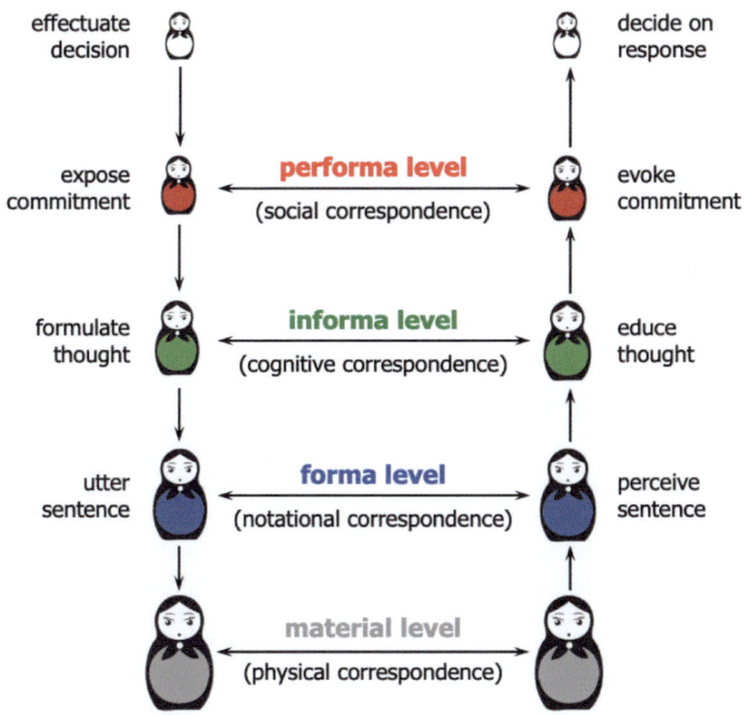

Fig. 4.10 Process of a communicative act

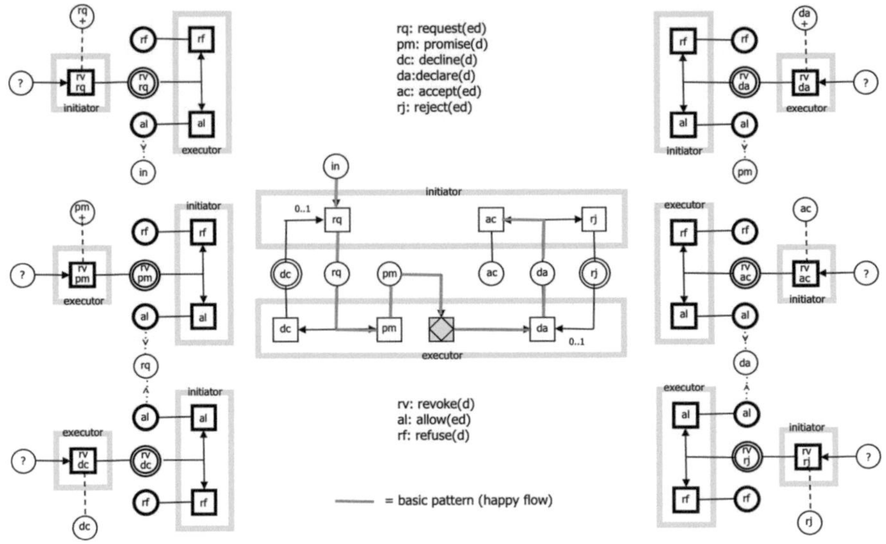

Fig. 4.11 Complete transaction pattern

The structure of a coordination act/fact is exhibited in Fig. 4.2. Examples of intentions are: request, promise, declare, and accept. An example of a product (or independent production fact) is ‘sale 1618 is completed’. As said, coordination acts occur in specific interaction patterns between two participants, called transactions. A transaction is successful if the (final) product is accepted. At that moment, the product starts to exist (comes into being). Figure 4.11 exhibits the complete transaction pattern, which is considered to be the universal pattern in all organisations. It consists of the standard pattern (middle part) and six revocations patterns. The green coloured path represents the basic pattern or happy flow, in which everything goes smoothly.

4.4.5 *The DELTA Theory*

The DELTA theory or EE systems theory (DELTA stands for *Discrete Event in Linear Time Automaton*), is a theory of discrete event systems, both from the construction and from the function perspective (cf. Section 4.4.1). According to Weinberg’s division of the realm of systems [18], organisations fall in the category of organised complexity: they are too organised for statistics and too complex for (mathematical) analysis. Bunge’s system definition [19] is adopted: a (homogeneous) *system* is a triple (C, E, S), where C (composition) is a set of elements of some category, E (environment) is a set of elements of the same category as the elements in C, and S (structure) is a set of influencing bonds among the elements in C and between them and the elements in E. Examples of categories are: physical, biological, and social. Organisations fall in the category of social systems.

Two sorts of conceptual systems are distinguished that may serve as models (cf. Section 4.4.2) of concrete systems: the *black-box* system and the *white-box* system. White-box models are suited to study the construction and operation of systems (cf. Section 4.4.3). Black-box models are suited to study their functionality and behaviour. Because black-box systems don't have an internal state, the grey-box system is introduced as a black-box system with internal state. Well-known examples of grey-box systems are the finite automaton (or finite state machine) and the discrete event system. For a deep and formal study of grey-box and white-box models, the PRISMA model is introduced. Three ways of mutual influencing between (the elements of) systems are distinguished, called *activating*, *restricting*, and *impeding*.

In the PRISMA *grey-box* model, all acts by the system, and their resulting facts, are divided in *production acts/facts* and *coordination acts/facts* (cf. Section 4.4.4).

The PRISMA grey-box model is defined as a tuple (**P**, **R**, **I**, **S**, **M**, **A**), where:

P is a partial function, called the *performance function.*
R is a set of C-fact types, called the *reaction base.*
I is a set of C-fact types, called the *impediment base.*
S is a set of P-fact types, called the *state base.*
M is a set of P-fact types, called the *mutation base.*
A is a set of C-fact types, called the *action base.*

$$\mathbf{P} \text{ is defined as} : \wp((\mathbf{A} \cup \mathbf{I}) * \mathrm{T}) * \wp(\mathbf{S} * \mathrm{T}) \rightarrow \wp(\mathbf{M} * \mathrm{D}) * \wp(\mathbf{R} * \mathrm{D})$$

where **Y** is the union of the extensions of $\mathbf{y} \in \mathbf{Y}$ (**Y** is **A**, **I**, **M**, **R**, or **S**); T is the discrete time scale and D is the set of (positive) time delays.

The PRISMA *white-box* model allows one to conceive systems as *prismanets*: networks of processors, channels, and banks. The complete prismanet model of a system is divided into the construction model and the operation model. The *construction model* of a system is the part that is expressed in the prismanet diagram, whose legend is shown in Fig. 4.12. The meanings of the various links between the basic shapes (box for processors, diamond for banks, and disk for channels) are expressed in an informal way. The *operation model* of a system consists of the action rules that constitute the performance function of the corresponding prisma. They reside in the processor that is the kernel of the prisma. The abstraction that is achieved through the notions of activating, restricting, and impeding makes the prismanet ontologically comprehensive. That is why it is called the *essential model* of the system.

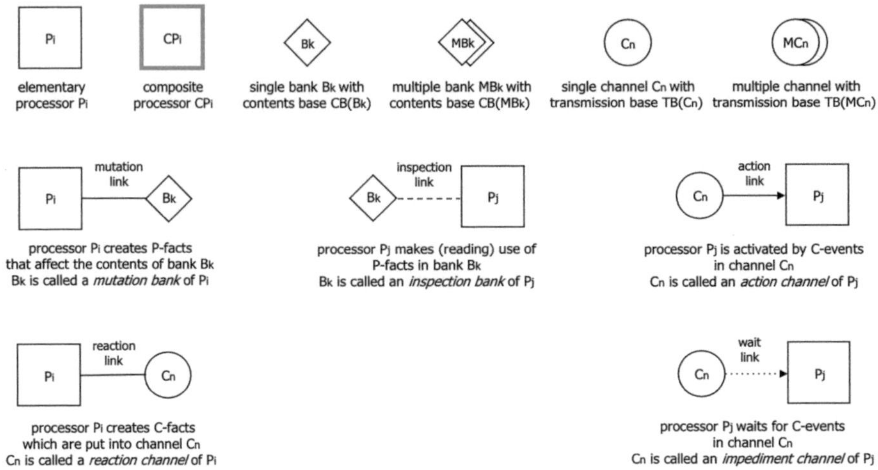

Fig. 4.12 Legend of the prismanet diagram

4.4.6 The OMEGA Theory

The OMEGA theory or EE organisational construction theory (OMEGA stands for *Organisational Modules Emerging from General Arrangements*) clarifies the coordination structures in which transactor roles are connected. Three basic structures are distinguished: interaction, interstriction, and interimpediment.

The *interaction structure* determines for every transactor role in the organisation which transactor roles are initiator in transactions of the corresponding transaction kind. It appears that the interaction structure of an organisation is always a set of tree structures. Consequently, the transaction kinds at any level of such a tree structure are enclosed in another transaction kind (except the 'root' of the tree) and do have enclosed transaction kinds (except the 'leaves' of the tree). The interaction structure is the inherent fundamental structure of business processes (which are commonly envisioned as flows, i.e. as sequences of events). In addition, it clarifies the responsibility ranges of actors in business processes, and thus notions like process ownership and data ownership.

The *interstriction structure* determines which transactor roles may inspect the history of the transactions of other transaction kinds. These other transaction kinds may be external to the organisation (or Scope of Interest). Actors do inspect the history of transaction processes because they need to take process facts into account when deciding on acts to perform. In this way, actors restrict each other's decision freedom.

The *interimpediment structure* determines whether actors in some actor role have to wait with performing specific acts until other transaction processes have reached a specific state. All three organisational structures are expressed in the *Coordination Structure Diagram* (CSD), of which Fig. 4.13 exhibits the legend. Figure 4.14

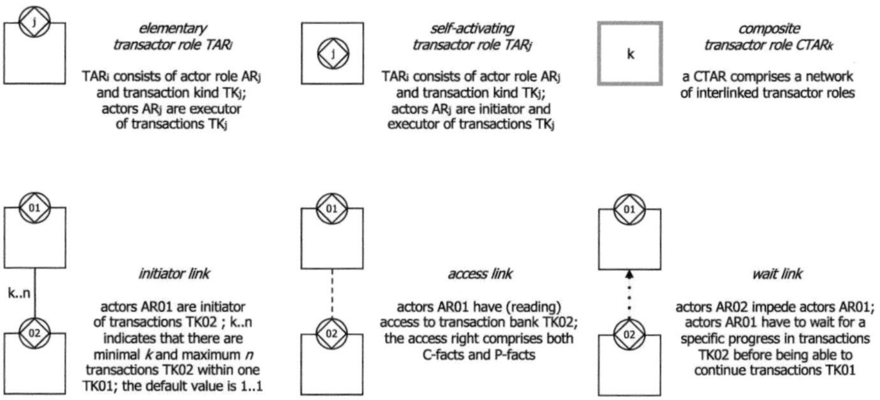

Fig. 4.13 Legend of the coordination structure diagram

illustrates them, using the GloLog case (cf. Chap. 19) as an example enterprise. The red colour of the diamonds indicates that the transactor roles belong to the O-organisation of the modelled enterprise (cf. Section 4.4.7). There are four interaction trees, also called *business processes*. The top of the left one is a composite transactor role. The initiator link with TAR01 expresses that it contains a (unknown) transactor role that initiates transactions TK01. The top of the other three structures is a self-activating transactor role. The light-grey colour of some boxes indicates that they belong to the environment of the focus within the Scope of Interest. Each of the four processes has its own case kind: client order, supply order, ship content, and container content, respectively. The evoked structural clashes [20] between them are resolved by the wait links. In addition, there are several inspection links. Figure 4.14 clearly shows the added value of product (tree) thinking in addition to flow thinking. There cannot be one 'seamless' process flow in GloLog. Instead, there are four autonomous processes, with their own process cycle, determined by their case kind. As alluded to in Sect. 4.4.5, no additional knowledge is needed to get a complete (ontological) understanding of the organisation, i.e. of the collective business processes, provided that the action rules for the transactor roles are also known. Therefore, this model is called the *essential model*.

There is a second kind of general arrangements that comes in addition to the ones above. It appears that every organisational structure is composed of a limited number of *reference patterns*, which often resemble legal patterns of action, like the transfer of property and the granting/obtaining of usufructuary rights.

4.4.7 The ALPHA Theory

The ALPHA theory or EE organisational essence theory (ALPHA stands for *Abstraction Layers in Production for Holistic Analysis*) is a theory about layers of transactor

19

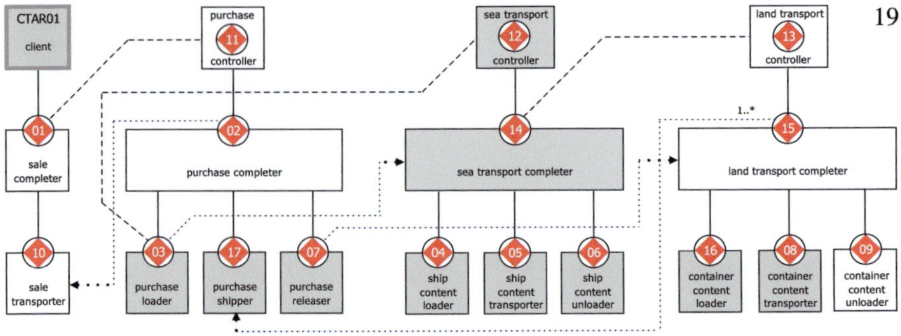

Fig. 4.14 CSD of the GloLog enterprise

roles that come in addition to the compositional trees from the OMEGA theory (cf. Section 4.4.6). These tree structures occur in four transactor layers, which are based on the distinction of four sorts of production acts: original, informational, documental, and material.

Original production acts bring about original production facts. Examples are devising, deciding, and judging (all of them dealing with intangible things), as well as manufacturing, transporting, and observing (all of them dealing with tangible things).

Informational production acts comprise remembering facts (in the state of the production or coordination world of an organisation), recalling (remembered) facts, and computing or deriving facts. Computing does not change the state of a world, it only leads to presenting the state in new, possibly more intelligible ways.

Documental production acts concern the signs (or data) that contain facts. They comprise saving, providing, and transforming (documents or datasets).

Material production acts concern the physical carriers of signs, commonly called files. They comprise storing, retrieving, copying, transmitting, and destroying (files).

Because original acts are the only acts that change the state of the production world of an organisation, they need to be performed by authorised and responsible actors, thus subjects in actor roles. Informational, documental, and material acts may be taken over by artefacts, notably ICT systems. However, as pointed out in Sect. 4.4.4, human actors are ultimately responsible and accountable.

Corresponding with the distinct sorts of production, the actors in an organisation can be partitioned in four layers: the *O-organisation* (O from original), the *I-organisation* (I from informational), the *D-organisation* (D from documental), and the *M-organisation* (M from material). The I-organisation supports the O-organisation by means of informational services (remembering and sharing facts), the D-organisation supports the I-organisation by means of documental services (saving and providing documents), and the M-organisation supports the D-organisation by means of material services (storing and retrieving files).

By the *realisation* of an organisation is understood the devising of the I-, the D-, and the M-organisation, given its O-organisation (cf. Figure 4.15). Conversely,

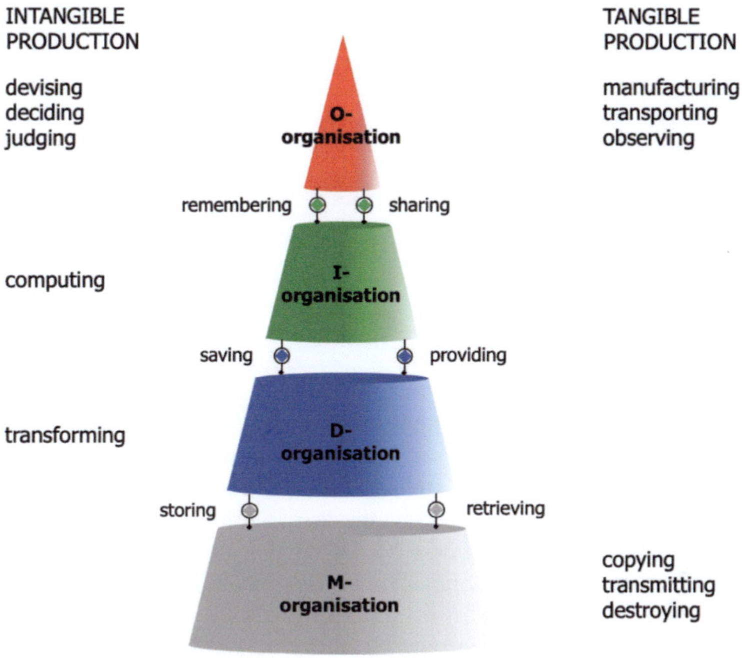

Fig. 4.15 Four aspect organisations

abstracting from realisation yields the O-organisation of an enterprise. The additional abstracting from implementation yields the ontological model of the O-organisation, also called the *essential model* of the (total) enterprise (cf. Section 4.4.5).

The 'pie chart' in Fig. 4.16 illustrates the correspondence between tangible production in the O-organisation and material production in the M-organisation. The adjacency of tangible original production and material production expresses that the sort of an act/fact may depend on the point of view taken: sending a letter by postal mail is a material documental act for the sender. Postal mail companies may consider the distinction between original and material production less interesting. Their business is to transport packages, including envelops, without much regard to their contents.

4.4.8 The BETA Theory

The BETA theory or EE design theory (BETA stands for *Building from Essence with Technology and Architecture*), is a theory about designing artefacts. Where the ALPHA theory tells one how to abstract from the concrete appearance of a system (realisation and implementation), the BETA theory guides one in designing a system

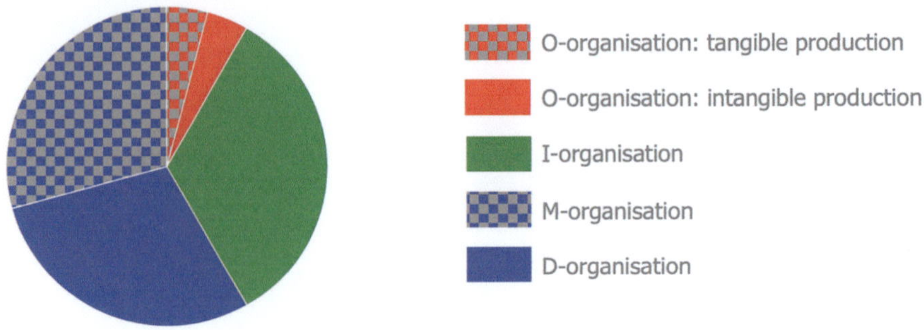

Fig. 4.16 Aspect organisations and sorts of production

and in making it concrete. First, Simon's notion of *design* [21] is discussed, understood as devising a situation that is considered preferable to the current situation, as well as Alexander's notion of *design process* [22], understood as a sequence of alternate analysis (of the problem) and synthesis (of a solution) steps. In Fig. 4.17, the *General System Development Process* (GSDP) is introduced. It is a general framework for understanding the development of an *object system* for the benefit of a *using system.*

With reference to the TAO theory (cf. Section 4.4.3), a clear and sharp distinction is made between the function and the construction of the object system, as well as between the function and the construction of the using system, thereby clarifying that the function of the object system supports the construction of the using system.

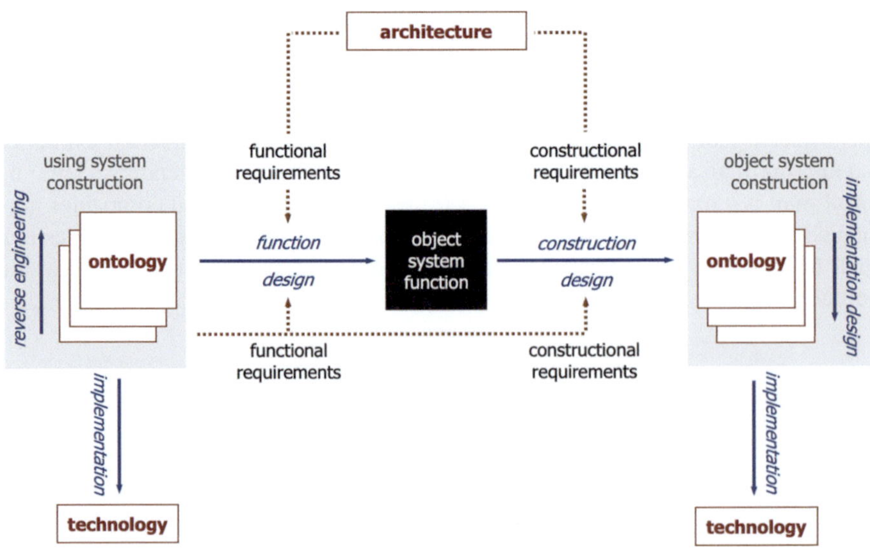

Fig. 4.17 General system development process

The three main phases in a development process are function design, construction design, and implementation design. *Function design* starts from the ontological model of the using system, which is commonly arrived at by reverse engineering (cf. Section 4.4.7), and ends with the specification of the object system function. There are two inputs: *functional requirements* determined by the using system construction and *functional requirements* determined by the applicable architecture. *Construction design* starts from the object system function, and ends with the ontological model of the object system. There are two inputs: *constructional requirements* determined by the using system construction and *constructional requirements* determined by the applicable architecture. *Implementation design* (also called *engineering*) starts from the ontology of the object system and ends with the fully detailed specification of a possible implementation, which can subsequently be implemented with appropriate technology. The inputs are the two kinds of constructional requirements.

A general problem in system development is the (too) large amount of design freedom that is left when all requirements are satisfied. Since time immemorial, the notion of *architecture* helps designers to use this freedom in a purposeful and systematic way. To exemplify this, the Metropolitan Opera in New York, the Sydney Opera House, and the Scala in Milan have the same basic function, namely to offer the facilities that are needed to perform operas. Yet, their appearances are very different. One only has to look at the photos of the respective buildings to see it. Thus, whereas the functional requirements for each of the opera houses are (for the largest part) the same, the applied architectures are quite different.

The *General Requirements and Architecture Framework* (GRAF) is introduced for expressing architecture in practicable design and implementation *principles*, which are basically understood as *generic requirements* that constrain system development in addition to the specific requirements.

4.4.9 The ETA Theory

The ETA theory or EE implementation theory (ETA stands for Engineering with Technology under Architecture), is a theory about the implementation of organisations. The word "engineering" is used here in its narrow sense: it is equal to implementation design. As expressed in Fig. 4.18, the ETA theory covers both the implementation design and the implementation itself, as defined in the BETA theory: it guides the enterprise engineer in establishing the implementation model, as well as in finding, justifying, and assigning technological alternatives for the actual implementation. The theory includes installation and operation, as the subsequent phases after implementation. The starting point is what has been stated already by the PSI theory: there are three technologies needed to implement an organisation: actor technology, production technology, and coordination technology.

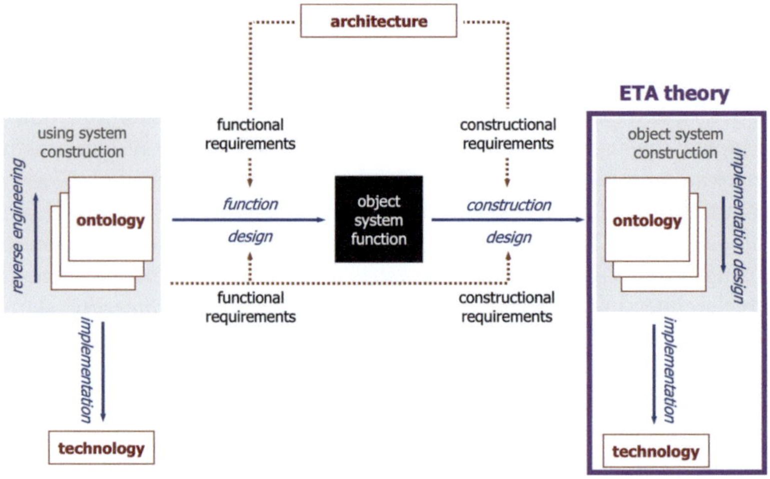

Fig. 4.18 Place of the ETA theory in the GSDP framework

4.4.10 The NU Theory

The NU theory or EE automation theory (NU stands for *Normalised Units*), is a theory about the construction of systems. It is complementary to the DELTA theory (cf. Section 4.4.5). Applying the NU theory in the development (cf. Section 4.4.8) of a system, results in a modular structure of the system that prevents unwanted side effects when the system undergoes changes. Figure 4.19 shows the part of the GSDP (cf. Figure 4.17) that is covered by the NU theory.

The EE automation theory (or NU theory) is a theory about the implementation design of organisations where ICT is the implementation technology. Its main contribution to software engineering or, more precisely, to enterprise information systems engineering, is the elaboration of the distinction between the information-centric and the communication-centric way of producing software, as proposed by the CIAO paradigm in Sect. 4.2. The traditional way of developing enterprise information systems is information-centric. It is characterised by having no suitable and accurate understanding of the supported organisation, and by eliciting system requirements through interviewing future users and other stakeholders. In addition, developed software systems are prone to deterioration in the long run, as convincingly brought to the floor by Lehman [23]. One of the current approaches to remedy this drawback is normalised systems [24].

Enterprise Engineering embraces the communication-centric point of view, by which the drawbacks of the traditional way of software engineering vanish. Three kinds of 'normalised units' are distinguished: transaction process steps (the organisational *atoms*), transactor roles (the organisational *molecules*), and business process kinds (the organisational *fibres*). Organisational models that are based on the communication-centric point of view can rather straightforwardly be automated and

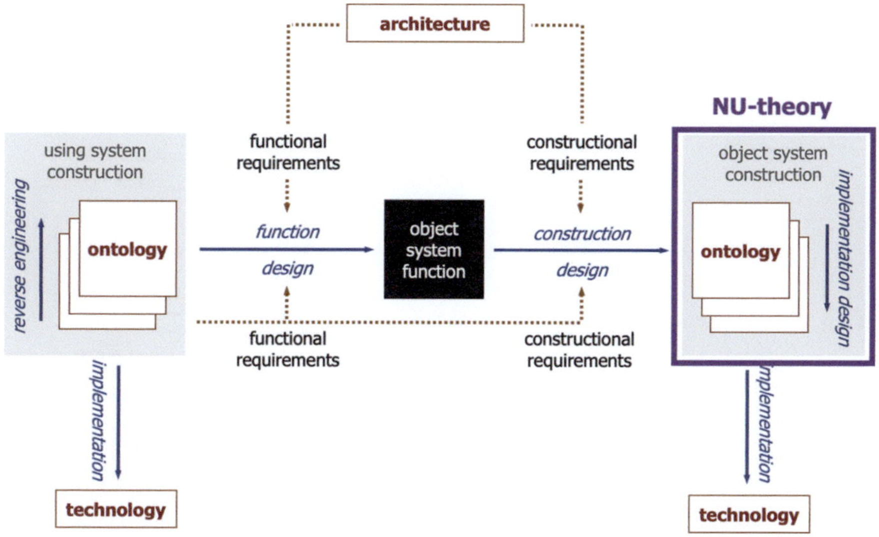

Fig. 4.19 Place of the NU theory in the GSDP framework

changed, without the drawbacks of the traditional way of software engineering. There are no combinatorial effects or other unwanted side effects.

4.4.11 The KAPPA Theory

The KAPPA theory or EE assignment theory (KAPPA stands for Competence-based Assignment of Professional Persons to Actor roles) is a theory about the assignment of actor roles to individual employees, based on the competences that are needed to fill the actor roles. The basic notions, both on the demand side and on the supply side of the labour market, are formally defined. The needed competence of an actor role is connected to the authority and the responsibility that role fillers are assumed to exert, as elaborated already by the PSI theory (cf. Section 4.4.4). It is complementary to the DELTA theory (cf. Section 4.4.5). Figure 4.20 shows the part of the GSDP (cf. Figure 4.17) that is covered by the KAPPA theory.

In the KAPPA theory the demand side and the supply side of the labour market are analysed and made more concrete, so that they can be matched on a scientific basis.

The advertisement of an actor role consists of three parts: authority, responsibility, and competence. The authority part is a list of authority elements. Examples of authority elements for ‘rental completer’ (AR01) in the Rent-A-Car enterprise (cf. [8] Chap. 15) are: promising a rental contract (TK01/pm), declaring a rental contract (TK01/da), and requesting the payment of the deposit of the rental (TK04/rq). The responsibility part in an advertisement would be a list of responsibility elements that

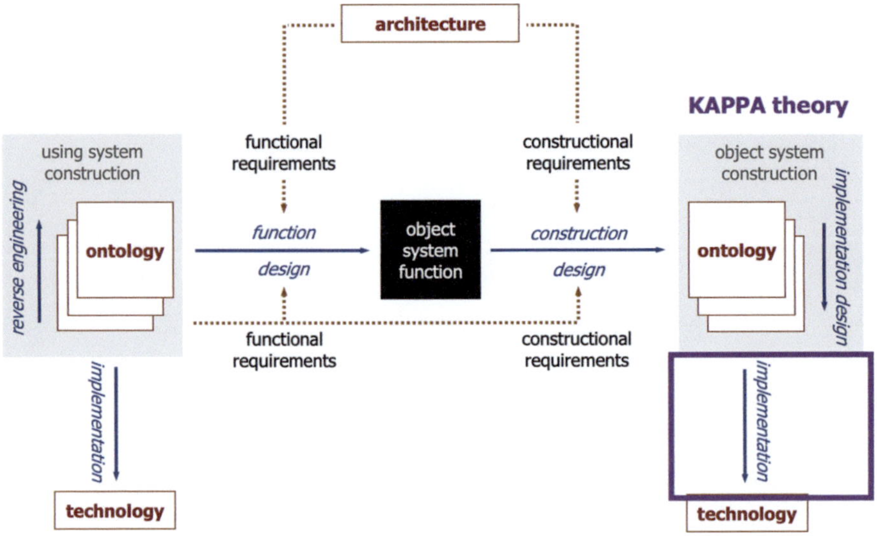

Fig. 4.20 Place of the KAPPA theory in the GSDP framework

looks similar to the list of authority elements, because authority and responsibility are the two sides of the same coin. Therefore, this list is left out. It is wise, however, to mention the autonomy of actor role fillers. The *competence* part of the advertisement is a list of competence elements, so both behaviour elements and knowledge elements. Regarding the example actor role of rental completer in the case Rent-A-Car, the behaviour part may be the most important one for the HR employee who is dealing with the vacancy. Examples of behaviour elements are social intelligence and logical intelligence at a certain level.

4.4.12 The SIGMA Theory

The SIGMA theory or EE governance & management theory (SIGMA stands for *Socially Inspired Governance and Management Approach*), is an ideological theory about how enterprises should be managed and governed in such a way that the people in the enterprise are maximally empowered. Traditional thinking about enterprises considers (executive) management the primary and exclusive custodians of enterprise performance. Employees, under management control, must behave instrumentally as parts of the enterprise machine. There is no employee variability: standard, predefined instrumental behaviour is required and expected. The SIGMA theory submits a fundamentally different perspective by arguing that variability in employee behaviour is crucial for operational and strategic performance. In our view, the instrumental approach to employee behaviour conflicts with moral and ethical considerations concerning employees and society at large. Current economic thinking, in which enterprises are merely seen as money-generating machines, reinforces the instrumental view on employees. It is argued that employee variability is an absolute prerequisite for aligning employee interests with enterprise performance interests. This unitarist perspective rejects any supposedly 'natural' opposition between them. The SIGMA theory is made operational through the notion of meaningful work, which is seen as an affordance (cf. Section 4.4.3): a relationship between employees with certain subjective needs and enterprises with certain objective properties of the work environment. The nature of these needs and properties is elucidated, clarifying at the same time that the theory is firmly grounded in the organisational sciences. The employee-centric nature of this theory aims to counteract the narrow economic theories advanced by many business schools. The discussion of these current ways of thinking reveals the fundamentally different perspective on enterprises that the SIGMA theory radiates.

4.4.13 The GAMMA Theory

The GAMMA theory or EE delegation theory (GAMMA stands for *General Automata and Machines Mastering Approach*), is an ideological theory about the delegation of (part of the) authority by an authorised filler of an actor role to somebody else. More specifically, the GAMMA theory discusses the delegation of authority to technological artefacts, thus automata and machines. It assembles the scattered pieces of text in [8] about the position of artefacts in EE. Although the distinction between responsible human beings (social individuals) and supporting artefacts is rather straightforward and clear, it seems still to be worthwhile to stress it, particularly in view of the latest kind of artefacts, AI systems. Artificial intelligence products appear to confuse people. Yet AI is what it is: artificial intelligence, nothing less and nothing more.

The GAMMA theory is classified as an ideological theory because in the end, it is up to the people, in enterprises, and in society at large, whether they consider ICT systems, notably AI systems, to be social individuals or not. Our position is clear, we just like to warn people.

4.4.14 The CHI Theory

The CHI theory or EE transaction cost theory (CHI stands for *Cost of Human Interactions*), is an ontological theory about the costs of transactions. It may be useful when one wants to insource or outsource a transaction. Bering based on the economic transaction cost theory, as for example developed by Williamson [25], specific emphasis is put on the loss of competence (cf. Chap. 5) when the decision is considered to outsource a transaction kind.

References

1. Dietz, J. L. G., & J.A.P. Hoogervorst, J. A. P. (2013). The discipline of enterprise engineering. *International Journal of Organisational Design and Engineering, 3*, 28.
2. Austin, J. L. (1962). *How to do things with words.* Harvard University Press.
3. Searle, J. R. (1969). *Speech acts: An essay in the philosophy of language* (Vol. vii, p. 203). Cambridge University Press.
4. Habermas, J. (1986). *The theory of communicative action.* Polity Press.
5. Weigand, H. (2006). Two decades of the language-action perspective. *Communications of the ACM, 49*(4).
6. Searle, J. R. (1995). *The construction of social reality* (Vol. xiii, p. 241). Free Press.
7. Dietz, J. L. G. (2012). *Red garden gnomes don't exist.* Sapio Enterprise Engineering.
8. Dietz, J. L. G., & Mulder, H. B. F. (2024). *Enterprise ontology: A human-centric approach to understanding the essence of organisation* (2nd ed., p. 475). The Enterprise Engineering Series. Springer Nature.
9. Mintzberg, H. (1979). *The structuring of organizations: A synthesis of the research.* (Vol. xvi, p. 512). Theory of Management Policy. 1979, Prentice-Hall International.
10. Weber, M. (1990). Legitimate authority and bureaucracy. In D. S. Pugh (Ed.), *Organization theory.* Penguin Books.
11. Weick, K. E. (2001). *Making sense of the organization* (Vol. xii, p. 483). Blackwell Publishers.
12. Laloux, F. (2014). *Reinventing organizations: A guide to creating organizations inspired by the next stage of human consciousness* (1st ed., Vol. xviii, p. 360).
13. Dietz, J. L. G., & Mulder, H. B. F. (2025). *Enterprise design fundamentals: Settling an enterprise business and devising the enterprise organisation.* (Vol. 1, p. 357). The Enterprise Engineering Series. Springer Nature.
14. Ogden, C. K., et al. (1923). The meaning of meaning: A study of the influence of language upon thought and of the science of symbolism. In International library of psychology, philosophy, and scientific method (Vol. xxxi, p. 544). K. Paul, Trench, Trubner & Co. Harcourt, Brace & Company, Inc.
15. Stamper, R. K. (1973). *Information in business and administrative systems* (Vol. 6, p. 362). Batsford.
16. Apostel, L. (1960). Towards the formal study of models in the non-formal sciences. *Synthese, 12.*
17. Gibson, J. J. (1979). *The ecological approach to visual perception* (Vol. xv, p. 332). Houghton Mifflin.
18. Weinberg, G. M. (1975). *An introduction to general systems thinking* (Vol. xxi, p. 279). Wiley Series on Systems Engineering and Analysis. Wiley.
19. Bunge, M. (1979). Treatise on basic philosophy ontology II: A world of systems. In *Treatise on basic philosophy* (Vol. 4). Reidel.
20. Jackson, M. A. (1975). *Principles of program design* (Vol. xii, p. 299). APIC Studies in Data Processing. Academic Press.
21. Simon, H. A. (1969). *The sciences of the artificial* (Vol. xii, p. 123). Karl Taylor Compton Lectures. M.I.T. Press.
22. Alexander, C. (1964). *Notes on the synthesis of form* (p. 216). Harvard University Press.
23. Lehman, M. M., & Belady, L. A. (1985). *Program evolution: Processes of software change* (Vol. xiii, p. 538). APIC Studies in Data Processing. Academic Press.
24. Mannaert, H., Verelst, J., & Bruyn, P. D. (2016). *Normalized systems: From foundations for evolvable software toward a general theory for evolvabler design.* Koppa.
25. Williamson, O. E. (2013). *The transaction cost economics project: The theory and practice of the governance of contractual relations* (Vol. xxiv, p. 417).

Chapter 5
The EE Assignment Theory

Abstract The EE assignment theory or KAPPA theory is a theory about the assignment of actor roles to individual employees. It is based on the competences that are needed to fill the actor roles. The basic notions, both on the demand side and on the supply side of the labour market, are formally defined. The needed competence of an actor role is connected to the authority and the responsibility that role fillers are assumed to exert, as elaborated in the PSI theory (Performing in Social Interaction).

5.1 Introduction

The EE assignment theory is also labelled K-theory. The Greek letter is pronounced as KAPPA, which is an acronym for Competence-based Assignment of Professional Persons to Actor roles (Note The Greek alphabet has no letter "c"; therefore we use the letter "k" as the first letter of "competence"). It is a theory about the assignment of actor roles to individual employees. The KAPPA theory only covers the implementation phase in the GSDP, as shown in Fig. 5.1. This means that it can be applied also in cases where there is no talk of redesign, like hiring people, or when otherwise actor roles are assigned to employees. So, compared to the ETA theory (cf. [1] Chap. 10), the KAPPA theory only concerns the actor technology, notably the Actor role Position Table or APT.

In Sect. 4.3, notably in Fig. 4.5, the KAPPA theory is classified as a technological theory. Technological theories can be predicated as rigorous and relevant. So, this is the way the KAPPA theory must be evaluated: is it rigorous and relevant? Does it help to assign human individuals to actor roles?

In [2] Sect. 8.3.3 the notion of *competence* is presented, in relationship to the notions of authority and responsibility. The unit of authority and responsibility is the actor role: the being executor in transactions of a certain kind. Assigning individuals to actor roles is based on the competences they appear to have to perform the production acts in transactions of the kind as well as the associated coordination acts. The most distinguishing characteristic of an actor role is the product kind in the transaction kind of which the role is executor. The competences that one acquires through

J. L.G. Dietz and H. B. F. Mulder, *Enterprise Governance and Management*, The Enterprise Engineering Series, https://doi.org/10.1007/978-3-032-24318-8_5

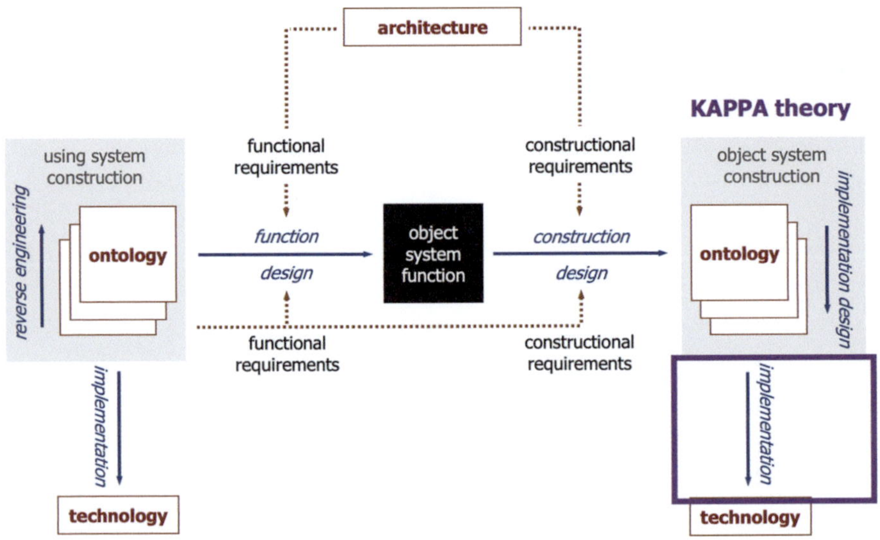

Fig. 5.1 KAPPA theory in the GSDP framework

education and experience are directed to the products that one will bring about. Commonly, competences are collected in professions. Examples of professions are baker, gynaecologist, and plumber.

Concerning coordination acts, the general idea is that in an educational programme or training course, one also learns how to collaborate with other people. Among other things, one learns to use one's autonomy to deal with exceptions. One may decline a request instead of promising, and one may later revoke the decline (and perform the promise act) when the reason for declining has been eliminated. Likewise, one may reject a declaration instead of accepting it, and one may later revoke the reject (and perform the accept act). In addition, one monitors the execution of transactions one has initiated and interferes if and when one feels the need to do so.

The remainder of this chapter is organised as follows. In Sect. 5.2 we lay the foundations of the KAPPA theory, thus the basic ideas we have in mind and consider valuable in order to discuss the assignment of actor roles to human individuals. The findings of Sect. 5.2 are elaborated in Sect. 5.3, such that the consequences of applying the KAPPA theory become lucid and convincing. Section 5.4 completes the chapter with a few conclusions.

5.2 Foundations

5.2.1 *Demand Side Concepts*

On the demand side of the labour market are the enterprises that have a need to hire people for the work that has to be done. In order to make this work more graspable, we start by defining the notion of *activity* and the notion of *mantle*. By the latter we mean such a distinction as between executing, managing, advising, and teaching. The concept of activity is specific for a professional field. For the profession of plumber one may distinguish leak diagnosing, leak repairing, faucet mounting, etc. For other professions these activities are generally different. Let us introduce the concept of *work element* and define it as the Cartesian product of activity and mantle; thus we consider pairs where one element is an activity and the other element is a mantle. We express this definition in GOSL (cf. [2] Chap. 6). The result is shown in Fig. 5.2.

Examples of work elements are thus 'executing leak repairing' and 'teaching faucet mounting'. Next, we add an additional concept, namely the *complexity degree* of a work element. It is expressed in values on an Ordinal Scale (cf. [1] Chap. 6), for example, the scale {high, average, low}. The aggregation of work element and complexity degree is called *performance element*. Its graphical definition is shown in Fig. 5.3. Examples of performance elements are 'executing leak repairing at a high level' and 'advising on leak repairing at an average level'.

Usually the demand side of the labour market wraps what it asks for in *functions*. By reading the description of an offered function, the job-seeker gets a global idea of what an enterprise is looking for. Examples of functions are Java programmer,

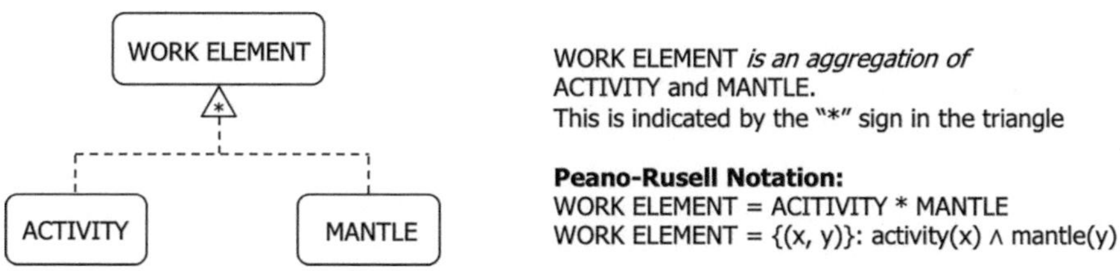

Fig. 5.2 Graphical definition of WORK ELEMENT

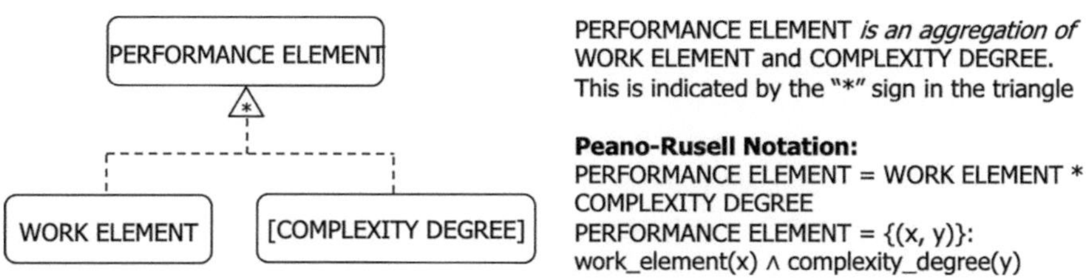

Fig. 5.3 Graphical definition of PERFORMANCE ELEMENT

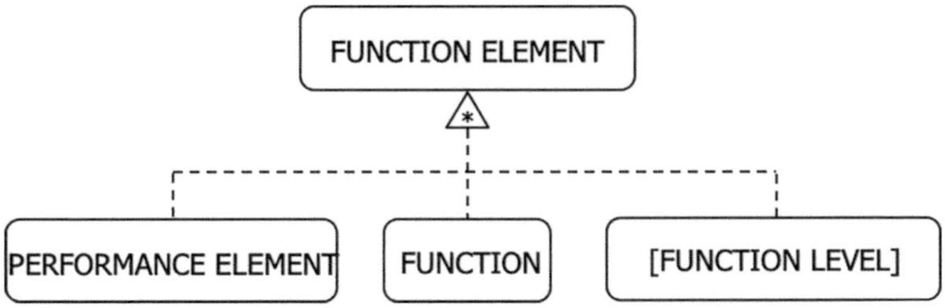

Fig. 5.4 Graphical definition of FUNCTION ELEMENT

salesperson, and purchaser. Usually, a *function level* is added in an advertisement. Function levels are values on an Ordinal Scale, for example, junior, senior, and expert.

We combine function, function level, and performance element into the aggregate concept of *function element*. Its graphical definition is exhibited in Fig. 5.4.[1] By advertising the function elements, one can more precisely specify what one is looking for. As an example, an enterprise may advertise these function elements: executing leak repairing at senior level, executing leak repairing at expert level, and advising faucet mounting at senior level.

5.2.2 *Supply Side Concepts*

In this sub section we will have a look at the concepts that seem to be useful on the supply side of the market. Thus the concepts that a job-seeker needs in order to specify her/his competences. The challenge is to devise concepts that help the job-seeker to clarify her/his competences in a better way than is commonly done. We start by looking at the concept of *intelligence*. Unlike in the old days, and thanks to the work of Howard Gardner [3], one nowadays distinguishes eight modalities of intelligence, namely kinaesthetic, social, linguistic, logical-mathematical, naturalistic, intrapersonal, spatial, and musical. Whether one possesses an intelligence and in which degree, is primarily a matter of heritability. When we add the concept of *intelligence level*, we can define the concept *behaviour element* as the aggregation of intelligence and intelligence level. In GOSL, the definition looks like what is exhibited in Fig. 5.5.

Examples of behaviour elements are possessing social intelligence at an average level, possessing kinaesthetic intelligence at a high level, and possessing musical intelligence at a low level. Next we introduce the concept of *knowledge kind*. Knowledge is something one can acquire through education, given one possesses the needed intelligences at the requested levels. We distinguish two knowledge kinds: basic knowledge and up-to-date knowledge. Basic knowledge is the kind of knowledge

[1] The reader is invited to produce herself/himself the corresponding Peano-Russell notation of the aggregation.

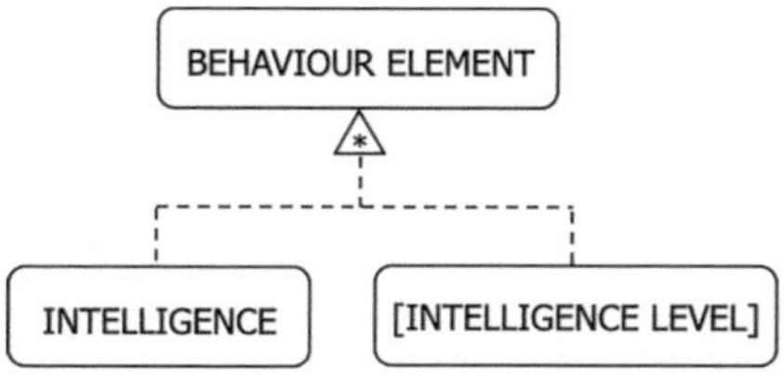

BEHAVIOUR ELEMENT *is an aggregation of* INTELLIGENCE and INTELLIGENCE LEVEL. This is indicated by the "*" sign in the triangle

Peano-Rusell Notation:
BEHAVIOUR ELEMENT = INTELLIGENCE * INTELLIGENCE LEVEL
BEHAVIOUR ELEMENT = {(x, y)}: intelligence(x) ∧ intelligence_level(y)

Fig. 5.5 Graphical definition of BEHAVIOUR ELEMENT

one usually acquires through (general or professional) education. Up-to-date knowledge is the kind of knowledge one acquires through reading professional literature and taking courses or workshops. It is also a side effect of experience, thus of practising a profession. Let us distinguish between these *knowledge levels*: low, average, high (like the other levels or degrees, these are values on an Ordinal Scale). We then are able to define the concept of *knowledge element* as the aggregation of knowledge kind, knowledge level, and work element (cf. Figure 5.6).

Behaviour elements and knowledge elements together constitute *competence elements*. The definition of the latter therefore is the generalisation of behaviour element and knowledge element. Graphically, it looks like what is exhibited in Fig. 5.7 expressed again in GOSL.

With the concept of competence element we have the key to match demand and supply. There is no need to go further on the supply side and to define, for example, the concept of profession. An enterprise that has established Enterprise Ontology and

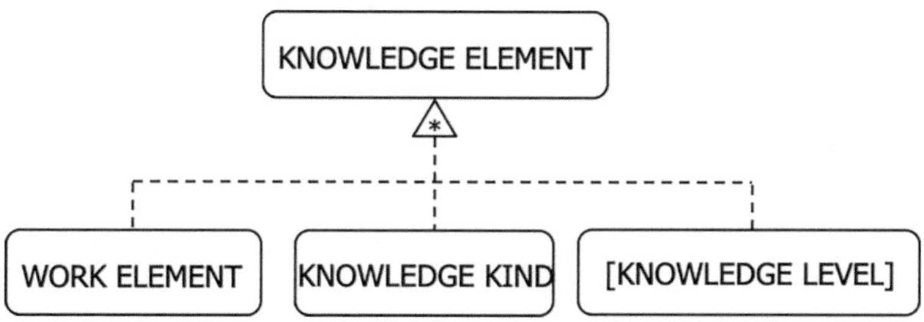

Fig. 5.6 Graphical definition of KNOWLEDGE ELEMENT

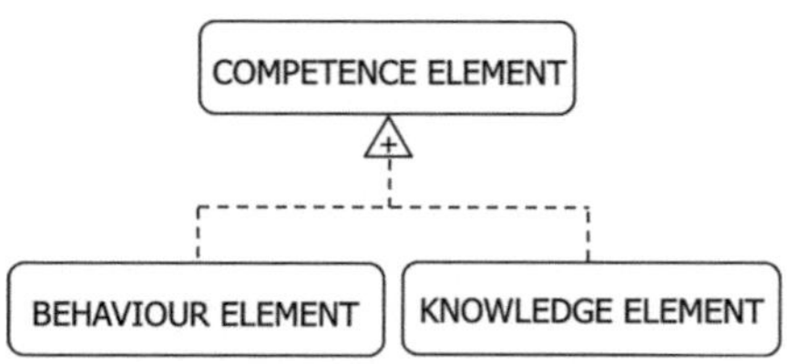

COMPETENCE ELEMENT *is the generalisation of* BEHAVIOUR ELEMENT and KNOWLEDGE ELEMENT. This is indicated by the "+" sign in the triangle

Peano-Rusell Notation:
COMPETENCE ELEMENT = BEHAVIOUR ELEMENT ∪ INTELLIGENCE LEVEL
∀x: competence_element(x) ⇒ behaviour_element(x) ∨ knowledge_element(x)

Fig. 5.7 Graphical definition of COMPETENCE ELEMENT

thus has determined actor roles, is able now to match candidates and actor roles on the basis of the competence elements that a candidate has to offer and the competence elements that are needed by the actor role that the candidate applies for. We will elaborate this in the next section.

5.3 Elaborations

Following up the conceptual framework that we have developed in Sect. 5.2, the competence that is associated with an actor role can now simply be defined as a set of competence elements, so of behaviour elements and knowledge elements. If the HR department of an enterprise has the need to hire new employees, this can be done by advertising the actor role(s) for which one seeks new fillers. The advertisement for an actor role consists of three parts: authority, responsibility, and competence.

The *authority* part is a list of authority elements. Examples of authority elements for 'rental completer' (AR01) in the Rent-A-Car enterprise (cf. [2] Chap. 15) are: promising a rental contract (TK01/pm), declaring a rental contract (TK01/da), and requesting the payment of the deposit of the rental (TK04/rq). In addition, one could mention that a rental completer has access to two information sources: the personal facts regarding the renter (or client) and the general facts of Rent-A-Car concerning the renting of cars, like the car kinds that are offered and the rental prices. The personal facts of a renter may already be available (if he/she has rented a car before) or they are entered by the rental completer to the collection 'persons facts'.

The *responsibility* part in the advertisement is a list of responsibility elements. As said in [2] Chap. 8, responsibility is generally understood as the exerting of assigned authority in the best possible way. Consequently authority and responsibility may be considered as the two sides of a coin: none of them can exist without the other. It may be wise to mention this general idea in the advertisement, as it may also be wise to mention the *autonomy* of the actor role filler, so the right (which in practice becomes an obligation!) to deviate from the current business rule (action rule) if the circumstances ask for it, for example, in case the rental completer has the strong suspicion that the renter is not going to pay the deposit.

Thus, it seems to make little sense to mention a list of responsibilities because this list would be similar to the already mentioned list of authorities. It does make sense, however, to state in the advertisement that one is held accountable for the way in which one exerts the assigned authority. This means that the rental completer may be asked by the head of the front office to provide justifications of a deviation from the existing business rule(s). The head of the front office is a managing actor role, thus an actor role of which the mantle of the main work element is 'managing' instead of 'executing' (cf. Figure 5.2).

The *competence* part of the advertisement is a list of competence elements, as discussed in Sect. 5.2, so both behaviour elements and knowledge elements. Regarding the example actor role of rental completer, the behaviour part may be the most important one for the HR employee who is dealing with the vacancy.

5.4 Conclusions

In this chapter we have tried to make the notion of actor role graspable for people who have to decide on the employment of persons in an enterprise. The presented KAPPA theory presupposes the establishment of actor roles in the enterprise, which may be a main obstacle for applying the theory.

Next to hiring new employees for actor roles, the theory also applies of course to the assignment of an actor role to already hired employees in order to increase the capacity of an actor role, that is the number of persons filling the actor role. To make this concrete, if there are many clients of Rent-A-Car who want to rent a car, the front desk manager may assign the role of 'rental completer' (AR01) to extra employees. As for the use of ICT artefacts to solve the capacity problem, we have discussed this issue in [2].

References

1. Dietz, J. L. G., & Mulder, H. B. F. (2025). *Enterprise design fundamentals: Settling an enterprise business and devising the enterprise organisation* (Vol. 1, p. 357). The Enterprise Engineering Series. Springer Nature.
2. Dietz, J. L. G., & Mulder, J. B. F. (2024). *Enterprise ontology: A human-centric approach to understanding the essence of organisation* (2nd ed.). Enterprise Engineering. Springer Nature.
3. Cavas, B., & Cavas, P. (2020). Multiple intelligences theory—Howard Gardner. In B. Akpan & T. J. Kennedy (Eds.), *Science education in theory and practice: An introductory guide to learning theory* (pp. 405–418). Springer International Publishing.

Chapter 6
The EE Delegation Theory

Abstract According to the PSI theory, delegation is the transfer of authority, and the corresponding responsibility, by some actor to another employee. In most cases, delegation regards only a subset of the steps in the complete transaction pattern. In current practice, and contrary to the PSI theory, delegation is considered to be the transfer of authority to ICT artefacts. The negation of the most important role of human beings in enterprises and in society as a whole, leads to poignant cases.

6.1 Introduction

The EE delegation theory is also labelled Γ-theory. The Greek capital letter is pronounced as GAMMA, which is an acronym for General Automata and Machines Mastering Approach. The word "mastering" should be taken here as "understanding", "grasping". The GAMMA theory is about how one should view the role of automata and machines in organisations. Although we thought initially that it would be an ontological theory, we have in the end classified it as ideological (cf. Figure 4.5) for reasons to become evident later. Ideological theories cannot be predicated as truthful (like philosophical theories) or as sound and appropriate (like ontological theories), nor as rigorous and relevant (like technological theories). They can only be predicated as *significant*. The significance of an ideological theory boils down to the usefulness that its supporters assign to the theory.

In [1] Chap. 8, we briefly discussed the delegation of actor roles, thus of authority and responsibility. Fully in line with the CIAO paradigm (cf. Sect. 4.2), we stated that human actors may use as many technological artefacts, notably ICT artefacts, as they deem appropriate, but that there is always a human actor responsible for what these artefacts bring about. In the meantime, the use of these artefacts has grown enormously. Specifically AI (Artificial Intelligence) artefacts are currently conquering the world. At the same time, a growing number of people sincerely think that these systems are taking over human decisions, because they are better equipped to decide (?). We warned already in 2020 for this serious flaw when discussing the chess game between Gary Kasparov and Deep Blue (cf. [1] Chap. 11). Despite

J. L.G. Dietz and H. B. F. Mulder, *Enterprise Governance and Management*, The Enterprise Engineering Series, https://doi.org/10.1007/978-3-032-24318-8_6

various attempts to resist the idea that ICT artefacts or other machines are taking over human decisions, like the one by Shakha Mirza in [1] Sect. 19.10, there is a growing conviction among modern professionals that artefacts, notably AI systems, are rightly taking over human decisions. We think that this growing misunderstanding among people of the role of technology in our modern societies is worth devoting a separate theory to the subject, namely the current EE delegation theory.

The remainder of this chapter is organised as usual. In Sect. 6.2 (Foundations), the basic concepts are presented and discussed that underlie the EE delegation theory. In Sect. 6.3 (Elaborations) these foundations are elaborated. Section 6.4 (Discussions) concludes the chapter.

6.2 Foundations

A growing number of people seem to have no problem with accepting non-human beings, especially AI-artefacts, as full-fledged social individuals. As an example, we mentioned in [1] Sect. 11.3.4.3 the decision by the government of Saudi Arabia to declare the robot Sophia to be a full-fledged citizen. More recently, the prime minister of Albania has appointed the AI-bot Diella to be the minister of Tenders. The idea is that in this way the government can fight effectively corruption. One forgets probably that the 'decisions' taken by AI-artefacts are mostly not transparent at all and often manipulated. It is questionable, therefore, that one can fight corruption in this way.

Ultimately, it is of course a decision of human beings to do these things or not. That's why we have classified the GAMMA theory as ideological. We can only warn of the danger of considering artefacts as fellow social individuals. First, as we have discussed in [1] Chap. 8, decisions are social acts. AI-artefacts, like all ICT systems, can only compute. They cannot decide for the simple reason that they are not social individuals. Second, artefacts can never enter into or comply with commitments. They can only fake to do so. The need of human beings in executing transactions becomes particularly apparent when an actor has violated the applicable business rules (for which there may be very good reasons, as we have seen in [1]). The actor will be held accountable for having deviated from the rule or the norm. Sanctions may be applied, depending on the severity of the deviation.

It thus are only human beings who can constitute nations. Within a nation there is legislation that (among other things) rules the social interaction between the nation's citizens. For unjust interactions, people get punished, up to being sentenced. Through these punishments people become aware that their social behaviour is unacceptable. How could one ever punish an artefact? But indeed, human beings may decide that artefacts are full-fledged fellow social individuals, as discussed above. We can only once more warn for the danger of doing this. We will not warn again.

In [1] Sect. 8.3.3, we have discussed the notions of authority, responsibility, and competence. Authority (and the corresponding responsibility) can be achieved by people in two ways: through authorisation and through delegation. Authorisation means that one is assigned an actor role as the product of a (assignment) transaction.

Anyone who has been assigned an authority is able to delegate the authority to another person. Usually, only some transaction steps are delegated. Good examples of such delegation can be found in the case Pizzeria (cf. [1] Chap. 14).

A delegate is always held accountable for the acts he/she performs. According to Mintzberg [2], authority can be delegated, but ultimate responsibility (which we prefer to call accountability) cannot be delegated. Delegation is accomplished through *vertical decentralisation*: decision-making power flows down the hierarchy, yet the superior retains final accountability. Mintzberg distinguishes also *selective decentralisation*, where authority is distributed to specific actor roles, but always with clear oversight by the delegator.

Related to accountability is the notion of *liability*, which means that an actor may be persecuted legally on the basis of the applicable Civil Code. Delegates are never liable for their deeds. Instead, the delegator always is.

6.3 Elaborations

A special issue in the discussion of responsibility, accountability, and liability is the position of legal persons. By this misleading name no persons are referred to but legal entities, like companies, associations, and corporations. The question is what it means when such entities are considered liable for the deeds of their employees. An example of such a case is the condemnation of the Lidl supermarket chain in France for the death of a sixteen-year-old teenager. The teenager could easily buy a bottle of vodka in one of the Lidl shops. After having emptied the bottle, he stepped on his scooter and crashed fatally into a pole.

The legal entity of Lidl in France was condemned to pay a fine. While a specific employee likely violated the law, the legal entity bore the sanction. Mintzberg's structural typology sheds light here: in divisionalised organisations, authority is dispersed, but accountability still mounts upward to the corporate level. Without clear delegation (and traceability of decisions), responsibility risks dissolving into the 'organisation' rather than being owned by individuals. Logically, a judge cannot do more than imposing a fine, for the simple reason that a legal entity cannot be put in jail. The point is of course that one of the employees should be held liable, because it is clear that this employee has acted against the law. Unfortunately, it will not be easy to find this employee, because when it comes to accountability and liability, most people try to escape their responsibility while they mostly seem proud of their authority.

Related to the previous issue is the subject of using artefacts, notably ICT artefacts, by responsible human actors. Currently, many enterprises employ such artefacts, especially in the first contact with customers, thus in responding to requests. If this response is a promise, customers will generally have no problem with the 'automatic' reply. But if the response is a decline, they may want to discuss the reasons for the decline with the authorised human actor. Too often this proves impossible. This practice reflects, according to Mintzberg [3], an excessive reliance on *standardisation* as a coordination mechanism. Standardisation is powerful for routine production work but dangerous when applied to social acts such as declining a request. By standardisation of coordination, decisions are reduced to impersonal algorithms, stripping away the possibility for contextual judgement. Mintzberg warns against blind reliance on formal techniques, arguing that even strategy requires a blend of clearheaded logic and vigorous intuition—both uniquely human capacities.

In current practice, it appears that most web applications supporting purchase/sale transactions do not connect the customer with a human actor. Worse, it often is very hard or impossible to get contact with the human actor who is responsible for the decline. Clearly, the current practice of employing ICT artefacts does not follow the PSI theory (cf. [1] Chap. 8), to the legitimate frustration of the customer. Poignant example is presented in Chaps. 12–14. At the core of this harrowing practice lies the adherence to the information-centric view on information systems (engineering), as presented in Sect. 4.2. It is hard to fight this technology-driven, inhuman view. One can only hope, in the interest of all humankind, that ICT people will see the light before it is too late.

6.4 Discussions

As pointed out in the preceding sections, the widespread misunderstanding of the important difference between human beings and their supporting tools (like automata and machines) prevails the current discussions about organisation and automation. Although modern AI systems can process information far beyond the limits of human mental capabilities, only human beings can make genuine social decisions and bear responsibility for them. As Mintzberg observed in [3], organisations risk becoming “slaves to their servants” if they let tools dominate rather than support human work. Machines can analyse, compute, and recommend, but they cannot bear responsibility. The best use of technology is to get a better basis for decisions, while keeping accountability firmly with human actors.

References

1. Dietz, J. L. G., & Mulder, H. B. F. (2024). *Enterprise ontology: A human-centric approach to understanding the essence of organisation* (2nd ed., p. 475). The Enterprise Engineering Series. Springer Nature.
2. Mintzberg, H. (1979). *The structuring of organizations: A synthesis of the research* (Vol. xvi, p. 512). Theory of Management Policy. Prentice-Hall International.
3. Mintzberg, H. (1989). *Mintzberg on management: Inside our strange world of organizations.* MIT.

Chapter 7
The EE Transaction Cost Theory

Abstract The transaction cost theory is an important economic theory, developed in the twentieth century by several economic researchers, like Coase, Dahlman, North, and Commons, and especially by Williamson. This economic theory is the basis for the EE transaction cost theory. The EE transaction is the central notion. Tracking all steps in the complete transaction pattern, the knowledge needed to perform responsibly the request act as well as the final accept/reject act, appears to be most crucial for the decision to outsource the executor role of a transaction kind.

7.1 Introduction

The EE transaction cost theory is also labelled X-theory. The Greek capital letter is pronounced as CHI, which is an acronym for Costs of Human Interactions. By "interactions" we mean especially the actagenic conversations, the corresponding factagenic conversations, and the production acts in between [1]. In short, the CHI theory is a transaction cost theory. It is about the costs of in and outsourcing of transactions, based on the economic theory of transaction costs, as put forward, among others, by Williamson [2]. Transaction costs are the total costs of carrying out a transaction, including the cost of planning, deciding, resolving disputes, after-sales, etc. The chapter is organised as follows: in Sect. 7.2 (Foundations), the theoretical foundations of the EE transaction cost theory are presented, which consists of the various contributions from the field of transaction cost economics. In Sect. 7.3 (Elaborations), the foundations are transformed into practical insights and guidelines. Section 7.4 summarises the conclusions from the foregoing.

J. L.G. Dietz and H. B. F. Mulder, *Enterprise Governance and Management*, The Enterprise Engineering Series, https://doi.org/10.1007/978-3-032-24318-8_7

7.2 Foundations

In the twentieth century, economists became interested in the cost of (economic) transactions, foremost of transactions between companies, later also of internal transactions. Among the many researchers that have published their research findings, four persons deserve being mentioned: John Commons, Carl Dahlman, Douglas North, and Oliver Williamson. The foundations of transaction cost economics, however, must be traced back to the seminal work of Ronald Coase [3], who was the first to raise the fundamental question why there is not a single enterprise doing all production, but instead a plurality of enterprises coexisting in markets with contractual transactions. His insight was that the scope of interest of an enterprise is determined by transaction costs.

Dahlman [4] distinguishes between three kinds of costs: search and information costs (such as which supplier has the lowest price), bargaining and decision costs (when there are multiple suppliers), and policing and enforcement costs (making sure that the other party sticks to the terms of the agreement).

North [5] states that these four factors determine transaction costs: measurement (of all aspects involved), enforcement (of negotiated deals), market size (impacting the partiality of transactions), and ideological issues (the values and perceptions of all parties involved).

Commons [6] considered transactions to be the basis of a new economic theory. According to him, transactions are the smallest unit of activity. Instead of exchanges of commodities, he considered transactions to be units of alienation and acquisition of the rights of property, which must be negotiated between the parties involved.

In accordance with experiences from the rapid enterprise design approach [7], these classical contributions are integrated under a governance perspective. The scope of interest is set by the elementary actors in an enterprise (cf. [1] Chap. 8). Transaction cost factors are thereby not only considered as abstract economic constructs but as practical conditions that influence the design and governance of an enterprise.

In EE, the notion of transaction is not the economic notion of transaction as discussed above. Yet, we will try to reconcile the two notions. The focus in EE is on the make or buy decision, thus on the decision to insource or to outsource a transaction kind. As an example, we discussed in [1] Sect. 11.4 the outsourcing of car transportation in the case Rent-A-Car. Let us start our research into the costs of EE transactions with distinguishing two kinds of costs: coordination costs and production costs, in full accordance with [1] Chap. 8.

Regardless of the in or outsourcing of the production of a transaction kind, an enterprise will always have to bear the coordination costs of the initiator of the transactions. For the sake of convenience, we reproduce the CTP in Fig. 4.11 as Fig. 7.1.

The costs of the initiator consist of the costs of performing the request, the costs of discussing a potential decline, the costs of accepting or rejecting a declare fact, the costs of discussing a reject, and the costs of dealing with any of the six possible revocations. The sum total of these costs in any transaction consists of the multiplication

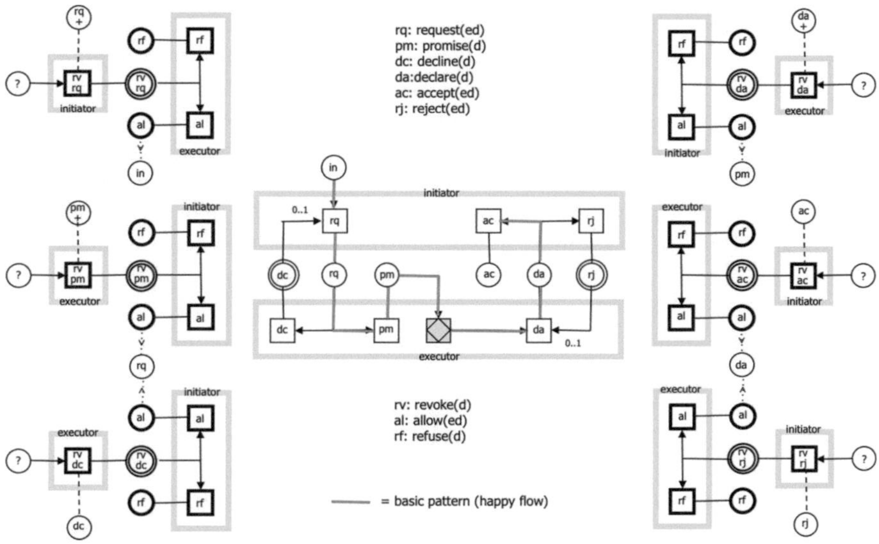

Fig. 7.1 Complete transaction pattern (CTP)

of the total amount of time units spent by the initiator and the costs per time unit of the person filling the role of initiator, plus the costs of the involved communication.

If the transaction kind is outsourced, then the transaction costs for the enterprise consist of the total costs as discussed above plus of course the price paid for the supplied product/service and the executor costs of the payment transaction. In addition, there may be costs of storing and transporting if the product regards tangible things.

If the transaction kind is insourced, then the transaction costs for the enterprise comprise the coordination costs of the initiator, the coordination costs of the executor, as well as the production costs. In case the product concerns intangible things, the production costs are limited to the costs of making the decision that the product is brought about. Otherwise, so if the product concerns tangible things, there may be costs of having production equipment and workspace, as well as goods storage and handling costs, next to labour costs.

7.3 Elaborations

In economics, the transaction theory is primarily concerned with the decision to in or outsource the production of a transaction kind. We adopt this point of view, but we will try to be more specific about the costs that are incurred when the decision is taken to outsource a transaction kind, that is to outsource the executor role. Such a decision seems to be straightforward when all identified cost elements, as mentioned in Sect. 7.2, are known. However, there is an element that is hard to assess but that can yet be most important to consider: the loss of competence at the initiator side.

Let us first look at the situation that transactions of the transaction kind are fully carried out internally, thus that the executor role is filled by employees within the enterprise. The initiator and the executor of a transaction then are colleagues. Problems regarding the formulation of the request, in particular the specification of the product properties, are easily solved, because the two actors can simply gather and discuss them. From these discussions the initiator learns which properties are most important for the executor and also why they are important. Although the initiator is not able to do the work of the executor (and doesn't need to be able to), he or she gets a proper idea about the production process for which the executor is responsible.

Similar remarks hold for the acceptance act by the initiator. Because he/she is quite knowledgeable about the ins and outs of the production process, he/she is perfectly able to assess the quality of the product once it is declared by the executor. This holds a fortiori in case there is no formal quality assurance procedure.

As soon as the executor role of such a transaction becomes outsourced, the relationship between initiator and executor changes, with possibly dramatic outcomes. In many cases, the persons that formerly filled the initiator role are replaced by other persons, namely people from the purchase department, because it is deemed wise in many enterprises to have all purchase activities concentrated in one department. The change is very dramatic indeed, because the new initiator is not knowledgeable about the production process. In practice it is often even worse: purchasers are commonly not praised for having this knowledge but for finding the best deal! And even if the former initiators are still involved in the purchase process, sooner or later they will be replaced by new people, and the same lack of knowledge will become apparent.

For the acceptance of the product, the consequences of outsourcing are equally dramatic, since it will be performed by people without proper knowledge of the products to be accepted (or rejected).

Thus, the decision to outsource an executor role should not be based on economic figures only. A transaction is first of all the communication between the initiator and the executor, in the order phase (the actagenic conversation) about the product to be brought about, and in the result phase (the factagenic conversation) about the product that is actually created. Both actors must be sufficiently knowledgeable about the production process, not only the executor. This insight, brought to the floor by the discipline of EE, and sharpened in the EE transaction cost theory, is most valuable.

7.4 Conclusions

The (economic) transaction cost theory, as developed in the twentieth century, and as particularly outlined by Williamson [2], is an important theory for decisions about in and outsourcing economic activities in enterprises. The EE transaction cost theory, which is based on it, sheds a missing light on outsourcing decisions. Although the main focus is of course on the executor role that is going to be outsourced, the initiators appear to be as important. Notably the fading knowledge in the enterprise about the outsourced production process, puts a challenge to performing adequate requests and accepts/rejects.

Above we have highlighted what outsourcing may imply and that caution must be taken in outsource decisions. In view of the SIGMA theory (cf. Chap. 8), such decisions are governance decisions.

References

1. Dietz, J. L. G., & Mulder, H. B. F. (2024). *Enterprise ontology: A human-centric approach to understanding the essence of organisation* (2nd ed., p. 475). The Enterprise Engineering Series. Springer Nature.
2. Williamson, O. E. (2013). *The transaction cost economics project: The theory and practice of the governance of contractual relations* (Vol. xxiv, p. 417).
3. Coase, R. H. (1937). The nature of the firm. *Economica, 4*(16), 19.
4. Dahlman, C. J. (1979). The problem of externality. *Journal of Law and Economics, 22*, 21.
5. North, D.C. (1992). *Transaction costs, institutions, and economic performance* (p. 32). Occasional Papers (International Center for Economic Growth). ICS Press.
6. Commons, J. R. (1934). *Institutional economics; its place in political economy* (Vol. xiii, p. 921). The Macmillan Company.
7. Mulder, H. B. F. (2006). Rapid enterprise design. In *Computer Science* (p. 160). Delft University of Technology.

Chapter 8
The EE Governance and Management Theory

Abstract The EE governance and management theory or SIGMA theory is a theory about the core notions of this book: governance and management. In current literature, a clear distinction between governance and management is not always made. These notions can, however, be distinguished and properly defined in EE on the basis of the essential model of an enterprise; when the model is changed, it is called governance, when the model is not affected, it is called management. A useful metaphor for understanding the distinction is the sailing of a ship. Setting the route is a governance act, keeping the ship on a set route, is a matter of management.

8.1 Introduction

The EE governance and management theory is also labelled Σ-theory. The Greek capital letter is pronounced as SIGMA, which is an acronym for Socially Inspired Governance and Management Approach. It is a theory about the core notions of this book: the notion of governance and the notion of management. Although some comments about governance and management have already been made in the two other books of the 'trilogy', Enterprise Ontology [1] and Enterprise Design Fundamentals [2], the notions need still to be addressed properly. The first two words of the acronym (Socially Inspired) refer to the human-centricity of Enterprise Engineering (EE), as articulated by the PSI theory (cf. [1] Chap. 8 or [2] Chap. 6). Particularly in Sect. 8.2.3 or Sect. 6.2.3, the most inner self of every subject or person is presented and discussed. There reside the wisdom and love that constitute the basis for deciding on how to comply with commitments (cf. [1] Fig. 8.5 or Fig. 6.5). It is an additional way to stress the important distinction between the *information-centric* and the *communication-centric* perspective on information systems (engineering), as discussed in [1] in Sect. 4.2.

In addition, we like to stress that the Five Ways Framework, to be discussed in Chap. 9, is actually not sufficient to fully address the current SIGMA theory. It should be extended with a Way of Learning and a Way of Leading, based on the most valuable insights into governance of W. Edwards Deming [3].

J. L.G. Dietz and H. B. F. Mulder, *Enterprise Governance and Management*, The Enterprise Engineering Series, https://doi.org/10.1007/978-3-032-24318-8_8

In Sect. 4.3, notably in Fig. 4.5, the SIGMA theory is classified as an ideological theory. Ideological theories cannot be predicated as truthful (like philosophical theories) or as sound and appropriate (like ontological theories), nor as rigorous and relevant (like technological theories). They can only be predicated as *significant*. The significance of an ideological theory boils down to the usefulness that its supporters assign to the theory. So, this is the way the SIGMA theory has to be judged: is it useful? Does it answer the questions we have about governance and management in a satisfying way? Does it seem applicable in practice?

As will become apparent, especially from the cases in part III, the answers to these questions will be positive. In EE, the human-centric approach, both to Enterprise Management and to Enterprise Governance are key. The arguments in favour of this approach are paramount, as discussed in [4], where it is called employee-centric. In order to connect to the current understanding and the current practice of management in the broad sense (which means including governance), we will address the ten roles of the manager, as discussed in Chap. 2.

In EE, the construction perspective on an enterprise, thus the *organisation* of the enterprise (cf. [1] Chap. 5) is constituted by authorised and responsible actors (cf. [1] Chap. 8) who use their inherent autonomy when filling actor roles. They may decline a request instead of promising, and later revoke the decline (and perform the promise act instead) when the reason for declining has been eliminated. In a similar vein, they may reject a declaration instead of accepting it, and later revoke the reject (and perform the accept act instead). Moreover, they monitor the execution of transactions of which they are the initiator and interfere if and when they feel the need to do so (cf. [1] Chap. 10).

We will stick to the distinction between management and governance as made in Chap. 3. Management is about controlling an organisation, about keeping the ship on a set route. Governance is about changing the organisation, about choosing another route for the ship, thus about navigating. Contrary to the main stream of addressing governance and management, we will basically consider all employees (the human beings that fill actor roles) to participate in Enterprise Governance and Management. Consequently, we will end up with a minimal need for separate manager roles.

At the same time, we want to emphasise that the being rooted of the SIGMA theory in EE, more specifically in Enterprise Ontology [1], means that several areas of management are already dealt with in the essential model of an organisation, as presented in [1], notably in Chaps. 8, 10, and 11. Consequently, there is no need that they be 'managed' by dedicated managers.

The remainder of this chapter is organised as follows. In Sect. 8.2 we discuss the notion of Enterprise Management in current practice. In a similar way, the notion of Enterprise Governance is covered by Sect. 8.3. In Sect. 8.4 we will discuss the separation between the two. The findings of Sects. 8.2–8.4 are elaborated in Sect. 8.5, such that the consequences of applying the SIGMA theory become lucid and convincing. Section 8.6 completes the chapter with a few conclusions.

8.2 Foundations of Enterprise Management

Enterprise Management is concerned with controlling the operations of an enterprise's organisation, so with keeping the ship on a set route. But what are the dimensions of controlling an enterprise, and what are the controlling instruments? On the basis of Enterprise Ontology (cf. [1] Chap. 8), we identify the next dimensions and corresponding instruments, following up on the discussion in Chap. 2, in particular concerning the ten roles of a manager, as distinguished by Henry Mintzberg.

The first dimension that we distinguish is the *production capacity* of an actor role. The instrument in the hands of the unit[1] manager is the assignment of less or more persons to the actor role. As a concrete example we take the case Rent-A-Car, which is presented and discussed in [1], Chap. 15. Apparently, Chiara is the team manager of the 'unit' rental completers. When more production capacity is needed, she may assign new persons (including herself) to the actor role 'rental completer'. When less production capacity is needed, she may revert these assignments. In doing so, she is filling the role of resource allocator, according to Mintzberg [5].

The second dimension is the *production time*, for example, the time needed to bring about a product of the kind '[rental] is completed' in the case Rent-A-Car. The team manager of the 'unit' rental completers can set or change the value of a parameter 'max production time'. The rental completers take this value into account because it appears in the action rules that they execute. Actors may have to give account of their actual production times (Note. The introduction of this parameter in the action rule is of course an act of governance, because it changes the essential model of Rent-A-Car). Introducing something like the maximum production time influences of course the behaviour of the executing actors.

The third dimension is the (intended) *settlement time*, for example, the time needed to respond to a request for a product of the kind '[rental] is completed' in the case Rent-A-Car. The notion of settlement time is extensively discussed in [1] Chap. 8. The team manager can set/change the value of a parameter 'max settlement time'. The actors take this value into account because it appears in the action rule. Actors may have to give account of their actual settlement times (Note. The introduction of the parameter is an act of governance, because it changes the essential model of Rent-A-Car). Introducing something like the maximum settlement time influences of course the behaviour of the executing actors.

Setting and changing the value of the parameters mentioned above (the maximum production time of a production act or the maximum settlement time of a coordination act), as well as assigning actor roles to employees, is done by actors who fill a generic actor role that we will call *Enterprise Manager* (EM). As one can deduce from the examples presented, this actor role is assigned to unit managers. In the case Rent-A-Car, the role will be assigned to Chiara, as the team manager of the rental completers. Of course, also other team managers can be assigned this actor role, for setting and changing the values of operational parameters.

---

[1] An organisational unit is a part of an enterprise's organisation, as discussed in Chap. 2, and as defined by Mintzberg.

In [1] Sect. 10.3.1, the notion of *responsibility range* is discussed, which has led to a precise definition of the notion of *process ownership*. Regarding the kind of management that we called process management there, we stated that the owner of a process is also the process manager. As notably clarified in [1] Fig. 10.12, the filler of an actor role is not only responsible for the executor part of the transactions in which he/she is the executor, but also for the initiator parts of the transactions on the next lower level of the transactor tree, thus the transactions he/she initiates and concludes. It means that a process manager may have to chase the executors of these transactions in order to achieve the set goals. As discussed in [1] Sect. 8.3, and exhibited in [1] Fig. 8.18, the addressee of every C-act knows the associated (intended) settlement time. If this time is exceeded, the process manager, thus the initiating actor, may decide to exhort the executing actors who fail to live up to their commitments. By this notion of process management, we avoid the allocation of a separate process manager to a business process, as is common practice nowadays. Concluding, we do exercise process management, but we do not need a separate process manager role.

Enterprise Management thus concerns reaching the goals as determined by the governors of the enterprise. It is executed partly by actors who are process owner of a transactor tree and partly by actors who are fillers of an actor role which we will call *Enterprise Manager* (EM). The instruments of these actors consist of the setting or changing of operational parameters that are taken into account by operating actors. Enterprise Managers are held accountable for the way in which they use these instruments. As explained in [1] Sect. 8.3, they are not responsible or accountable for the performance of business processes. Instead the process owner is. For example, in the case Rent-A-Car, the team manager (Chiara) is responsible for setting and changing the values of operational parameters, but only the rental completers are responsible for the process of completing a rental.

8.3 Foundations of Enterprise Governance

In this section, we introduce the notion of Enterprise Governance, and relate it to the notions of enterprise design and the operation of enterprises, as discussed respectively in [1, 2]. In order to explain clearly the role of governance, we introduce another metaphor. To refer to the operation of an enterprise we speak of "running the mill", to refer to enterprise design we speak of "changing the mill", and to refer to Enterprise Governance we use the expression "steering the mill". The mill may of course be substituted by any (other) enterprise.

By "running the mill" we have more specifically in mind the being operational of the essential model of an enterprise organisation, thus the ontology of its O-organisation, as discussed in [1] Chap. 11 or [2] Chap. 8. The other organisational layers will be operational when needed by the O-organisation. So, the mill is running as long as O-actors respond to coordination events. These O-actors can perfectly well deal with small disturbances in the operating process, for example, by using their autonomy to deviate from the applicable business rule, as discussed in [1] Chap. 8.

Unfortunately, in many contemporary enterprises, such a discretionary authority is not part of the job anymore. Employees have to act as robots (as they actually often are). Any exception has to be decided upon by their manager, who will normally not allow a deviation from the applicable rules, from fear of being held accountable (which cannot be the case anyhow). Where this misunderstanding of management can lead to is convincingly discussed in Chaps. 10–12.

In Sect. 8.1 we have stated that every change in the ontological model of any of the organisational layers (cf. [1] Chap. 11) is an act of governance. To accommodate the execution of these acts, we introduce the generic actor role *Enterprise Governor* (EG). As one can deduce from the examples presented, this actor role is assigned to unit managers, as distinguished in Chap. 2. The highest Enterprise Governor is often a group of people: the Board of Directors. Note that the members of the board fill the actor role (EG) collectively, as discussed in [1] Chap. 8.

In large enterprises, there may be the need to distinguish one or more additional management layers between the (lowest) layer of unit managers and the (highest) layer of the Board of Directors, because the span of control could become too large.

The most important thing to keep in mind is that only on the lowest level, managers, fill the actor role EM. At all levels above the lowest one, they exclusively fill the actor role EG. The lowest level is called the *operational* level. Consequently, we speak of operational managers. In management literature, one commonly also discerns the *strategic* level above the operational level. However, the distinction between these levels is often imprecise; therefore, we will not adhere to this habit.

Concluding, the governance in an enterprise is executed by Enterprise Governors (the fillers of the actor role EG). They have the exclusive authority (and responsibility) to incite changes that affect the essential model of the enterprise.

8.4 The Distinction Between Management and Governance

If one thing is clear from studying the vast amount of literature on (enterprise) management and (enterprise) governance, it is that there is no general agreement about the distinction between governance and management. Probably for this reason respectable researchers, like Henry Mintzberg, avoid to make a distinction and just call all roles above the operational level management roles. Consequently, every organisational change, whether a control action to keep 'the ship' on the route or a change of the route, is an act of management.

Fortunately, it is possible to clarify the scope of a change on the basis of Enterprise Ontology (cf. [1]). To illustrate this, we will hereafter present four different change proposals: two internally originated changes and two changes that originate from outside the enterprise. In all cases, there is a change of the organisation, thus of the essential model of the enterprise. Therefore, all changes are by definition a matter of governance. Let us have a look at how enterprises currently deal with them.

An example of a *small internally* originated change is a change of the work instruction for a specific production act (cf. Chap 9), entailing, for example, that the production act can be performed in less time than before. An example of a *large internally* originated change is the automation of the means of communication between actors: instead of exchanging paper forms, the actors will communicate coordination facts by means of electronic devices (cf. [1] Chap. 8).

An example of a *small externally* originated change is an increase in the VAT percentage on invoices to customers. An example of a *large externally* originated change is to operationalise the requirement for certification of the quality of a service.

In the first case (the reduction of the production time of a production act), the Work Instruction Specification (WIS) of one production act kind (in one of the four organisational layers, not necessarily the O-organisation) has to be changed (cf. Chap. 9). Commonly such a change is brought up and discussed in a meeting of a team of workers with the team manager. Because the impact of this change is restricted to the scope of the team, we consider the decision to implement the change to be a *management* act.

The second case (the automation of the communication between actors) affects the coordination acts/facts in all organisational layers, as distinguished by the ALPHA theory (cf. [1] Chap. 11 or [2] Chap. 8). The best way to explain what has to be done is by referring to Fig. 8.5 in [1] or Fig. 6.5 in [2] (the process of a coordination act). At the 'grey' level, so the level of the physical transmission of the coordination fact from the 'sender' to the 'receiver', there is a big change: the sentence to be transmitted is not inscribed any more on paper but instead in electronic media. Presumably, every symbol (letter or punctuation mark) is inscribed in a bit pattern (using ASCII or some other standard) and subsequently transmitted. As said, this change does not only affect the M-organisation, but all layers, because there are coordination acts in every layer: the O-, the I-, the D-, and the M-organisation. Such a change proposal may be brought up in a team management meeting, but the scope of a team manager is in principle too narrow to deal with it autonomously. Therefore, he/she will pass it through to the Board of Directors (or some other next management level). Therefore, we consider this change to be a matter of *governance*.

In the third case (the increase of the VAT percentage), some redesign has to be performed, be it on a small scale: the VAT percentage that is used in one or more action rules in the O-organisation has to be updated. It implies ideally the update of the value of a shared constant, and at worst a redesign of one or more action rules (if the VAT percentage is designed as a shared constant; then no action rule has to be changed). Setting/changing the value of the VAT percentage is the responsibility of some actor role. It may even not need to be brought up in a team meeting. Therefore, we consider this change to be a matter of *management*.

In the fourth example (the need of certification of the quality of a service), a major redesign is needed: a new O-transaction kind has to be defined (let us call it "certification providing") and consequently a new executing O-actor role (which we will accordingly call "certification provider"). The initiator role lies with one (or more) of the existing actor roles in the O-organisation. We will not elaborate the consequences for the O-organisation nor for the other organisational layers. Because the implications of such a change are beyond the scope of a team, we consequently consider this change to be a matter of *governance*. It will normally be decided upon by the next management level, presumably the Board of Directors.

Concluding, in current practice both managers and governors are dealing with changes in the operations of an organisation, although basically every change is an act of governance. The distinction between governance and management we have made above is a practical one. Although bringing about the changes are governance acts, we consider the two small ones to be addressed by management. Only the two large changes are true governance cases.

8.5 Elaborations: The Ten Roles of Mintzberg

In this section, we will discuss the ten management roles that are distinguished by Henry Mintzberg in [5], which we summarised in Chap. 2, in view of the definitions of management and of governance that are presented above.

The roles of *figurehead*, *leader*, and *liaison*, together called the interpersonal roles by Mintzberg, have been ignored up to now. The reason is quite clear: they seem, at least in first instance, not needed to set or change the route of the ship, nor to keep the ship on a set route. Or, using the other metaphor, filling these roles does not affect the mill, at least not in the short term. But in order to make well-informed decisions (as entrepreneur, disturbance handler, or resource allocator), filling these roles in a proper way is definitely necessary. Consequently, when looking for fillers of the role EG, one has to make sure that the candidates have the competencies for filling the interpersonal roles, thus for being figurehead, leader, and liaison.

The roles of *monitor* and *disseminator* are covered by the notion of interstriction as discussed in [1] Chap. 8. In current practice, most monitoring and disseminating is actually performed by ICT systems. The third informational role of Mintzberg, thus *spokesperson*, has to be filled by a human being. In our view, the competences that are needed to fill this role must be added to the ones being mentioned earlier, thus *monitor* and *disseminator*. The same holds for the roles of *entrepreneur* and *negotiator*. We consider them necessary, but they do not have short-term effects on the enterprise.

As for the remaining roles of *disturbance handler* and *resource allocator*, the competences needed to fill them properly have to be added to the requirements of both the actor role EM and the actor role EG. When the essential model of the enterprise is not affected, the necessary actions are taken by someone filling the actor role EM. Otherwise, someone filling the role of EG is needed.

To conclude this section, we like to spend some additional thoughts to the role of leader. In [6], Theo Mulder introduces leadership styles. He distinguishes between goal-driven entrepreneurs, people-oriented commanders, and detail-focused stewards, culminating in the archetype of the "combi-leader" who balances vision and operational insight. Mulder stresses that leadership style is not freely chosen but deeply rooted in personality, shaping both a leader's approach to uncertainty and her/his informational needs. This point of view seems to be crucial for determining the needed competences of governors and managers. Leaders do not replace managers but complement them. Where managers plan and coordinate within complexity, leaders drive change, motivation, and meaning. Hopefully therefore, these leaders are managers.

Lastly, governance is a deeply human and style-dependent activity, not the exclusive domain of formal authority but the expression of legitimate and authentic leadership. In every enterprise, there are natural leaders. Let them grow to become the future Enterprise's Governors.

8.6 Conclusions

The notions of governance and management in current practice are quite blurred, as we discovered already in Chaps. 2 and 3. In current practice, it will not be easy to introduce the simple, but well-founded, ideas that are developed and discussed in the current chapter. The vast, and ever increasing, amount of 'professional' managers, mostly shaped by 'business schools', will certainly block any progress that is to their disadvantage. Nevertheless, the current tsunami of 'professional' managers has to stop somehow some time, if alone for becoming too costly. The number of management positions in enterprises has increased exponentially in the past century.

The ideas as presented in this chapter are particularly interesting for enterprises that want to resist the current management hype and are able to be 'headstrong'. Among these enterprises are the SME's that are not for the largest part funded by external investors, as well as all governmental agencies. Concluding, we need brave innovative leaders. What we did not touch in the SIGMA theory is the culture of an enterprise. In EE this aspect is not addressed explicitly at all. Yet it is, but implicitly: human-centric implies being democratic and transparent. Considering people as the pearls of an organisation leaves no room for whatever kind of discrimination.

What the SIGMA theory does not cover is the kind of governance that is expressed in the next examples. One is the decision by the Board of Directors of a company to cut the number of employees by a substantive percentage, for example, 20%. Often it is the first act of a new Chief Executive Officer (abbreviated to CEO). Usually, such a decision is 'pushed' down the management hierarchy to the level of the foreman (cf. Chap. 2), before people raise the important question "How can we do his?"

Another example is the need for a number of hospitals that are located close to each other, to operate more efficiently and more professionally, thereby offering more cost-effective medical services as a cluster to the region. In first instance, this is also a cost-driven change, but now one that must be executed in collaboration.

Both cases start with a function-oriented perspective on the enterprise, or cluster of enterprises (cf. [1], Chap. 7). After some time, having arrived at an 'operational' level of management, the focus shifts to the construction of the new enterprise. Obviously, because any functional change is the effect of a constructional change, as discussed and exemplified in [1], Chap. 7. At some point in the process, this transition has to be made, much like step 2 in the DAO method (cf. [2], Chap. 11).

References

1. Dietz Jan, L. G., & Mulder, H. B. F. (2024). *Enterprise ontology—a human-centric approach to understanding the essence of organisation* (2nd ed., p. 475). The Enterprise Engineering Series. Springer Nature.
2. Dietz, J. L. G., & Mulder, H. B. F. (2025). *Enterprise design fundamentals—settling an enterprise business and devising the enterprise organisation.* The Enterprise Engineering Series. (Vol. 1, p. 357). Springer Nature.
3. Deming, W. E. (2018). *The new economics for industry, government, education* (3rd ed.). MIT Press.
4. Hoogervorst, J. A. P. (2017). *Foundations of enterprise governance and enterprise engineering* (p. 574). Springer International Publishing.
5. Mintzberg, H. (1973). *The nature of managerial work* (Vol. 13, p. 298). Harper & Row.
6. Mulder, T. J. (1990). *Leiders en informatiesystemen.* Academic Service.

Part III
Applications

I hear and I forget
I see and I remember
I do and I understand
—Confucius

Part III is about the application in practice of the theories from Part II. Chapter 9 contains an extensive sum-mary of the DEMO methodology, including the DEMO specification language (diagrams, tables, and formal textual specifications). In Chaps. 10 and 11 exercises are presented to dive into governance and management in current practice. These exercises are particularly suited as course material. In Chap. 12, practical applications of DEMO in diverse industrial areas are reported.

Chapter 9
The DEMO Methodology

Abstract DEMO (Design and Engineering Methodology for Organisations) comprises a Way of Thinking (WoT), a Way of Modelling (WoM), and a Way of Working (WoW). The WoT consists of a number of theories. The WoM consists of an integrated whole of four aspect or sub models: the Cooperation Model (CM), the Action Model (AM), the Process Model (PM), and the Fact Model (FM). The CM of a Scope of Interest (SoI) is the ontological model of its construction, thus of the identified transactor roles and the coordination structures among them: the interaction structure, the interimpediment structure, and the interstriction structure. The AM of an SoI is the ontological model of its operation. For every actor role in the focus (of the SoI), it provides the rules that guide the role fillers in doing their work. The guidelines for responding to coordination events are called action rules, the ones for performing production acts are called work instructions. The PM of an SoI is the ontological model of the state space and the transition space of its coordination world. It contains the existence laws and occurrence laws for all transaction kinds in the SoI. The FM of an SoI is the ontological model of the state space and the transition space of its production world. It contains the existence laws and occurrence laws for all identified entity types, value types, property types, attribute types, and event types. For producing essential models of enterprises, the WoW of DEMO offers the OER method (Organisational Essence Revealing). It consists of a number of steps in which the four DEMO models are produced, preferably in a spiral way. For (re) developing organisations as well as for developing enterprise information systems, DEMO offers the DAO method. The name is an acronym of Designing under Architecture from Ontology. Lastly, for devising and establishing governance and management, DEMO offers the HOS method. The name is an acronym of Human-centric Operating and Steering.

J. L.G. Dietz and H. B. F. Mulder, *Enterprise Governance and Management*, The Enterprise Engineering Series, https://doi.org/10.1007/978-3-032-24318-8_9

9.1 Introduction

Everyone who understands the EE theories, as discussed in Chaps. 5 through 8, and in [1] Chaps. 5 through 11, disposes of the intellectual ability to analyse organisational problems and to solve them accordingly. Yet, most people appear to be uncomfortable with only theories in their toolbox, even if they agree with Kurt Lewin's adage "Nothing is more practical than a good theory". They like to have more concrete bridges to their practical work. With reference to the CIAO tree in Fig. 4.1, they like to have methods that guide them in doing the work.

By a *method* is commonly understood a systematic procedure for accomplishing a task. Examples are teaching methods, learning methods, methods to develop software, and methods to make lasagna. Next to "method", there is the word "methodology". By a *methodology* is commonly understood a system of methods, used in a particular area of study or activity, whereas the original meaning is: doctrine or principles of methods, specifically concerning scientific research. We will adopt the first meaning while requiring in addition that a methodology is firmly rooted in theoretical foundations, like the trunk of the CIAO tree in Fig. 4.1 is firmly rooted in the EE theories. In Fig. 9.1, the so-called Five Ways Framework is presented, as an aid to discuss methodologies. It is an adapted version of the one in [2].

The core of every methodology is a Way of Modelling (WoM) and a Way of Working (WoW). By a WoM is meant a collection of meta models (cf. [1] Chap. 6) that guide one in understanding a system. The WoW comprises the methods that are used for producing the models that constitute this understanding, as well as the methods for bringing about devised changes.

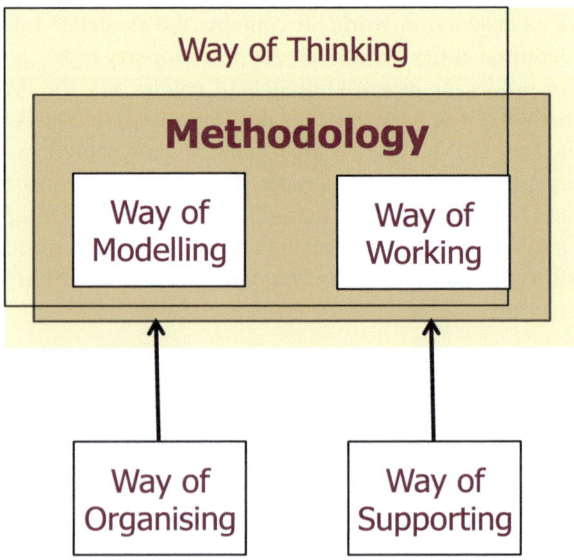

Fig. 9.1 Five ways framework

The WoM and the WoW must firmly be rooted in a common Way of Thinking (WoT), thus in a theoretical foundation that is coherent and consistent, and that is appropriate for the subject matter. Consequently, a *methodology* is defined as a matching triple WoT, WoM, and WoW. It may be supplemented by a Way of Organising (WoO) and a Way of Supporting (WoS). The WoO regards the organising and managing of applying the methodology, and the WoS comprises (software) tools that support both the WoM and the WoW.

In the next sections, DEMO, the principal methodology in Enterprise Engineering, is introduced. In Sect. 9.3, the (meta) models, comprising together the WoM, are summarised. The WoW for revealing the essential model of an enterprise is discussed in Sect. 9.4. This OER method is needed when one has to produce the ontological model of an organisation through reverse engineering (cf. Fig. 9.11). In Sect. 9.5, the DAO method is presented. It is the method one needs for (re)developing organisations and for developing EISs. In Sect. 9.6, the HOS method is presented and discussed. Section 9.7 contains the conclusions of the chapter.

9.2 DEMO—Essence and Simplicity

DEMO (Design and Engineering Methodology for Organisations) is the result of scientific research, constantly fed by practical applications, from 1990 till 1994 at the University of Maastricht, and from 1995 till 2009 at Delft University of Technology. Since 2010, its development takes place within the worldwide DEMO community. From the late 90s on, courses in DEMO are taught under the auspices of the Enterprise Engineering Institute (EEi).[1] Next to commercial courses, the methodology is taught at several member institutes of the Ciao Network,[2] as well as at universities and polytechnic schools outside the network.

The motto of DEMO is "essence and simplicity". The notion of *essence* is specifically discussed in the PSI, DELTA, OMEGA, and ALPHA theories (cf. Chap. 4). It refers to the essential model of the organisation that one wants to study, in order to get deep insight into the problems one is facing, and subsequently to solve them by means of redesign, re-engineering and re-implementation. In addition to presenting the essence of a problem situation, it is crucial for a methodology to follow Ockham's razor[3] and keep things as simple as possible. This is of paramount importance for intellectually managing the complexity of a problem situation, and of enterprises in general. In [1] Sect. 9.4.1, five intellectual techniques are presented that offer help in achieving both essence and simplicity. These techniques, for mnemonic reasons called *sapiences*, are summarised in Fig. 9.2.

---

[1] For more information, visit www.ee-institute.org.

[2] The Ciao Network is an international group of researchers and practitioners who develop and practise the discipline of Enterprise Engineering. For more information, visit www.ciaonetwork.org.

[3] https://en.wikipedia.org/wiki/Occam%27s_razor.

Fig. 9.2 Five sapiences

Separation of concerns
Use of **a**bstraction
Devising **p**roper concepts
Verification by **i**nstantiation
Validation from **o**ntology

Examples of the first sapience, *separation of concerns*, are making the distinction between function and construction (cf. [1] Chap. 5), distinguishing between production and coordination, and distinguishing between the O-, the I-, the D-, and the M-organisation of an enterprise (cf. [1] Chap. 11). Examples of the second sapience, *use of abstraction*, are abstracting from the implementation of a system and in doing so arriving at its ontology, as well as additionally abstracting from the realisation of an enterprise and in doing so arriving at its essential model (cf. [1] Chap. 11). Examples of the third sapience, *devising proper concepts*, are the transaction concept as well as concepts like membership, flight, sale and purchase, in formulating uniquely identifiable products. We owe the three techniques above to Edsger Dijkstra, who provides convincing applications of them in [3]. The fourth sapience, *verification by instantiation*, is an indispensable intellectual technique for making sure that one really understands a conceptual model at the schema (or meta model) level (cf. [1] Chap. 6). It serves to convince oneself that a produced model is a correct model in the applied methodology. The technique has been articulated by Sjir Nijssen for the field of information systems engineering [4]. The fifth sapience, *validation from ontology*, serves to make sure that a produced ontological model is a faithful conception of the system (organisation, information system, data/document system) that one wants to understand. It does so by systematically checking for every ontological element whether it has a counterpart in reality. It is also a valuable technique for discovering errors in the realisation and implementation of an ontological model.

The development of DEMO was triggered by the dissatisfaction with the state-of-the-art in requirements determination in the 80s and 90s, when the information-centric view was dominant. A satisfying solution of this problem had to wait for the communication-centric view being conceived (cf. Chap. 4). Once DEMO was under construction, it became clear that it could provide more benefits than only solving the requirements determination problem. As an illustration, DEMO is (also) considered a coordination based business process modelling approach [5]. Therefore, the original reading of the acronym (Dynamic Essential MOdelling) was replaced, around the year 2000, by the current one (Design and Engineering Methodology for Organisations).

Up to now, DEMO is used almost exclusively as the methodology for producing ontological models of organisations and for improving organisations based on these models [1]. In this book, DEMO is applied to the governance and management of

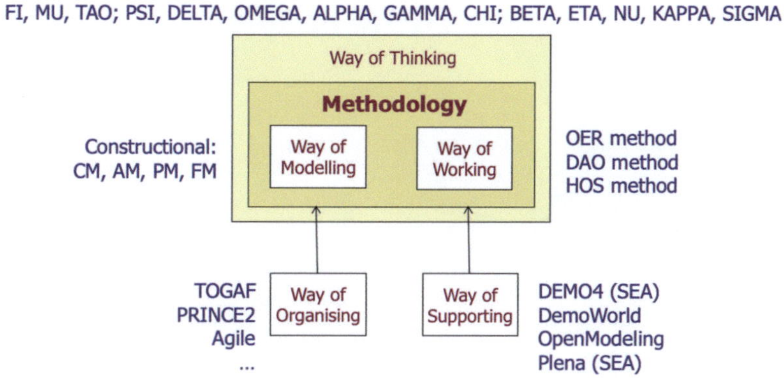

Fig. 9.3 DEMO in the five ways framework

organisations. Consequently, the Way of Thinking (WoT), the Way of Modelling (WoM), and the Way of Working (WoW) have to be extended.

Figure 9.3 exhibits the new position of DEMO in the framework of Fig. 9.1 (new compared to its position in [1]). The WoT comprises ten EE theories; the new ones are the KAPPA theory (Chap. 5), the GAMMA theory (Chap. 6), the CHI theory (Chap. 7), and the SIGMA theory (Chap. 8). The WoM comprises the four constructional models (CM, AM, PM, and FM). The WoW comprises three methods now: the OER method (cf. [1] Chap. 12), the DAO method (cf. [6] Chap. 11), and the HOS method, to be presented hereafter. Together they offer the support to (re)develop enterprises. The methodology does not include a specific WoO. Therefore, Fig. 9.3 just shows a few candidate project management methods. As for the WoS, several existing tools are listed. The list is not exhaustive since new tools may become available in the course of time. An overview of current tools can be found on www.ee-institute.org.

Since the early 90s, DEMO has been applied in thousands of practical projects, and its further development is nurtured and steered by the feedback from these experiences. Indeed, next to assisting the elicitation of requirements for information systems development in an objective way, DEMO has proven to provide effective help in organisational changes of any kind, from business process redesign and re-engineering up to enterprise transformations, like mergers and acquisitions. The key to exploring these, originally unanticipated, application areas, is the insight and overview that DEMO models offer, due to the unprecedented reduction of complexity that is made possible by being firmly rooted in the EE theories. Because of this quality, DEMO has evidently shown to be virtually indispensable in major enterprise change projects, such as the post-merger integration of the cargo divisions of Air France and KLM [7] and the organisation of large civil engineering projects [8], where the DEMO-based VISI method[4] is an ISO approved standard.

[4] https://www.crow.nl/thema-s/bouwwerkinformatie/visi.

Fig. 9.4 How DEMO reduces complexity

In Chap. 1, three generic goals are presented for the discipline of Enterprise Engineering: intellectual manageability, organisational concinnity, and social dedication. The focus of DEMO is on *intellectual manageability*, understood as achieving and maintaining insight and overview concerning enterprises and enterprise changes, in order to master the complexities of the phenomena one faces. It is achieved by a systematic *reduction of complexity*. Figure 9.4 illustrates this: the detailed description of the business processes of an insurance company, laid down in a document of over 200 pages is 'compressed', by applying DEMO, into an A3 size graphical representation of the cooperation model of the company (cf. Sect. 9.3.3.1). The reduction of complexity is notably achieved by the combined application of the PSI, OMEGA, and ALPHA theories (cf. [1] Chaps. 8, 10, and 11).

First, by virtue of the transaction concept, a universal pattern is imposed on the operational activities of an enterprise, yielding a reduction of complexity of at least 80% on average, since 19 concepts are replaced by one concept, as illustrated by the complete transaction pattern (cf. [1] Fig. 8.10). Second, the mind-bending railroad yard images of flow-based business process models that most current process modelling approaches come up with, are replaced by simple tree structures of transactor roles. This replacement offers a substantial additional reduction of complexity, estimated at 80%. Third, by systematically abstracting from implementation (i.e. from functionaries and departments, and from coordination and production technology), as well as from realisation (i.e. from the I-, the D-, and the M-organisation), another considerable reduction of complexity is achieved, also estimated at 80%. So, an overall reduction of well over 95% (in terms of the size of model expressions) is achieved. The resulting most important asset of DEMO to practitioners is their readiness in unravelling the ever more obstinate tangle called reality.

9.3 Way of Modelling

In modelling the construction of a system, we distinguish between its implementation independent ontology and the implementation dependent construction. The latter is the outcome of the implementation design phase (cf. Chap. 6).

The ontological model of an organisation in DEMO consists of the integrated whole of four aspect models, each taking a specific view on the organisation: the Cooperation Model (CM), the Action Model (AM), the Process Model (PM), and the Fact Model (FM). Models constitute one's understanding of a system or a situation, as discussed in [1] Chap. 9. Here, we will describe the four models only briefly.

The relationships between the four models is presented in Fig. 9.5. As illustrated by the triangular shape, and the division of this shape into the four sub models, the CM and the AM cover both coordination and production, while the PM regards only coordination and the FM only production. The PM connects the CM and the AM as far as the coordination between actors is concerned. In a similar way, the FM connects the CM and AM as far as production is concerned. The AM is the solid foundation on which the other three models are standing. In a sense, they are already 'contained' in the AM, they only need to be 'extracted'. Lastly, there is nothing 'above' the CM.

The *Cooperation Model* (CM) of an organisation is a model of its *construction* (cf. [1] Chap. 12), thus of the identified transactor roles and the coordination structures between them. A CM is expressed in a coordination structure diagram, supplemented by a transaction product table and a bank contents table.

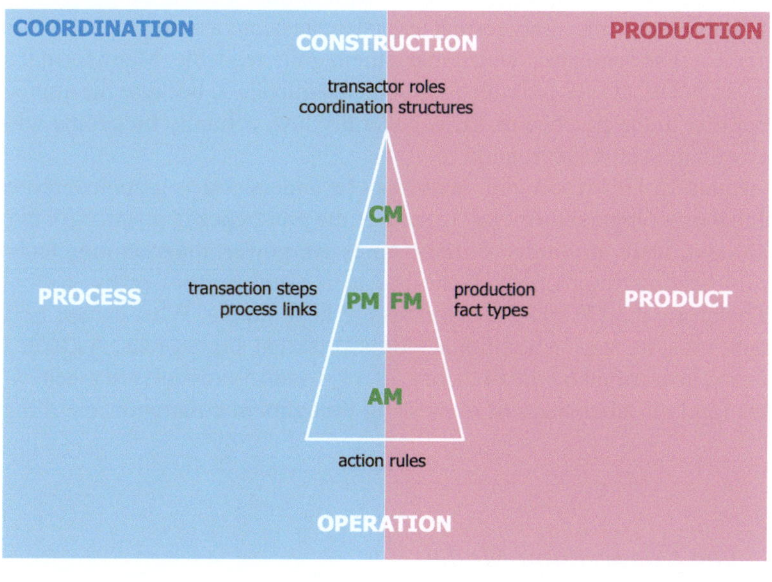

Fig. 9.5 Integrated ontological aspect models

The *Action Model* (AM) of an organisation is a model of its *operation*, thus the manifestation of the construction in the course of time (cf. [1] Chap. 12). An AM is represented by action rule specifications. They guide actors in performing coordination acts.

The *Process Model* (PM) of an organisation is a model of the (business) *processes* that take place as the effect of acts by actors. In systemic terms, it is a specification of the state space and the transition space of the coordination world (cf. [1] Chap. 12). A PM is expressed in a process structure diagram, optionally supplemented by a number of transaction process diagrams and a create use table.

The *Fact Model* (FM) of an organisation is a model of the *products* of the organisation. In systemic terms, it is a specification of the state space and the transition space of the production world (cf. [1] Chap. 12). An FM is expressed in an Object Fact Diagram, supplemented by Derived Fact Specifications, if applicable.

9.3.1 The DEMO Specification Language

In order to represent DEMO models, the DEMO Specification Language (DEMO-SL) is developed [9]. The distinction between models and representations is crucial (cf. [1] Chap. 6); they constitute respectively the semantics and the syntax of the language in which the models are expressed. Expressions in DEMO-SL are basically formal textual descriptions. Therefore, its syntax is defined in the Extended Backus-Naur Form (EBNF), the international standard syntactic meta language (ISO/IEC 14977). At the same time, these formal textual expressions are intuitive: they look like structured English sentences, which make them quite readable. Many formal textual expressions in DEMO-SL have also a graphical equivalent, because the appreciation of formal text in the practice of EE is generally low, certainly by people without a logical/mathematical background.

Consequently, DEMO-SL diagrams must be understood as graphical representations of first order logical formulas. In spite of the preference in practice for diagrams to formal text, there are limits to their expressive power: diagramming techniques can easily become impractical if one has to remember (too) many symbols and rules. Therefore, the DEMO-SL diagrams are kept simple. What cannot be said in a diagram, must be said in additional (formal) textual expressions. As indicated in Fig. 9.5, and as clarified by the FI theory (cf. [1] Chap. 5), models are green, whereas diagrams (and all other ways of expressing thoughts in communicable things) are 'blue'.

9.3.2 The Cooperation Model

The Cooperation Model (CM) of an SoI is the ontological model of its construction, thus the identified transactor roles and the coordination structures among them. Actor roles within an SoI are called internal. Transaction kinds of which both the initiator and the executor are internal actor roles, are called internal. If one of the actor roles is not internal, the transaction kinds are called border transaction kinds and the actor role is called environmental. There are three coordination structures among transactor roles: the interaction structure, the interimpediment structure, and the interstriction structure. The ways in which these structures can be expressed is presented in [9].

The *interaction structure* consists of initiator links between transactor roles and transaction kinds (Note: the executor links are implicitly specified by the notion of transactor role). Through this structure, trees of transactor roles emerge, as illustrated by Fig. 9.6, which is a reproduction of Fig. 18.11 in [1]. The initiator links are expressed by solid lines between actor roles and transaction kinds. A cardinality range (k..n) indicates how many transactions are enclosed (cf. Fig. 9.7).

The *interimpediment* structure consists of wait links from actor roles to transaction kinds. A wait link expresses that actors in the connected actor role have to wait for a specific progress in transactions of the connected transaction kind before they can

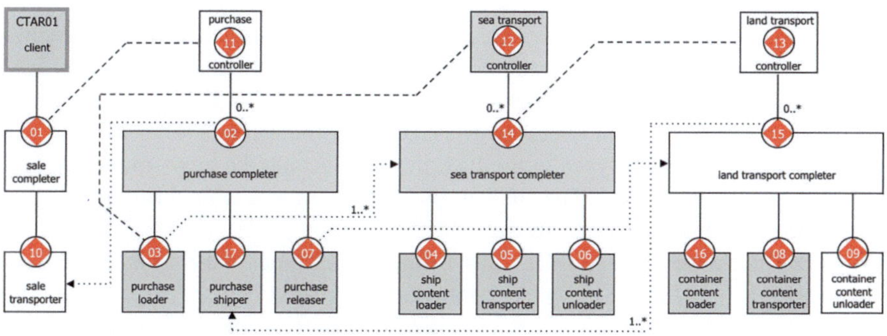

Fig. 9.6 Three coordination structures in the GloLog enterprise

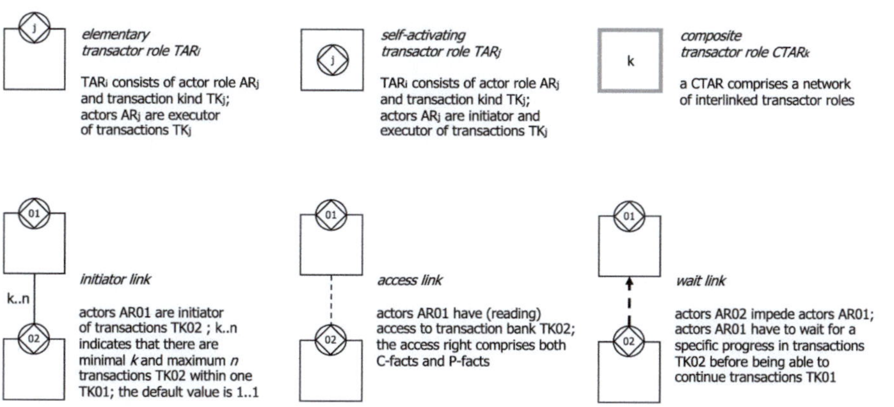

Fig. 9.7 Legend of the coordination structure diagram

proceed in their own transactions. In other words, the initiators or executors of these transactions impede actors in the connected actor role to carry on as long as the wait condition holds. A wait link is expressed by a dashed arrow from a transaction kind to the impeded actor role. For example, the wait link in Fig. 9.6 from TK02 to AR10 expresses that actors AR10 are impeded (hold up) in carrying out a transaction TK10 until a particular progress is made in a transaction TK02.

If one abstracts from the realisation of the O-organisation of an SoI, and thus aims at producing its essential model (cf. [1] Chap. 11), a third coordination structure comes on the scene. This *interstriction*[5] structure consists of access links from actor roles to transaction kinds, which are now conceived as transaction banks (cf. [1] Chap. 10). Access links are the ontological abstraction of the sharing transaction kinds between the O-organisation and the I-organisation of the SoI (cf. [1] Chap. 11). An access link expresses that actors in the connected actor role have reading access to the contents of the transaction bank (both to the C-facts and to the P-facts). Access links are represented by dashed lines between actor roles and transaction kinds. For example, the access link in Fig. 9.6 from AR11 to TK01 expresses that actors AR11 are allowed to inspect the contents of the bank TK01.

The CM of an organisation is expressed in a *Coordination Structure Diagram* (CSD), supplemented by a *Transactor Product Table* (TPT), and a *Bank Contents Table* (BCT). The TPT is a list of the identified internal and border transaction kinds, their product kinds and their executor roles. Because the product kinds are identical to the independent P-fact types in the FM, the TPT is called a cross-model table; it bridges the CM and the FM. The BCT is also a cross-model table, bridging also the CM and the FM, but in a different way.

The BCT of an organisation is a list of the P-fact types, both independent and dependent (cf. [1] Chap. 8), whose instances are created or used by the initiators and executors in transactions of the identified transaction kinds. They are grouped according to the transaction banks in which they are stored. P-fact types whose instances are used within the organisation but created outside it are also listed in the BCT. Because one commonly doesn't know the single transaction banks in which they reside, these banks are combined into multiple transaction banks (cf. [1] Chap. 10).

The legend of the CSD is exhibited in Fig. 9.7, which is identical to Fig. 10.4 in [1]. The upper part shows the three different sorts of transactor roles: elementary, self-activating and composite. As said, the interaction structure of an organisation consists of a number of tree structures. By definition, the top of these trees is a self-activating transactor role. The organisation of an enterprise, or any other SoI, commonly covers parts, i.e. subtrees, of such trees. If this is the case, then the cut-off upper part of the tree is represented by a composite transactor role, as discussed in [1] Chap. 10. Most business processes in enterprises originate in this way from the environment. The shapes and constructs are considered to be sufficiently explained in Fig. 9.7.

---

[5] "Restriction" originates from the Latin verb "stringere", meaning trimming, curtailing. The word "interstriction" expresses that actors restrict each others' decision freedom or 'play area'.

Figure 9.8 exhibits the CSD and Table 9.1 shows the TPT of the Volley organisation, resulting from applying the OER method to the case description (cf. Sect. 9.4). The red colour of the diamonds indicates that the transactor roles, as well as the external transaction kinds, belong to the O-organisation of Volley. Table 9.2 exhibits the corresponding BCT. In the second column, the entity types and value types are indicated in capital (so actually as object classes, cf. [1] Chap. 5), and the event types by (unary) predicates concerning entity types. The dependent fact type indications are indented. Variable names are placed between "[" and"]" as discussed in [9]. Note that the BCT can only be completed when the FM is produced.

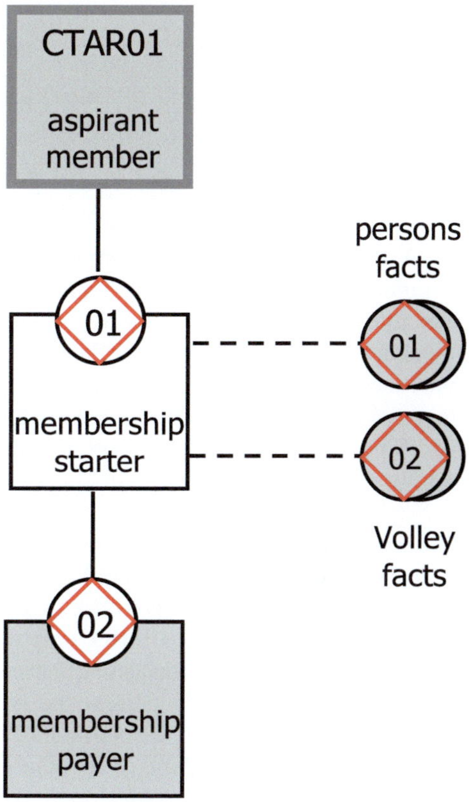

Fig. 9.8 CSD of the Volley organisation

Table 9.1 TPT of the Volley organisation

Transaction kind	Product kind	Executor role
TK01 membership starting	PK01 [membership] **is** started	AR01 membership starter
TK02 membership paying	PK02 **the** first fee **of** [membership] **is** paid	AR02 membership payer

Table 9.2 BCT of the Volley organisation

Bank	Independent/dependent facts
TK01 membership starting	MEMBERSHIP [membership] **is** started **the** starting day **of** [membership] **the** member **of** [membership] **the** amount to pay **of** [membership]
TK02 membership paying	**the** first fee **of** [membership] **is** paid **the** amount paid **of** [membership]
MTK01 persons facts	PERSON **the** day of birth **of** [person]
MTK02 Volley facts	YEAR **the** minimum age **in** [year] **the** annual fee **in** [year] **the** max members **in** [year]

9.3.3 The Action Model

The Action Model (AM) of an organisation or SoI is the ontological model of its operation (cf. [1] Chap. 8). It contains for every internal actor role, thus for every actor role in the focus, the rules that guide the role fillers in doing their work. The guidelines for responding to coordination facts (C-facts) are called *action rules*, the guidelines for performing production acts (P-acts) are called *work instructions*. They are respectively expressed in *Action Rule Specifications* (ARS) and *Work Instruction Specifications* (WIS). Because work instructions are usually enterprise specific, we will not elaborate them. One should consider them as the detailed instructions for accomplishing a certain production task, like the concluding of a rental contract or the baking of an apple pie. Although work instructions are often expressed in work flows, these work flows do not represent business processes, because business processes only exist in the coordination world. Instead, such work flows represent processes in the production world. In DEMO, only the final effect of production processes is modelled: the resulting products of the transaction processes (cf. [1] Chap. 8).

Therefore, we will only present the specification of action rules hereafter. In current practice, these rules are commonly called *business rules*.[6] In principle, there is an action rule for every kind of agendum (cf. [1] Chap. 8) that actors in a specific actor role have to deal with, while looping through their actor cycle (cf. [1] Chap. 8). The 'exception' states (declined, rejected, and the states in the revocation patterns) are mostly ignored, because the response is too dependent on the topical situation. Consequently, the standard practice is to specify only action rules for responding to events in the basic transaction pattern, in Fig. 9.9 indicated by the green line in the Complete Transaction Pattern (CTP), so for the events (rq), (pm), and (da). Actors are basically autonomous in deciding how to respond to coordination events, as well

[6] To be precise, they are the imperative business rules, as opposed to the declarative rules, which consist of existence laws and occurrence laws (cf. In this chapter).

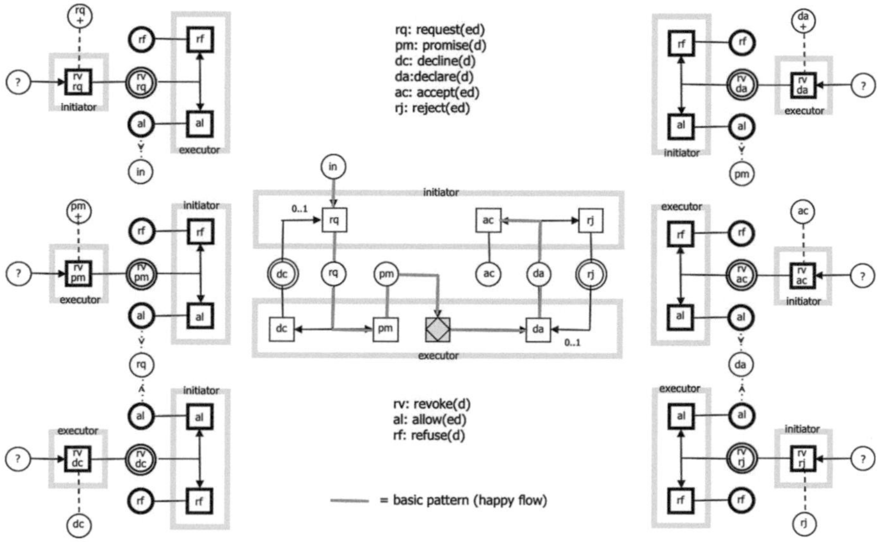

Fig. 9.9 CTP with the transaction states for which action rules are commonly specified

as how to perform production acts (cf. [1] Chap. 8). As a consequence, the ARS may be incomplete or even absent. In such cases, the actors are supposed to base their decisions on their professional and general knowledge.

The specification of an action rule is divided into three sequential parts: event part, assess part, and response part. As an example, Fig. 9.10 exhibits an action rule from the case Volley [10], following from the analysis of the case description in Sect. 9.4. To emphasise the differences between the three parts, the event part is coloured light-blue, the assess part light-tangerine, and the response part light-green. The formal definition of action rules in EBNF is presented in [9].

The *event part* comprises a when-clause, optionally supplemented by a given-clause and a while-clause. In the when-clause one states the type of the C-event (the agendum) that is going to be settled; in the example it is the being requested of the starting of a (new) membership of the tennis club. The product of such a transaction consists of the independent P-fact '[membership] **is** started' and a number of dependent P-facts. Two of these dependent P-facts are specified in the given-clause: the person who will be the member, and the day on which the membership will start (Note that this is an explicit specification of the operative time of the transaction's product, cf. [1] Sect. 8.3.1). The optional while-clause specifies the event that impedes settling the event in the when-clause. Then the rule cannot be executed until both events have occurred. Thus, there may be several action rules for the same kind of event, but each of them with a specific impeding event kind, like ARS-5 and ARS-7 in [1] Chap. 15. There cannot be two or more action rules that have the same when-clause and while-clause. Otherwise said, actors never have to choose what rule to execute, there will at most be one.

when	membership starting **for** [membership] **is** requested		(TK01/rq)
	given	**the** member **of** [membership]	
		the starting day **of** [membership]	
assess	*rightness:*	**the** performer **of the** request **is the** member **of** [membership];	
		the addressee **of the** request **is a** membership starter;	
	sincerity:	* the member complies with the Volley Regulations *	
	truth:	**the** starting day **of** [membership] **is the** first day **of some** month;	
		the age **of the** member **of** [membership] **on the** starting day **of** [membership] **is equal to or greater than the** minimum age **in the** year **of the** starting day **of** [membership];	
		the number of members **on the** starting day **of** [membership] **is less than the** max members **in the** year **of the** starting day **of** [membership];	
if	*performing the action after* ***then*** *is considered justifiable*		
then	promise	membership starting **for** [membership] **to** **the** performer **of the** request	[TK01/pm]
else	decline	membership starting **for** [membership] **to** **the** performer **of the** request * justification of decline *	[TK01/dc]

Fig. 9.10 Example of an action rule specification (ARS)

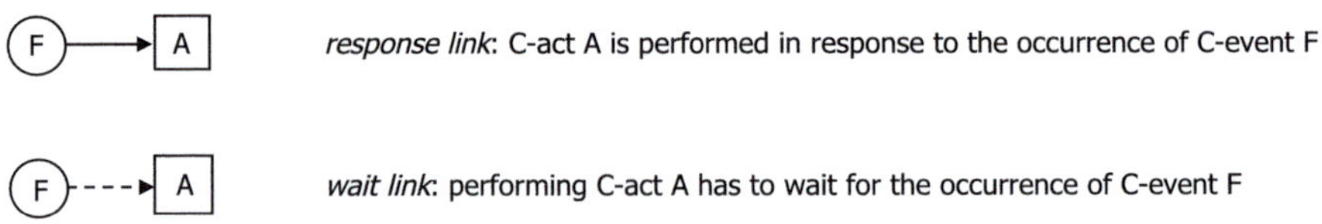

Fig. 9.11 Legend of the links in the PSD

The *assess part* consists of a number of propositions whose truth value must be determined. The propositions are divided in three, according to the three validity claims in Habermas' theory of communicative action (cf. [1] Chap 8): rightness, sincerity, and truth. In the *rightness* division the conditions are specified that must apply to the participating actors, and that serve to ensure that they have the proper authority. In the given example, the performer of the request must be the person who is mentioned as member in the with clause of the event part, and the addressee must be someone who is authorised to fill the actor role 'membership starter'. The first condition may look redundant, but it is not. If it would be omitted, anyone could make the request. In addition, it forbids that the (aspirant) member delegates her/his authority. Because the claim to sincerity is specific for the individual fillers of the actor roles, it seems hard to make the *sincerity* division more precise than checking that they seem to be trustworthy. However, if (formal) terms and conditions exist, one can explicitly assess the compliance with these rules. Lastly, the propositions in the *truth* division always regard the state of the production world. They serve to check the possible violation of existence and occurrence rules in the production world. The ones that are presented in Fig. 9.10 can easily be deduced from the case description.

The *response part* starts with the most distinctive condition in DEMO action rules, compared to other business rules approaches: *'if performing the action after* ***then*** *is considered justifiable'*. This sentence expresses the fundamental autonomy of the executor to decide what is the best response, given the specific case he/she is dealing with. As discussed in Sect. 8.3, there may always be circumstances that play a role but could not have been foreseen when the action rule was designed. As an example in the Volley organisation, someone could have applied for membership who is still younger than the minimum age, but well-known already for her talent. What is a wise decision then? Declining, thereby strictly following the business rule? Or promising, a decision that could probably very well be justified with the board.

At the right side in Fig. 9.10, the C-acts/facts in the CTP are indicated (cf. Chap. 8). The combination of a C-act and its resulting C-fact is a (transaction) *process step.*

9.3.4 The Process Model

The Process Model (PM) of an organisation is the ontological model of the state space and the transition space (cf. [1] Chap. 12) of its coordination world. Regarding the state space, the PM contains, for all internal and all border transaction kinds, the process step kinds as well as the applicable existence laws, in full accordance with the CTP (cf. Fig. 9.9). Regarding the transition space, the PM contains, for all internal and all border transaction kinds, the process step kinds as well as the applicable occurrence laws, including the cardinalities of the occurrences, in full accordance with the CTP. The PM of an organisation connects its CM and AM, as far as coordination is concerned (cf. Fig. 9.5).

A PM is represented in a *Process Structure Diagram* (PSD), optionally supplemented by *Transaction Process Diagrams* and a *Create Use Table.* A PSD shows the inter-transaction occurrence laws, thus the laws that hold between transactions of different kinds. They are expressed in two kinds of process links: *response links* and *wait links.* The legend of these links is explained in Fig. 9.11. Figure 9.12 exhibits the PSD of the business process kind that is constituted by the transactor roles CTAR01, TAR01, and TAR02 in Fig. 9.8. We will use it to explain the legend of a PSD in general.

The left part of Fig. 9.12 shows the tree structure from Fig. 9.8, but now in the 'click' mode. The PSD in the right part of the figure is directly derived from this representation. The disks of the transaction kind shapes are 'stretched' horizontally, thus becoming sausage-like shapes. One must consider these shapes to contain the complete transaction pattern. In particular, one must imagine that the sausage shapes contain the standard pattern (in the middle of Fig. 9.9). In addition, one must imagine a non-linear time axis from left to right in the sausage shapes. All coordination acts in the order phase of a transaction are contained in the part of a sausage shape to the left of the diamond. All coordination acts in the result phase of a transaction are contained in the part of a sausage shape to the right of the diamond. The diamond itself represents the execution phase.

The bold grey lines 'behind' the sausage shapes separate the responsibility area of the initiator (above the line) from the responsibility area of the executor (below the line). Only the coordination acts and facts that take part in the interactions between

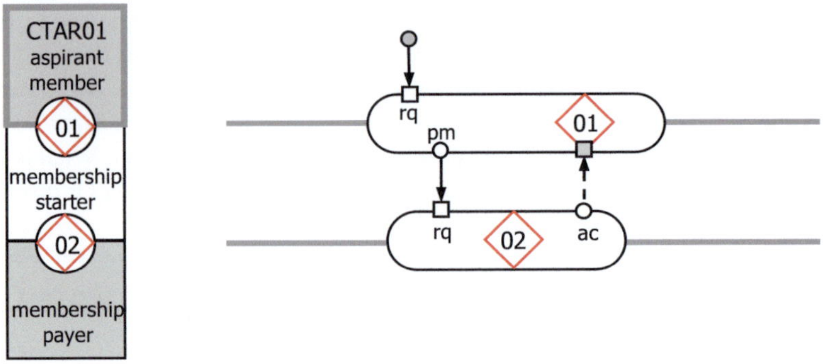

Fig. 9.12 PSD of the membership process in Volley

the participating actors are drawn, always on the edge of the sausage shape. For example, an aspirant member in the case Volley, thus a person in an elementary actor role inside the composite transactor role CTAR01, performs a [TK01/rq] in response to some (basically unknown) state in some (basically unknown) transaction. This initial state is represented in Fig. 9.12 by the small grey-filled disk, and the C-act is represented by the small box labelled "rq" on the edge of the shape of TK01. As follows from the actual operations in Volley or, more specifically, from the action rule in Fig. 9.10, the addressed actor AR01 performs a [TK02/rq] after having promised to carry out the TK01. This is represented by the response link from (TK01/pm) to [TK02/rq]. The actor AR01 will then wait until the transaction TK02 is completed, thus until the state (TK02/ac) is reached. This condition is represented by the wait link from (TK02/ac), expressed by the dotted arrow from the small disk labelled "ac" on the edge of the sausage shape of TK02 to [TK01/ex]; this is the P-act in transactions TK01. The small box is coloured light-grey in order to indicate that it is a P-act, whose performing is basically unknown to the initiator of the transaction TK01. All possible connections between transaction kinds in a PSD are exhibited in Fig. 9.13. In order to show that response links and wait links can apply both to the order phase and to the result phase, they are drawn on both sides of the diamond (u, v, w for the order phase, and x, y, z for the result phase).

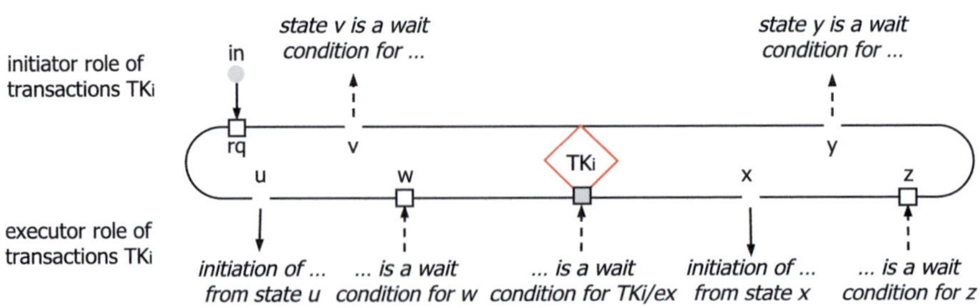

Fig. 9.13 Possible connections between transaction kinds in a PSD

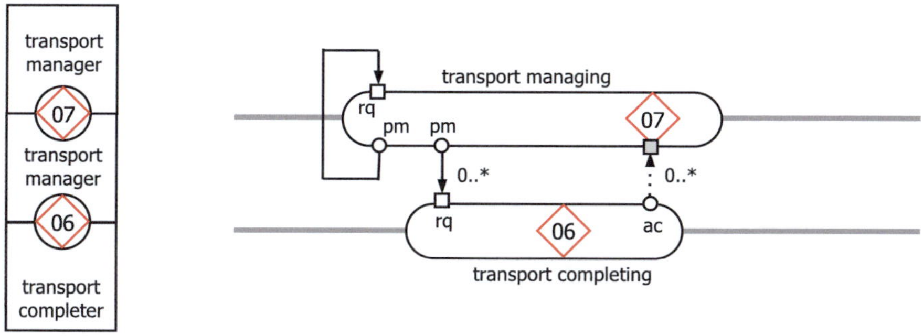

Fig. 9.14 PSD of the car transportation process of Rent-A-Car

Both to response links and to wait links, cardinality constraints may apply. A cardinality range k..n for a response link means that the C-act at the arrow side is performed a minimum number of times k and a maximum number of times n. The default value of k and n is 1; they are not indicated in a PSD. So, for example, the cardinality ranges that hold for the response link from (TK01/pm) to [TK02/rq] in Fig. 9.12, and for the wait link from (TK02/ac) to [TK01/ex] are the default ones.

Figure 9.14 shows examples of non-default cardinality ranges, namely the range 0..*, which means that the act to perform or the state to wait for can occur not at all or an indeterminate number of times. The figure exhibits the PSD of the car transportation process in the case Rent-A-Car (cf. Chap. 15). It also shows how self-activating transaction kinds and actor roles are represented in a PSD. As follows from the case description, transactions TK07 are carried out daily. During the carrying out of a TK07, a number (possibly zero) of transactions TK06 are initiated. When they are all completed, the corresponding transaction TK07 can be completed.

As said, the PSD of a business process kind can be supplemented by one or more transaction process diagrams and a create use table. A *Transaction Process Diagram* (TPD) may be helpful to discuss the exact connections between two transaction processes. Figure 9.15 exhibits an example from the case Volley. In tangerine, the connections between the patterns of transaction kinds TK01 and TK02 are shown. In response to reaching the state TK01/pm, the act TK02/rq is performed. The performing of the P-act (TK01/ex) has to wait for the occurrence of TK02/ac, thus for the completion of the payment of the first fee (cf. Fig. 9.12).

A *Create Use Table* (CUT) shows in which transaction steps instances of the fact types in the FM (cf. Sect. 9.3.5) are created (as an effect of performing the step) and in which steps they are used (in order to settle the agendum). The CUT is a cross-model table. It connects the PM and the FM. Note that the contents of a CUT is fully determined by the AM of the considered organisation. As an example, Table 9.3 shows the CUT for the case Volley. All fact types, so entity types, value types, event types, property types and attribute types, that occur in the FM are listed in the first column of the table. In the second column one indicates the acts by which facts of the type in the left column are *created*. In the third column one indicates the agenda

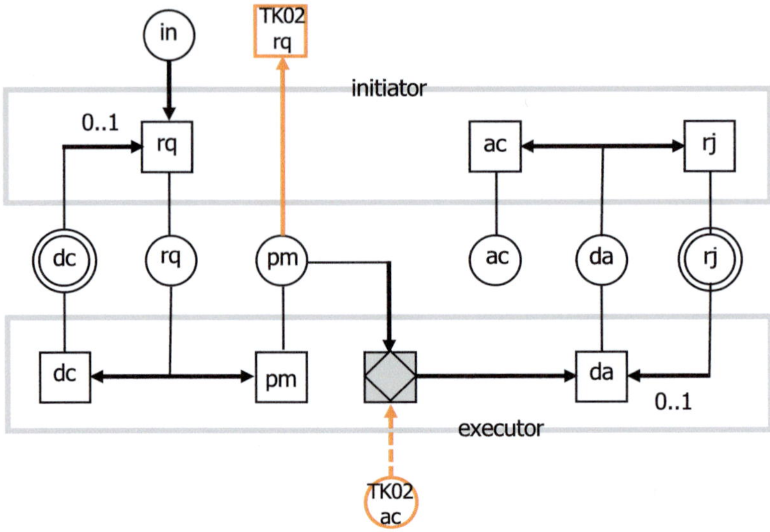

Fig. 9.15 TPD of (the standard pattern in) transaction kind TK01 of Volley

in whose settling facts of the type in the left column are *used*, except for the entity and value types since they are already indirectly used in the property and attribute types.

For fact types whose instances are accessible in external transaction banks, the indication in the second column is "<given externally>". They are listed in the BCT

Table 9.3 CUT of the Volley organisation

P-fact type	Created in performing	Used when settling
MEMBERSHIP	TK01/rq	
PAID MEMBERSHIP	<derived>	
PERSON	<given externally>	
YEAR	<given externally>	
[membership] **is** started	TK01/ac	
the first fee **of** [membership] **is** paid	TK02/ac	TK01/pm
the member **of** [membership]	<provided as par.>	TK01/rq, TK01/pm
the payer **of** [membership]	<provided as par. >	TK01/rq, TK01/pm, TK01/da
the starting day **of** [membership]	<provided as par. >	TK01/rq
the day of birth **of** [person]	<given externally >	TK01/rq
the minimum age **in** [year]	<given externally >	TK01/rq
the max members **in** [year]	<given externally >	TK01/rq
the annual fee **in** [year]	<given externally >	TK01/rq
the amount paid **of** [membership]	TK02/rq	TK02/da
the first fee **of** [membership]	<derived >	TK01/rq, TK02/da
the number **of** members **on** [day]	<derived >	TK01/rq
the age **of** [person] **on** [day]	<derived >	TK01/rq

(cf. Table 9.2), and they are inspected in the assess part of the action rules (cf. Fig. 9.10). For fact types whose instances are provided as parameter values in the given-clause of a when-clause in an action rule concerning the C-event type in the third column (cf. Sect. 9.3.3), the indication in the second column is "<provided as parameter>". Derived fact types are indicated by "<derived>". They have to be included in the Derived Fact Specifications, as part of the FM.

9.3.5 The Fact Model

The Fact Model (FM) of an organisation is the ontological model of the state space and the transition space of its production world. Regarding the *state space*, the FM contains entity types, value types, property types, and attribute types that are relevant for the modelled organisation as well as the existence laws that apply. An FM is the conceptual schema of the production world of the modelled organisation, as far as the state space is concerned. Regarding the *transition space*, an FM contains the event types and the occurrence laws that apply. The FM of an organisation connects its CM and AM, as far as production is concerned (cf. Fig. 9.5).

An FM is expressed in an *Object Fact Diagram* (OFD), supplemented by (textual) *Derived Fact Specifications* (DFS). If needed, (textual) existence laws, and (textual) occurrence laws may be added. Set theory and mathematical function theory help in understanding the relationships between the schema level and the instance level of the conceptual model of a world. The common way of representing sets in set theory is the Venn diagram. In such a diagram, the shape of a set is an oval; symbols within the oval represent the elements of the set. The common way of representing functions (or binary relations in general) is to extend the Venn diagram with connections between the elements of two sets. One set is called the domain of the function, the other one the range. A function maps the elements in the domain to the elements in the range. Figure 9.16 exhibits an extended Venn diagram, representing the function 'has as renter', having as domain the class RENTAL and as range the class PERSON. The figure is considered to be self-explaining.

The mappings between these classes represent property types or attribute types, depending on the kind of the range. *Property types* are expressed by lines between classes. As an example in Fig. 9.17, the property type '**the** member **of** [membership] **is** [person]' is a function that maps the class MEMBERSHIP to the class PERSON. One should imagine that the line between the round angles represents the bunch of connections between elements in MEMBERSHIP and elements in PERSON. The ">" indicates that MEMBERSHIP is the domain of the function and PERSON the range.

Attribute types can be represented in a simpler way, because they represent pure (mathematical) functions, i.e. functions of which the cardinality range at the domain side is 0..*, and at the range side 1..1. Moreover, the range is always a value class. The name of the attribute type is written in the round angle of the class that is its domain. To the right of it, the name of the value class that is the range of the function

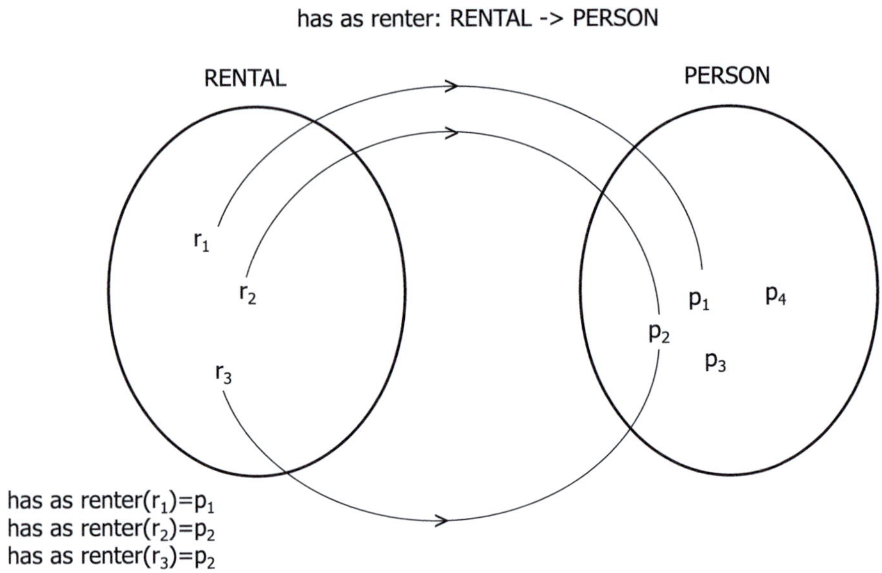

Fig. 9.16 Venn diagram notation of a (mathematical) function

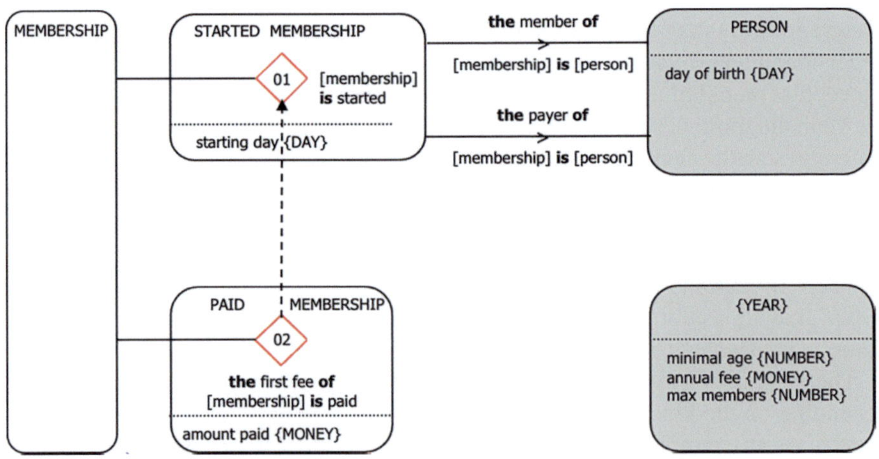

Fig. 9.17 OFD of the Volley organisation

is written, between "{" and"}". As an example, the day of birth of a person is an attribute type that has the object class PERSON as its domain and the value class TIME as its range. The measuring unit is 'day'. Instead of writing "day of birth {TIME: day}" in Fig. 9.17, the shorthand notation {DAY} is used [9].

Production *event types* are represented by diamonds, the universal symbol of production (cf. Chap. 8). They are represented as unary predicates concerning an entity type or class. For example, the event type '**the** first fee **of** [membership] **is** paid' concerns the entity type membership (or the entity class MEMBERSHIP). An event type in the FM is identical to a product kind in the CM. Therefore, the product kind identifier (e.g. PK02) is written in the diamond.

Derived entity types can often be specified graphically, as is done in Fig. 9.17 for started membership and paid membership. They allow precise specifications of the attribute types 'starting day' and 'amount paid': they are functions with as domain the entity classes STARTED MEMBERSHIP and PAID MEMBERSHIP respectively. Standard value classes like DAY and MONEY are assumed to be implicitly present in every OFD. The value class YEAR is explicitly included in the OFD in Fig. 9.17 because of the attribute types that have to be specified, and that have YEAR as their domain: 'minimum age', 'annual fee', and 'max members'.

An OFD also exhibits the *existence laws* that can conveniently be specified graphically. For example, the OFD in Fig. 9.17 shows that the domain of the property type '**the** member **of** [membership] **is** [person]' is the class MEMBERSHIP and that the range is PERSON. In addition it shows that every membership has exactly one person as its member, whereas a person can be member in 0, 1 or many memberships. This follows from the (default) cardinality range. Existence laws that cannot be specified graphically, must be specified textually (cf. Chap. 6). Moreover, an OFD exhibits the *occurrence laws* that can conveniently be specified graphically (expressed by a dashed arrow). For example, the OFD in Fig. 9.17 exhibits that the occurrence of an event of the type '**the** first fee **of** [membership] **is** paid' precedes the occurrence of the corresponding event of the type '[membership] **is** started'.

To complete the explanation of the OFD, the name of an entity class and the list of attribute types that have this entity class as domain, are separated by a dotted line. Lastly, external entity classes are coloured light-grey. Thus, PERSON is an external entity class. It means that persons are created outside the scope of the modelled organisation, but it must be possible to inspect their existence and to use their properties or attributes, like the day of birth. All standard value classes, as presented in [9], are external and thus also coloured light-grey. They are always available.

Derived (fact) types, of all kinds, that cannot be specified graphically, must be specified textually. As follows from the CUT in Table 9.3 and the OFD in Fig. 9.17, there are three attribute types in the case Volley that have to be specified textually, as is done in Fig. 9.18. In this figure, days are values in the Julian time dimension. So, the age of a person is expressed in the number of days that the person exists; it may be transformed to years in the Gregorian calendar. The cardinality of a set is the number of its elements. New members pay the proportional part of the annual fee in the year that the membership starts.

Figure 9.18 also contains the business laws that apply to Volley, in systemic terms called existence laws. They are the *declarative* counterparts of the (imperative) business rules [9] or action rules that are discussed in Sect. 9.3.3. The reader is invited to check that these business laws are correctly accommodated in the action rule in Fig. 9.10.

Derived Fact Specifications

the age **of** [person] **on** [day] ≡ [day] **minus the** day of birth **of** [person]
the number of members **on** [day] ≡ **the cardinality of** STARTED MEMBERSHIP **on** [day]
the first fee **of** [membership] ≡ (12 **minus** (**the** month **of the** starting day **of** [membership]) +1) **times the** annual fee **in the** year **of the** starting day **of** [membership]

Existence Law Specifications

[membership] **is** started **on** [day] **implies that** [day] **is the** first day **of some** [month] **and** [month] **is equal to or greater than** «current month»
[membership] **is** started **on** [day] **implies that the** age **of the** member **of** [membership] **is equal to or greater than the** minimal age **in the** year **of** [day]
[membership] **is** started **on** [day] **implies that the** number of members **on** [day] **is less than or equal to the** max members **in the** year **of** [day]

Fig. 9.18 Derived fact specifications and existence laws of the Volley organisation

9.4 Way of Working

9.4.1 The OER Method

The method in DEMO that supports the making of essential models is called the OER method (cf. Fig. 9.3). OER is an acronym of Organisational Essence Revealing. The notion of revealing is crucial. One does not devise an essential model or create it in some other way; the operational essence is already present in the organisation under consideration, it only has to be revealed. But how does one proceed to reveal the essence of an organisation effectively and efficiently? We come close to the answer by observing the organisation through the glasses that are constituted by the Way of Thinking as presented above.

Recognising that the essence of an organisation inheres in the actors, the best way of working is to address these people and to reveal the essence together with them. By involving them, they will also feel appreciated and they will most likely support your proposals to improve the organisation later. You will need them anyhow in the end for validating your models. The second best option is to rely on written documentation of the operational processes. It is second best for two reasons. First, there is most likely a difference between the descriptions in the documentation and reality. Second, you miss the positive effects of involving the ‘shop floor’ from the beginning. Yet, the second best option is by far the most widely spread approach in practice.

Hereafter, we present the OER method as one would use it for producing the ontological model of an organisation through reverse engineering (cf. Fig. 9.25, step 0). As the example organisation we take the O-organisation of (a part of) the Ford company, as presented in [11]. Our starting point is a narrative description of the case and a picture of the accounts payable process.

9.4.1.1 OER Step 1: Distinguishing Performa-Informa-Forma

The first goal of applying the OER method is to determine the transaction kinds and the actor roles (or the transactor roles for short) in the O-organisation of the enterprise (cf. [1] Chap. 12). A very helpful aid in achieving this goal is to distinguish carefully between the performa, informa, and forma shapes. Figure 9.19 resumes these human abilities both for coordination and for production. It is a copy of Fig. 12.19 in [1].

The innermost ability (the 'blank' me) is added to emphasise the humanness of actors. OER step 1, also called the PIF analysis (PIF from Performa-Informa-Forma), consists of traversing the available documentation and marking pieces of text as expressing performa or informa or forma matters. For illustrating the PIF analysis, we take the case Ford, as discussed in the seminal paper by Michael Hammer, titled "Reengineering Work: Don't Automate, Obliterate" [11]. The paper evoked a variety of endeavours that were all directed to improving the effectiveness of information systems engineering. It was published in 1990, after a decade of fruitless attempts to decrease the costs of automating business processes. People didn't understand business processes nor how automation could improve them. There was only the feeling that automating existing processes was not enough; there was more to be gained.

In the early 1980s, when the American automotive industry was in a depression, Ford's top management put Accounts Payable under the microscope in search of ways to cut costs. In North America alone, Accounts Payable employed more than 500 people. Management thought that by rationalising processes and installing new

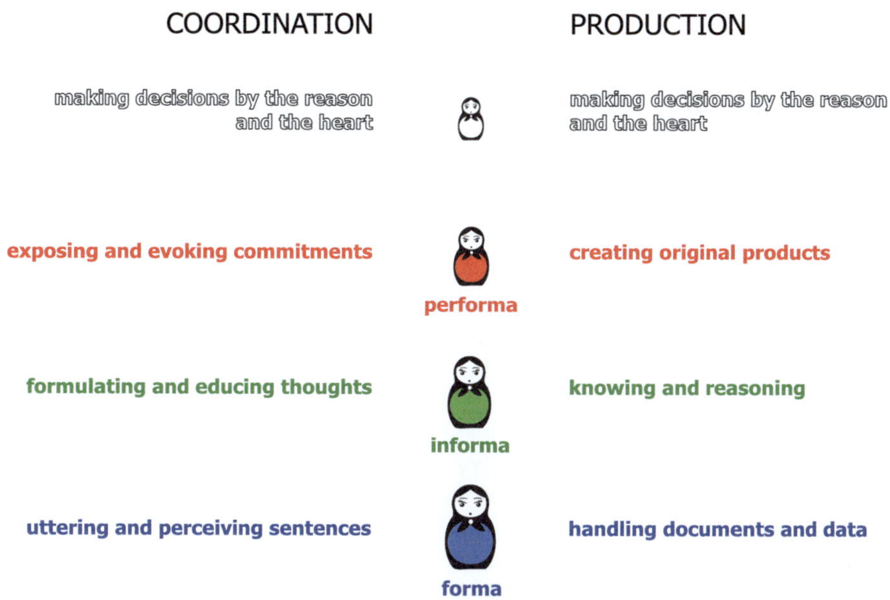

Fig. 9.19 Human abilities in coordination and production

computer systems, it could reduce the head count by some 20%. Ford was enthusiastic about its plan to tighten accounts payable until it looked at Mazda, where the accounts payable organisation consisted only of 5 people. Even after adjusting for Mazda's smaller size, Ford figured that its accounts payable organisation was five times the size it should be.

The current way of working in the accounts payable organisation is illustrated in Fig. 9.6. It is taken from [11]. *When Ford's purchasing department wrote a purchase order, it sent a copy to Accounts Payable. Later, when Goods Receiving received goods of the purchase, it sent a copy of the receiving document to Accounts Payable. Meanwhile, the vendor sent an invoice to Accounts Payable. It was up to Accounts Payable then, to match the purchase order against the receiving document and the invoice. If they matched, payment was issued.*

The department Accounts Payable spent most of its time on mismatches, instances where the purchase order, the receiving document, and the invoice disagreed. In these cases, an accounts payable clerk would investigate the discrepancy, hold up payment, generate new documents, and all in all gum up the works.

In applying OER step 1 to the case Ford, the first thing is to mark those pieces of text that seem to express the performa, informa, or forma level in coordination or in production. Doing this yields the result below. The uncoloured pieces are considered to be irrelevant for our purpose. They include specifically the first paragraph, which is meta text concerning accounts payable.

In the early 1980s, when the American automotive industry was in a depression, Ford's top management put Accounts Payable under the microscope in search of ways to cut costs. In North America alone, Accounts Payable employed more than 500 people. Management thought that by rationalising processes and installing new computer systems, it could reduce the head count by some 20%. Ford was enthusiastic about its plan to tighten accounts payable until it looked at Mazda, where the accounts payable organisation consisted only of 5 people. Even after adjusting for Mazda's smaller size, Ford figured that its accounts payable organisation was five times the size it should be.

The current way of working in the accounts payable organisation is illustrated in Fig. 9.6. *It is taken from* [11]. *When Ford's purchasing department wrote a purchase order, it sent a copy to Accounts Payable. Later, when Goods Receiving received goods of the purchase, it sent a copy of the receiving document to Accounts Payable. Meanwhile, the vendor sent an invoice to Accounts Payable. It was up to Accounts Payable, then, to match the purchase order against the receiving document and the invoice. If they matched, payment was issued.*

The department accounts payable spent most of its time on mismatches, instances where the purchase order, the receiving document, and the invoice disagreed. In these cases, an accounts payable clerk would investigate the discrepancy, hold up payment, generate new documents, and all in all gum up the works.

Although the main goal of the PIF analysis is to find the performa parts, colouring also the informa and forma parts may help in finding them. It is certainly most helpful in the beginning. After one has got experience, it will suffice to use only the red marker. At the same time, one must be cautious. In particular, one must be attentive to avoid the so-called *blue trap*. Sometimes, a piece of text expresses a forma level P-act, but is at the same time the forma level of a C-act. A good example is the piece "sent an invoice to accounts payable" in the second paragraph. Next to being 'blue' production (right side of Fig. 9.19), it expresses the 'blue' way in which a request is done to get payment (left side of Fig. 9.19). To indicate the additional performa meaning, the text is underlined. From now on, we consider the text thus as being 'red'.

As said, the main goal is to find the performa parts in a description. Nevertheless, being aware of the 'green' and 'blue' parts may help to achieve this goal.

9.4.1.2 OER Step 2: Identifying Transaction Kinds and Actor Roles

The second step of the OER method is to find the relevant transaction kinds, the corresponding product kinds, and the executing actor roles, based on the'red' results of the PIF analysis.

Part of the case description is Fig. 9.20, in which the flows are indicated that are related to the work of accounts payable. In Fig. 9.21, we have put transactor roles (so transaction kinds and their executor roles) on Fig. 9.20. The parts of the figure that are covered by the actor role boxes are considered to be the filler(s) of the actor roles.

So, we have identified three transaction kinds and consequently three executing actor roles. They are specified in the TPT in Table 9.4. TK03 (purchase shipping) is added to cover the physical transport of goods from the vendor to Ford. The result

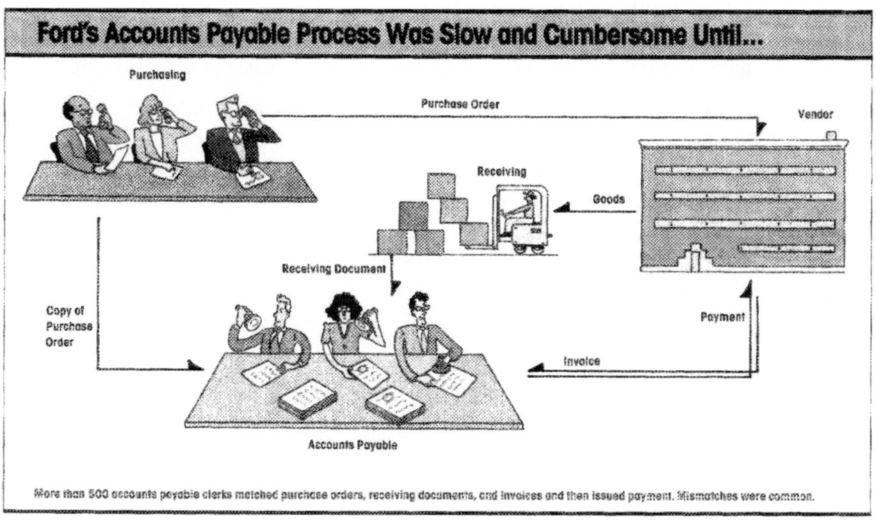

Fig. 9.20 Accounts payable work and related information flows

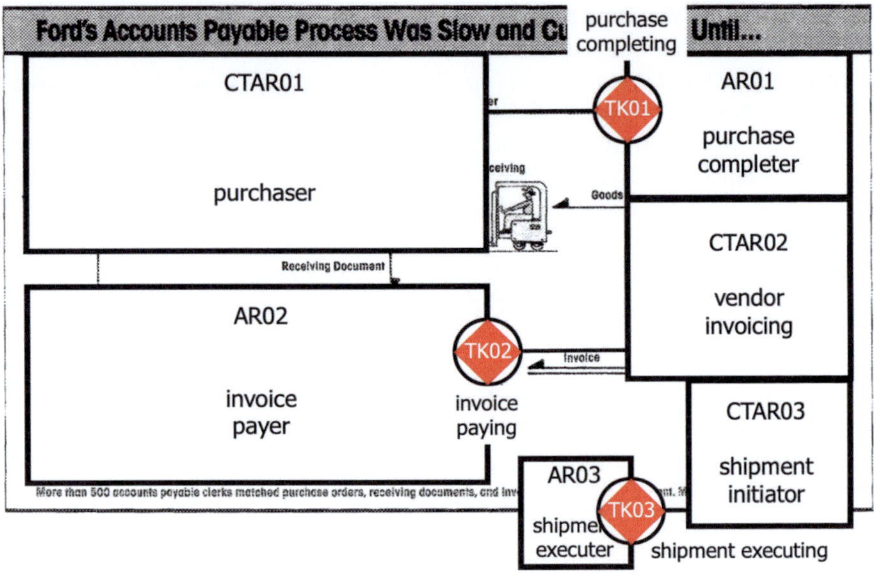

Fig. 9.21 Drawing of the identified transactor roles on Fig. 9.6

of a transaction TK03 is the delivery of the goods of a purchase to the receiving department of Ford.

The words "purchase", "invoice" and "shipment" between "[" and "]" represent the variable in the product kind. It is instantiated by the individual purchases, invoices, and shipments. In Fig. 9.22, the transaction acts are indicated that are performed in the 'red' flows in Fig. 9.20. The green lines represent information flows. They regard the contents of the purchase orders and the receiving documents.

The key problem of Ford is perfectly expressed by the TPT in Table 9.1. It is that purchases, shipments, and invoices are only loosely connected. Shipments are about some purchase, as invoices are, but they may be only about a part of a purchase. It can easily occur that a vendor responds to a purchase order for 1000 tyres of some brand and model by sending an invoice for 500 tyres, expecting that this quantity can be delivered now and the rest next week. But when loading the truck to ship the tyres, there appear to be only 497 in stock. Consequently, the workers in the accounts payable department are quite busy in trying to match the three flows: copies of purchase orders, received shipments, and invoices. From Fig. 9.8, it is clear

Table 9.4 TPT of the case Ford (old)

Transaction kind	Product kind	Executor role
TK01 purchase completing	PK01 [purchase] **is** completed	AR01 purchase completer
TK02 invoice paying	PK02 [invoice] **is** paid	AR02 invoice payer
TK03 shipment executing	PK03 [shipment] **is** executed	AR03 shipment executer

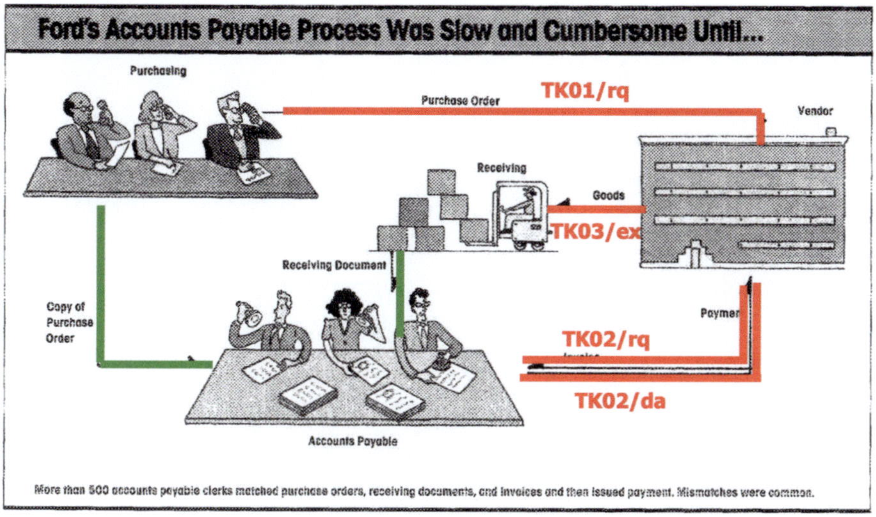

Fig. 9.22 Identified transaction acts in the case Ford (old)

that the workers in the Receiving Goods department accept all shipments, for the simple reason that they don't know the purchase orders. Therefore, they forward all Receiving Documents to Accounts Payable.

9.4.1.3 OER Step 3: Composing the Ontological Model

After having completed OER step 2, one has basically identified all transaction kinds and their executing actor roles in the organisation. It is now time to build the DEMO model of it. Figure 9.23 summarises the ways in which the four sub models of an organisation are expressed, in diagrams, tables, and (formal) texts (cf. [1] Chap. 12).

After having identified the transaction kinds TK01, TK02, and TK03, and subsequently the product kinds PK01, PK02, and PK03, as well as the executing actor roles AR01, AR02, and AR03, we can produce the CSD (Coordination Structure Diagram). It is presented in Fig. 9.24. Together with the TPT in Table 9.1, it represents the CM of the case Ford in the 'old' situation. Note that the three actor roles on the vendor side (AR01, CTAR02, and CTAR03) are all mapped on the vendor shape.

CTAR01 (Ford purchasing) belongs to the Ford organisation, whereas transactor role TAR01 (purchase completer) is part of the vendor. CTAR02 (vendor invoicing) and CTAR03 (vendor shipping) belong to the vendor organisation, whereas TAR02 (invoice payer) is part of Ford. TAR03 can be part of the vendor organisation, but it can also be a third party. The access links from AR02 to TK01 and TK03 represent that actors AR02 get copies of the purchase orders and the receiving documents.

Because the three trees of transactor roles are only 'loosely' coupled, there is little sense in producing also the other aspect models: the AM, the PM, and the FM.

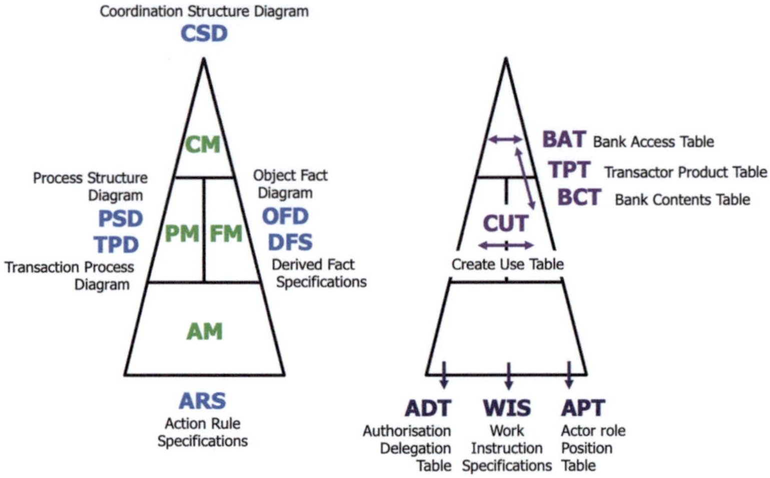

Fig. 9.23 Ways of representing the four sub models

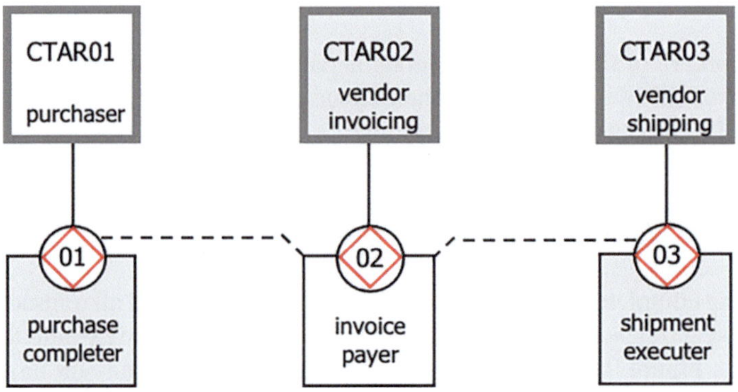

Fig. 9.24 CSD of the case Ford 'old'

9.4.1.4 OER Step 4: Validating the Essential Model

In the previous steps of the OER method we have applied the first four sapiences (cf. Fig. 9.2): *separation of concerns* (taking exclusively the construction perspective), *use of abstraction* (applying in particular the PSI, OMEGA, and ALPHA theories), *devising proper concepts* (notably in Sect. 9.4.3), and *verification by instantiation.* It is time now to practice the fifth sapience: *validation from ontology.* Where verification of a model ensures that the model is correct according to the applied methodology, validation ensures that a model offers a faithful understanding of the modelled piece of reality. The reader is referred to [1] Chap. 12 for a discussion of OER step 4.

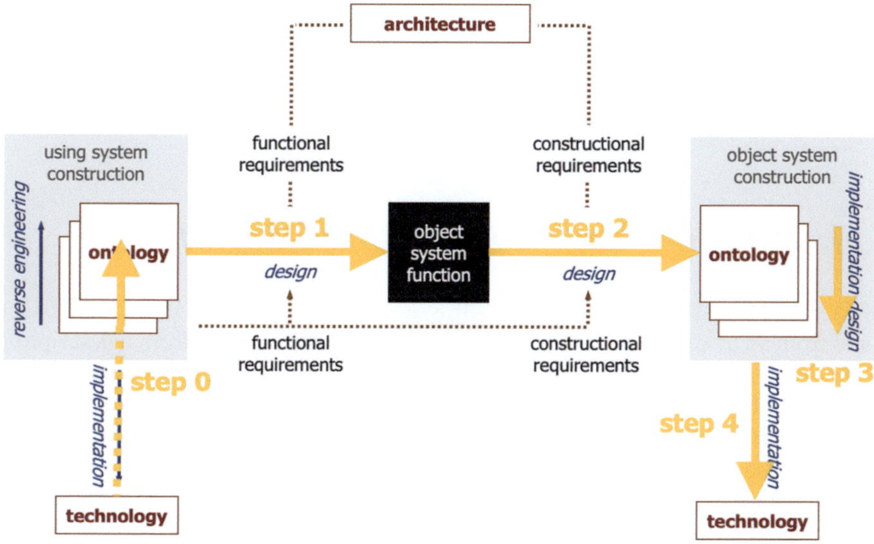

Fig. 9.25 GSDP with the five DAO steps

9.5 The DAO Method

The method in DEMO that guides the (re) development of organisations is called the DAO method (cf. Fig. 9.3). DAO is an acronym of Designing under Architecture from Ontology. DAO is also the name of a river in Portugal.[7] As brought to our knowledge by the ancient Greek philosopher Heraclitus,[8] rivers are never the same. So are organisations. New facts to base a purchase decision on, admitting a new vendor or hiring a new employee, are all changes of an enterprise. Not always does a change imply redesign. Only the first example leads to a change in the ontological model of the enterprise's O-organisation. The others are only implementational changes.

Figure 9.25 shows the distinct steps of the DAO method. Step 0 is added for the sake of completeness. It is actually what the OER method brings about. As we did in Chap. 8, "using system" is abbreviated to "US" and "object system" to "OS".

Both the GSDP (General System Development Process) and the GRAF (General Requirements and Architecture Framework) are crucial intellectual tools of the DAO method. They are presented in Sect. 8.2.5. Hereafter we will discuss how the distinct steps in the GSDP are performed and how the GRAF is used in performing a step, if applicable. As hinted at already in Sects. 8.3.1 and 8.3.2, the DAO method is applied to the (re) development of O-organisations and to the development of enterprise information systems (EISs). Applying the DAO method to the development

[7] By referring to the DAO river, we want to pay tribute to our Portuguese colleagues in the Ciao! Network, who always have been loyal to the cause of Enterprise Engineering, and who have contributed immensely to its development and spreading.

[8] One of the famous sayings of Heraclitus is "panta rei", "everything flows".

of O-organisations is presented in Sects. 9.5.1 through 9.5.5, with the case Ford for illustration. The application of the DAO method to the development of an EIS is presented in Sect. 9.5.6. Steps 1 and 2 are steered by the BETA theory (cf. In this chapter). Steps 3 and 4 are steered by the ETA theory (cf. Chap. 10).

9.5.1 DAO Step 0: Producing the Essential Model of the US

DAO step 0 consists of applying the OER method, as discussed in Sect. 9.3. One starts from an available lower level constructional model, or even from a description of the implementation itself (like the case descriptions in Chaps. 11 through 14), and reveals the ontological model of the US. If the OS is an O-organisation, then the model of the US is mostly an informal description of the future customers of the enterprise, as discussed in Sect. 8.3.1. This step needs only be performed if the ontological model of the US (using system) is needed but missing.

Fortunately, the description of the case Ford in [11] provides us with pictures of the constructional models of the US and the OS. In Sect. 9.4.1 we have discussed the revealing of the ontological model of the US of the case Ford.

9.5.2 DAO Step 1: Defining the Function of the OS

In DAO step 1, the function of the OS is defined. The important distinction between the construction of a system and the functionality it may offer to any other system is discussed in Chap 5 (the TAO theory). This functionality is completely based on the construction of the US. It is also expressed in terms of this construction, as we exemplified for a sales department in this chapter.

We distinguish between two sources of input: the functional requirements that are provided by the actors in the US, and the functional requirements in the applied architecture (cf. Fig. 9.11). In order to discuss and analyse the needs for change, we dispose of the BMC and the SCP approaches (cf. Chap. 3).

The most important change goal in the case Ford is to reduce costs, specifically through a 75% reduction of the staff working in Accounts Payable. The formulated change mission is what Ford calls 'invoiceless processing'. In [11], this change is articulated by the slogan "Ford's old rule: we pay when we get the invoice. Ford's new rule: we pay when we get the goods". It entails more, however: incomplete deliveries would just be sent back. This has enormous impact on the daily operations of Ford. The last paragraph of the case description reads:

The department accounts payable spent most of its time on mismatches, instances where the purchase order, the receiving document, and the invoice disagreed. In these cases, an accounts payable clerk would investigate the discrepancy, hold up payment, generate new documents, and all in all gum up the works.

Based on this text, we formulate the next QoS (Quality of Service) indicators. The quantities (20, 5 and 5) are chosen quite arbitrarily:

The time delay between receiving and paying an invoice is less than 20 days.
The number of refused invoices per month is less than 5.
The number of refused goods deliveries per month is less than 5.

9.5.3 DAO Step 2: Creating the Ontological Model of the OS

The starting point of the *ontological design* step is the object system function, thus the outcome of DAO step 1. Because of the fundamental difference between function and construction, as explained in Chap. 5, this design step is the most creative step: a construction must be conceived in the mind of the designer that, once put into operation, offers the required functionalities to the distinguished stakeholders.

Next to the specification of the object system function, the constructional designer has to satisfy two groups of (constructional) requirements. One is provided by the stakeholders of the US, the other one is provided by the applicable architecture (cf. Fig. 9.11). Both groups of requirements are discussed in Chap. 9. Conceiving a construction of the OS within the restrictions that are set by the functional model and the constructional requirements is the greatest challenge in designing things of any kind. Fortunately, the designer can rely on proven practices, like design patterns in software engineering [12], in addition to her/his skills. One should at the same time be aware that relying on proven practices may have its drawbacks, as our discussion in Sect. 3.2 of the design of the one-whole kettle in [13] convincingly demonstrates.

Concluding, constructional design is the hardest part of every design effort. The key element is the creativity of the designer, who also has to find a balance between reasonable requirements and feasible specifications [14]. In the case Ford, the design of the new construction of the enterprise's organisation has been done already. The board of directors of Ford has decided that the main goal, namely the reduction of the staff of Accounts Payable by 75%, will be achieved by the introduction of what they call 'invoiceless processing'. It means that deliveries of goods that do not fully match an issued purchase order, are refused, and that the acceptance of matching deliveries will count as having received the corresponding invoice.

The new situation is perfectly expressed in the TPT in Table 9.5. Instead of the three core entity types in Table 9.4, there is only one now, namely the purchase. The loosely coupled three processes, as shown in Fig. 9.24 are now strongly coupled, as shown in the CSD in Fig. 9.26. We also produce the other aspect models.

On the right side of Fig. 9.13, the corresponding PSD (Process Structure Diagram) is shown. In a PSD, the shape of a transaction kind is stretched out horizontally to a 'sausage'. It shows that a transaction TK02 is initiated from the state promised of a transaction TK01, and that the executing actor AR01 has to wait with performing the production act (represented by the small grey-coloured box) until the TK02 is accepted, which means that it is successfully carried out. A similar reasoning holds for transaction kind TK03. As soon as both the enclosed transaction TK02 and

Table 9.5 TPT of the case Ford (new)

Transaction kind	Product kind	Executor role
TK01 purchase completing	PK01 [purchase] **is** completed	AR01 purchase completer
TK02 purchase paying	PK02 [purchase] **is** paid	AR02 purchase payer
TK03 purchase transporting	PK03 [purchase] **is** transported	AR03 purchase transporter

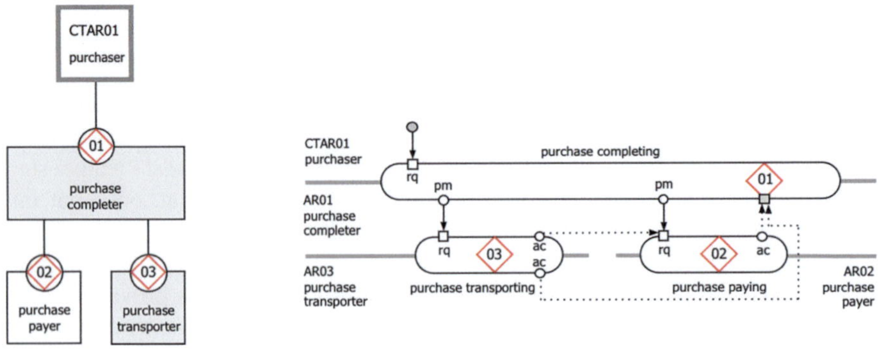

Fig. 9.26 CSD and PSD of the case Ford (new)

the enclosed transaction TK03 are finished, [TK01/ex] can be performed. Next, the transaction TK01 can be finished by performing the [TK01/da] and [TK01/ac].

In the new situation, delivering the goods of a purchase to Ford, also counts as performing the C-act [TK02/rq] (invoiceless processing). In the PSD this expressed by the wait link from (TK03/ac) to [TK02/rq]. Like it holds for the case Pizzeria (cf. Chap 12), the acceptance of goods deliveries, so the act [TK03/ac] is (implicitly) delegated to the people in Goods Receiving. In a similar way, [TK03/da], thus the delivery of goods, also counts as [TK01/da], which is the completion of the purchase by the vendor. By accepting this, so by performing the act [TK01/ac], Ford agrees with the completion. This act is performed tacitly.

The picture of the new situation in [11] is shown in Fig. 9.27. Mapping the three transaction kinds on Fig. 9.27 yields Fig. 9.28. Note that the difference with Fig. 9.7 is (only) in actor role AR01.

Like we did for the situation before re-engineering, we now indicate the main transaction kind steps in the picture of the new situation. This yields Fig. 9.29. Because of the new policy of Ford, receiving goods now counts as performing [TK03/da] and [TK02/rq]. As discussed, it also counts as performing [TK01/da]. There is no separate communication between actors AR01 and AR00.

In the foregoing discussion, we have seen several instances of delegation. They can be expressed conveniently in an ADT (Authorisation Delegation Table). Table 9.5 exhibits the delegations, both in the old (left side) and the new situation (right side). They appear to be the same. The delegation of [TK01/ac] from the purchaser to the goods receiver is a classical one: purchasers in a company are generally not accepting

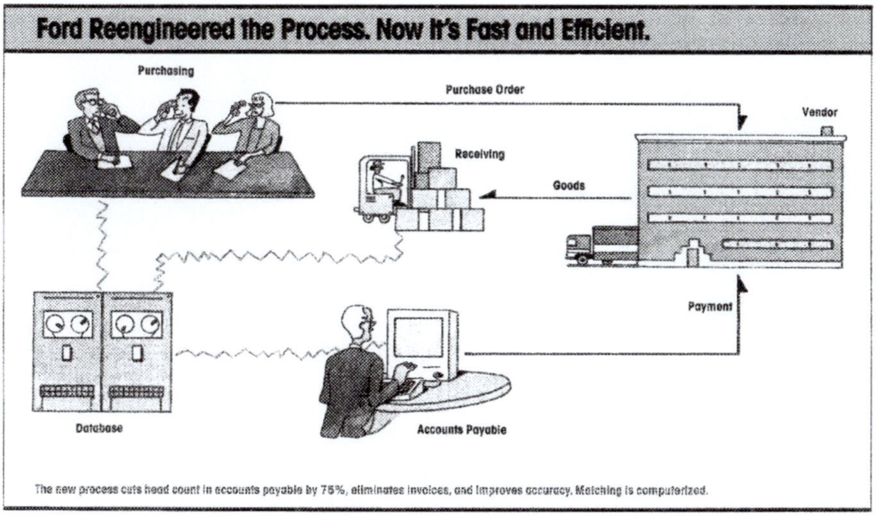

Fig. 9.27 Picture of the new situation

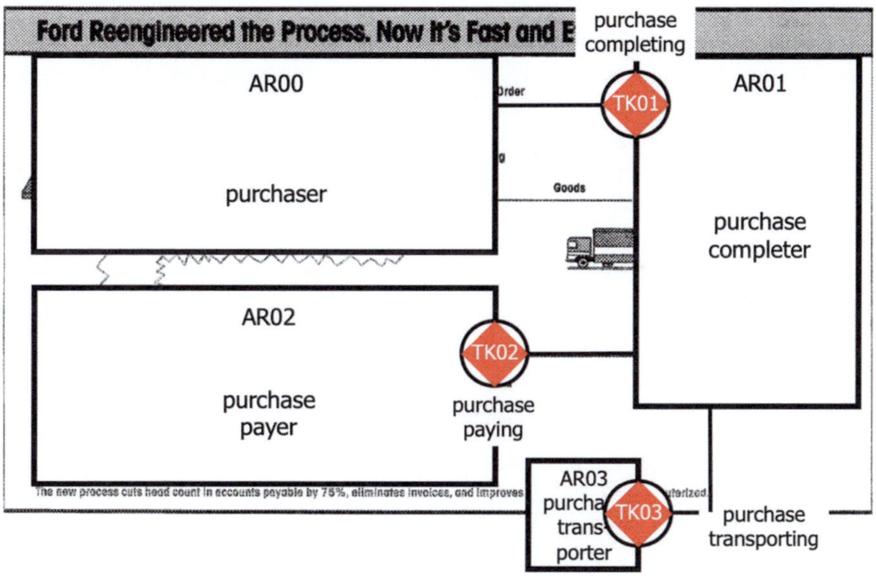

Fig. 9.28 Drawing of the identified transactor roles on Fig. 9.27

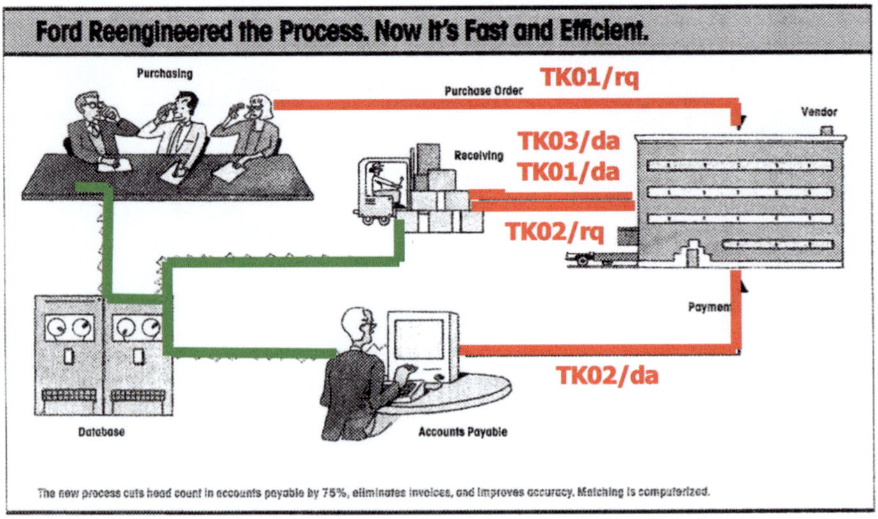

Fig. 9.29 Identified transaction acts in the case Ford (new)

the results of their purchasing, although as a consumer in a flower shop, they do. The delegation of [TK03/ac] has purely logistic reasons: one cannot expect the vendor, who anyhow initiated the transaction TK03, to be present at the site of Ford where the goods are delivered and received.

In Fig. 9.30, the OFD (Object Fact Diagram) of the case Ford is presented. Recall that the event types '[purchase] **is** completed', '[purchase] **is** paid', and '[purchase] **is** transported' are identical to respectively the product kinds PK01, PK02, and PK03.

9.5.4 DAO Step 3: Creating the Implementation Model of the OS

The starting point of the *implementation design* step is the ontological model of the object system (OS). In general, we distinguish between three kinds of technologies in the implementation of an ontological model: actor technology, production technology, and communication technology. The process of engineering (implementation design) is clarified by the ETA theory in [6] Chap. 10. Hereafter, we demonstrate DAO step 3, thus the design of the implementation model to the case Ford.

The CM of the case Ford is represented in the CSD in Fig. 9.26, left side, and the TPT in Table 9.5. The corresponding PM is expressed in the PSD in Fig. 9.26, right side. The AM is expressed in the action rules in Tables 9.6 and 9.7 and the FM is expressed in the OFD in Fig. 9.30. These model expressions are sufficient to start designing the implementation of the new situation at Ford.

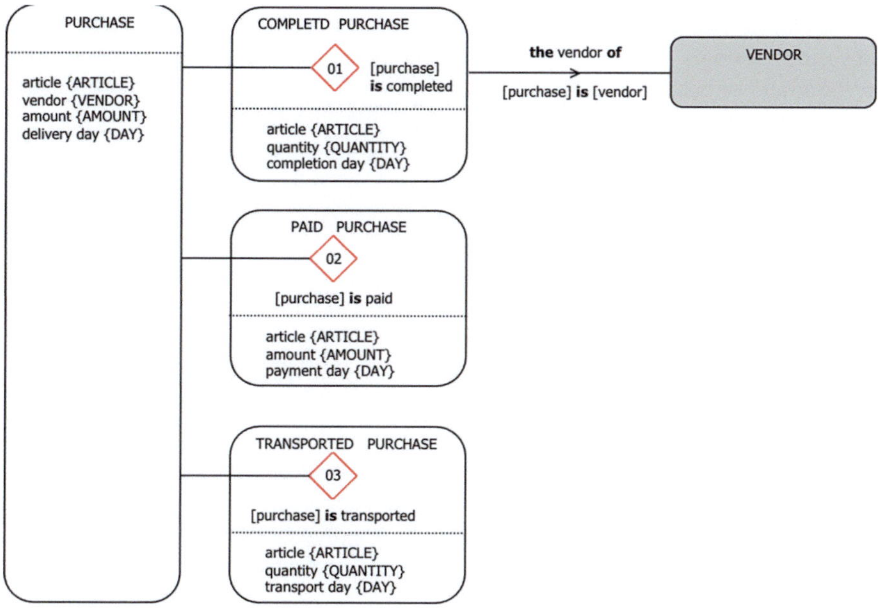

Fig. 9.30 OFD of the case Ford

Table 9.6 ARS01

when	purchase completing **for** [purchase] <u>is promised</u>		(TK01/pm)
	while purchase transporting **for** [purchase] <u>is accepted</u>		
	given	**the** payer **of** [purchase]	
assess	*rightness:*	**the** <u>performer</u> **of the** <u>promise</u> **is the** purchase completer **of** [purchase]	
		the <u>addressee</u> **of the** <u>promise</u> **is the** purchaser **of** [purchase] ;	
	sincerity:	< no specific condition >	
	truth:	< no specific condition >	
if	*performing the action after **then** is considered justifiable*		
then	<u>request</u>	purchase paying **for** [purchase]	[TK02/rq]
	to	**the** payer **of** [purchase] ;	
	with	**the** <u>requested</u> amount **of** [purchase]	

Table 9.7 ARS02

when	purchase paying **for** [purchase] <u>is declared</u>		(TK02/da)
	given	**the** <u>declared</u> amount **of** [purchase]	
assess	*rightness:*	**the** <u>performer</u> **of the** <u>declare</u> **is the** payer **of** [purchase] ;	
		the <u>addressee</u> **of the** <u>declare</u> **is the** purchase completer **of** [purchase] ;	
	sincerity:	< no specific condition >	
	truth:	**the** <u>declared</u> amount **is equal to the** <u>requested</u> amount **of** [purchase];	
if	*performing the action after **then** is considered justifiable*		
then	<u>accept</u>	purchase paying **for** [purchase]	[TK02/ac]
	to	**the** <u>performer</u> **of the** <u>declare</u> ;	
else	<u>reject</u>	purchase paying **for** [purchase]	[TK02/rj]
	to	**the** <u>performer</u> **of the** <u>declare</u> ;	
	* justification of rejecting *		

The employees in purchasing are the fillers of actor role CTAR00 (purchaser) and the various vendors (presumably the sales persons within the vendor organisations) are the fillers of actor role AR01. C-acts [TK01/rq] are performed through sending purchase orders (on paper by postal mail or digital/electronically). C-acts [TK01/pm] are performed tacitly, which means that there is no evidence of having performed them, as explained in Chap. 6. The delivery of the goods of a purchase is the act [TK03/da]. It counts also as performing the [TK01/da] of the same purchase and of the corresponding [TK02/rq] (cf. Fig. 9.29).

The embodiment of [TK02/rq] is the forwarding of the (electronic) receiving document of the purchase to Accounts Payable. The employees in this department are the fillers of actor role AR02 (purchase payer). They respond to C-acts [TK02/rq] by an implicit promise [TK02/pm] and an explicit [TK02/da]. Presumably, the vendor becomes aware of these acts through receiving the payment slips from the bank. The acceptance [TK02/ac] is performed tacitly.

The actors in Purchasing, who issued the purchase orders (and thus performed the C-acts [TK01/rq]), should actually respond also to the events (TK01/da). They won't however, as we have discussed above. Apparently, they have delegated this authority to the workers in Goods Receiving, but the question is whether they are aware of this.

Transactions TK03 (purchase transporting) are necessary but there are no Ford actors involved in carrying out these transactions. The delivery of the goods of a purchase is the effect of performing the P-act TK03/ex, but the [TK03/da] is directed to the transporter or shipper. For logistic reasons, we consider the act being addressed to the goods receivers in Ford. Consequently, these people are considered to have the delegated authority to respond to acts [TK03/da], as shown in the ADTs in Table 9.8.

Lastly, refusing a shipment of goods, because it does not (fully) match a purchase, means two things. First, the goods are sent back to the vendor straight away (the people at Ford just refuse to receive them). Second, there is no performing of C-acts, neither of a [TK03/da] nor of a [TK02/rq]. There is also no performance of a [TK01/da], which means that the TK01 is still alive. It can only be ended in the way as described above.

Table 9.8 Delegations in the case Ford

Agendum/Position	TK01/da	TK03/da
Purchaser	A	
Goods receiver	D	D
Shipper		A

Agendum/Position	TK01/da	TK03/da
Purchaser	A	
Goods receiver	D	D
Shipper		A

Table 9.9 APT for the Ford organisation

Actor role/position	AR02
Accounts payable officer	X

9.5.5 *DAO Step 4: Implementing the OS*

The implementation of the object system is carried out according to the ETA theory, as discussed in Chap. 10. By implementing is understood the assignment of actor technology, production technology, and communication technology to the elements of the implementation model, thus to the outcomes of DAO step 3. To these outcomes belongs also the assignment of actor roles to (organisational) positions, which is presented in an Actor role Position Table (APT). Table 9.9 shows these assignments for the Ford organisation.

Since our focus is Accounts Payable, we only care about transactor role TAR02. The fillers of actor role AR02 are the officers in the Accounts Payable department. The production technology that they use in order to execute transactions TK02 is only their minds: they decide on the payments they do. Regarding the coordination technology that actors AR02 use in carrying out transactions TK02, the implementations of the coordination acts are discussed already in Sect. 9.5.4 (DAO step 3).

9.6 The HOS Method

In this section, we discuss the HOS method. HOS is an acronym of Human-centric Operating and Steering organisations. The HOS method guides one in establishing governance and management in an organisation, as well as in deciding how to go about changes. As we have discussed in Chap. 8, such a decision is sometimes a matter of management and sometimes of governance. As the example SoI we take the part of the Ford company that we have used already above.

9.6.1 *HOS Step 1: Establishing Management*

As we discussed in Chap. 8, when presenting the SIGMA theory, the metaphor for management is keeping the ship on a set route. The route itself is determined by the precise shape of the enterprise's essential model, in particular by the ontological model of the O-organisation. Although this model does not contain management transactor roles, we have identified situations in which a manager is needed to decide upon the number of employees that fill an (operational) actor role simultaneously. When looking at the Ford case above, the three departments involved, so Purchasing, Accounts Payable, and Receiving, need such a manager in order to deal with the fluctuating demand on the resources, including the human fillers of the operational actor roles. These managers decide about the capacities needed on a regular basis, probably daily, but it could also be shorter or longer than a day.

In order to focus on the management tasks it turns out that we need to extend the ontological model of Ford's O-organisation with a (self-activating) transactor role TAR04, a (self-activating) transactor role TAR05, and a transactor role TAR06, as shown in Fig. 9.31. The addition of TAR04 means that we assume that purchasers act independently of other actors and that they periodically decide to place a purchase order, presumably after having inspected the current stock of the goods to be replenished. The purchase manager decides on who is filling role A04 and on the (maximum) production time of a TK04. Setting the production time of transactions TK01 as well as setting the settlement time of transaction steps TK01/rq is considered to be the responsibility of actors AR04.

Regarding the receiving of goods and their storage in the warehouse, we need to add transactor roles TAR05 and TAR06. Employees in the Receiving department fill actor role AR06. The filler of actor role AR05 is most likely the manager of the Receiving department. He/she thus controls the Receiving employees. This actor role also determines the number of employees that fill actor role AR06 simultaneously. In addition, he/she may decide on the (maximum) production time of transactions TK06 as well as on the (maximum) settlement time of the transaction steps TK06/rq. Figure 9.31 applies to the old and for the new situation at Ford. In other words, the extensions also hold for the CSD in Fig. 9.26. Note that transaction kinds TK03 and TK06 are different. The effect of a transaction TK03 is that goods are delivered

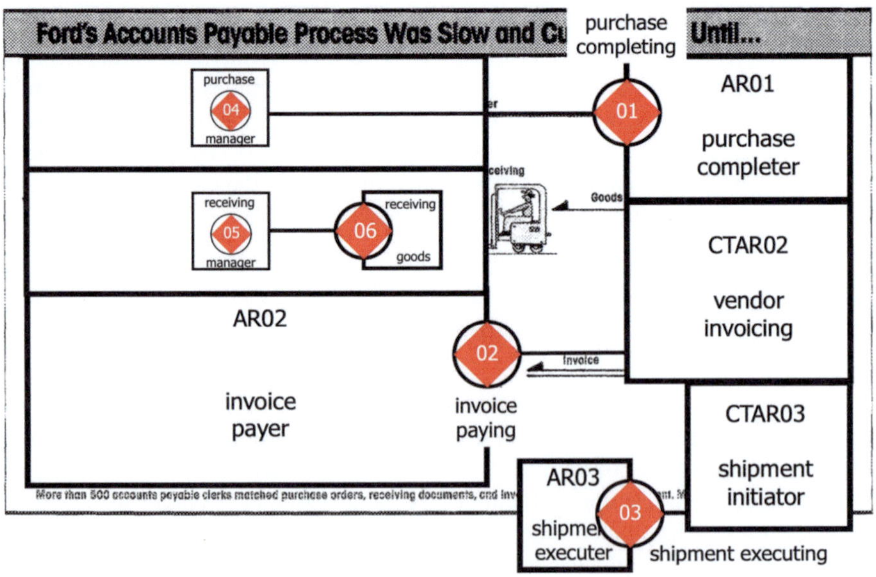

Fig. 9.31 Adapted CSD of the Ford organisation

at a warehouse of the Ford company. The effect of a transaction TK06 is that specific delivered goods are picked up and stored in the warehouse.

Concluding, we have introduced two new management transactor roles: a *Purchase Manager* and a *Receiving Manager*. The first one manages/controls the employees in the Purchase department, the second one does the same for the employees in the Receiving department.

9.6.2 HOS Step 2: Establishing Governance

As discussed when we presented the SIGMA theory in Chap. 8, every employee of an enterprise is involved in the governance of the enterprise. It means that everyone is encouraged to submit change proposals that improve the overall performance of the Ford company, be it on short or on long term. As also discussed in Chap. 8, namely in Sect. 8.4, decisions to change are sometimes 'clear' governance matters, but sometimes they are considered management acts. This is the case when a change proposal is brought up and decided upon within a 'lowest level' team of workers, and when the scope of the change is limited to the team. In principle, however, every change proposal that affects the route of the ship, is a governance issue. In order to make this rule practical, we have stated that any change of the essential model of the SoI under consideration, is a governance issue.

The human-centric character of the HOS method (and of Enterprise Engineering in general) is practised by involving every employee in the governance of the enterprise. This is not something easily established. Compared to the (still dominant) Taylorian view on workers, it implies a huge cultural change. The number of enterprises that have succeeded in bringing about this change is still small. The resulting pleasure and proud of the workers, however, has no precedent. Several enterprises have succeeded in implementing a human-centric organisation. The most well-known example is the company Semco in Brazil [15]. The characteristics of the Semco model are its being human-centric and democratic. Similar ideas are discussed in [16]. In The Netherlands, there are several examples of enterprises that have based their organisation on the Semco model. Among the most well-known are Buurtzorg (www.buurtzorg.com) and ZorgAccent (www.zorgaccent.nl). A software (ERP) company that has implemented Enterprise Ontology in its organisation is Mprise (www.mprise.nl).

9.6.3 HOS Step 3: Identifying Governance Decisions

In Sect. 9.5.3 (DAO step 2), we discussed already the decision that the staff in the Accounts Payable department should be reduced by 75%. This decision was taken by the Board of Directors of Ford, thus by the 'highest' governance actor. The directors think that this goal can be achieved by taking a number of measures, which they collectively call 'invoiceless processing'. It entails primarily that deliveries which do not fully match a purchase order, are completely refused, and that the acceptance of a delivery counts as having received the corresponding invoice. Hence the term "invoiceless", which thus only means that the vendor doesn't need to send a separate (paper) invoice. Although the executing actor of transaction TK03 thus the filler of actor role AR03, is external to Ford, creations of PK03 which do not match exactly a PK01, will not be allowed, i. e. such deliveries are refused on the spot or will be sent back later.

Although the ontological model of the O-organisation of Ford seems not to have changed when comparing the CSDs in Figs. 9.20 and 9.28, there has been an important mental/conceptual change, namely the conceiving of the purchase as the new unit of thinking about the formerly rather unrelated processes of purchasing, shipments delivering, and invoice paying. A quick comparison of the TPTs in Table 9.4 and 9.5 elucidates what we intend to convey. Goods deliveries are only accepted if they match exactly a purchase order. Therefore, the decision to go for 'invoiceless processing' is undoubtedly a governance decision: it changes the ontological model of the O-organisation of Ford.

The changes in the I-organisation, the D-organisation, and the M-organisation that come along with it, are also considerable. As pictured in Fig. 9.27, all three departments, thus Purchasing, Receiving, and Account Payable, are impacted by the automation of the communication between them. Most likely, a new department is established. Let us call it ICT Systems.

Concluding, the decision by the Board of Directors of Ford to go for 'invoiceless processing' is without any doubt a governance decision. Because of the considerable impact of the decision (at least three departments are involved), it seems proper that it is taken at the level of the Board of Directors.

9.6.4 HOS Step 4: Identifying Management Decisions

As explained in Chap. 8, management decisions are basically characterised by the property that they do not change the ontological model of the O-organisation. Consequently, all decisions to bring about such changes are considered management acts. However, there are decisions that do change the ontological model of the O-organisation, but are still considered management acts. This exception is made for decisions that are taken at the lowest management level, that is the level of the foreman as depicted by Mintzberg in Fig. 2.1, and that have no impact outside the team.

In general, management decisions are confined to keeping the ship on the set route, as discussed in Sect. 9.6.1. The control instruments of the manager are discussed in Sect. 8.2. They are the assignment of employees to actor roles, the setting of the (maximum) production time of the transactions they execute, and the setting of the (maximum) settlement time of the requests these actors perform.

9.7 Conclusions

In this chapter, we have presented the DEMO methodology: the Way of Thinking, the Way of Modelling, and the Way of Working. We have demonstrated how the essential model of an enterprise can be produced by applying the OER method to the implementation of an organisation, like the narrative description of the case Ford. Next we have demonstrated how a new organisation can be designed by applying the DAO method, using the case Ford again for illustration. In addition, we have shown how an EIS (enterprise information system) can be developed by applying the DAO method.

As discussed in [11], the organisation of Ford has been re-engineered and the results are astonishing: a reduction of the staffing of Accounts Payable with 75% is achieved! From the discussion in [11], it has also become evident that the re-engineering approach of Michael Hammer lacks a theoretical basis. Therefore, it is hard to reproduce the outcome or to transfer the approach to other organisations. Based on their experiences, Michael Hammer c.s. formulated several 'principles of reengineering', which are included in the cited paper. These principles were revolutionary at the time, when most companies were organised according to the divisional ideas of Frederic Taylor [17]. As discussed in [18], Taylor actually ignored the human nature of workers. One could even say that Taylor invented the assembly line, where the workers are actually robots instead of human beings who have autonomy in decision-making.

In particular through the tree-thinking approach (cf. Chap. 7), DEMO clarifies the distinct responsibilities in the Ford organisation. They have been discussed in the preceding sections, specifically those of the HOS method.

Let us conclude this chapter by emphasising five crucial properties of the DEMO methodology. First, DEMO is at the same time a process modelling approach, a data modelling approach, a business rules modelling approach, and a business product modelling approach. Moreover, these approaches are fully and properly integrated. In addition, DEMO offers the overarching Cooperation Model, something that none of the current approaches to enterprise modelling incorporates.

Second, producing DEMO models is to a large extent a straightforward undertaking. The essential model of an organisation is not the outcome of a creative action nor something that one can have differences of opinion about. The essence of every organisation is 'hidden' in its implementation, it only has to be revealed. By applying the OER method properly, one gets it, irrespective of the person(s) who produce(s) it. If two knowledgeable professionals would get the task of producing the essential model of the same SoI, they will deliver the same model. If not, one of them (or both) has made one or more mistakes. Modelling approaches without such a solid and proper theoretical foundation allow for subjectivity and consequent boundless discussions about the correctness and rightness of a model.

Third, next to offering full confidence regarding the correctness (through verification) and rightness (through validation) of a model, applying the OER method assures one of the most valuable approval and support by the actors in the organisation, the people 'on the shop floor'.

Fourth, because of its firm rooting in the BETA theory (cf. [6] Chap. 9), notably the GSDP, DEMO's way of working that is called DAO method can be applied quite straightforwardly. It supports both the (re) design of organisations and the development of (automated) EISs. The latter has become a guaranteed successful endeavour because of its firm rooting in the ALPHA theory (cf. [1] Chap. 11).

Fifth, the HOS method provides the handles one needs to instal governance and management according to the theories that are applicable. These theories are the central SIGMA theory (cf. Chap. 8), as well as the supporting KAPPA theory (the EE assignment theory), GAMMA theory (the EE delegation theory), and the CHI theory (the EE transaction cost theory). Thanks to the CIAO paradigm (cf. Chap. 4) and the notion of Enterprise Ontology that is based on it [1], it is just natural that all employees in an organisation are involved in governance. Moreover, many management tasks are already taken account of by the ontological model of an organisation.

References

1. Dietz, J. L. G., & Mulder, H. B. F. (2024). *Enterprise ontology—A human-centric approach to understanding the essence of organisation* (2nd ed., p. 475). The Enterprise Engineering Series. Springer Nature.
2. Seligmann, P. S., Weijers, G. M., & Sol, H. G. (1989). Analyzing the structure of IS methodologies—An alternative approach. In *First Dutch conference on information systems*. Amersfoort.
3. Dijkstra, E. W. (1976). *A discipline of programming* (Vol. 17, p. 217). Prentice-Hall series in automatic computation. Prentice-Hall.
4. Nijssen, G. M. (1976). *Modelling in data base management systems: Proceedings of the IFIP working conference on modelling in data base management systems* (p. 418). North-Holland Pub. Co.
5. Keen, P. G. W. (1997). *The process edge: Creating value where it counts* (Vol. 17, p. 185). Harvard Business School Press.
6. Dietz, J. L. G., & Mulder, H. B. F. (2025). *Enterprise design fundamentals—Settling an enterprise business and devising the enterprise organisation* (Vol. 1, p. 357). The Enterprise Engineering Series. Springer Nature.
7. Op't Land, M., Zwitzer, H., Ensink, P., & Lebel, Q. (2009). Towards a fast enterprise ontology based method for post merger integration. In *SAC'09* (pp. 245–252). ACM.
8. Pluijmert, N. J. (2017). VISI revisited. In: *Lecture notes in business information processing* (Vol. 284, pp. 89–98).
9. Dietz, J. L. G. (2019). *DEMO-4 Specification language*. Enterprise Engineering Institute.
10. Perinforma, A. P. C. (2015). *The essence of organisation*. Sapio Enterprise Engineering.
11. Hammer, M. (1990). *Reengineering work: Don't automate, obliterate*. Harvard Business Review.
12. Marcinak, J. J. E. (2002). *Encyclopedia of software engineering*. Wiley.
13. Alexander, C. (1964). *Notes on the synthesis of form* (p. 216). Harvard University Press.
14. Dietz, J. L. G. (2009). *Architecture: Building strategy into design*. SDU Publishing.
15. Semler, R. (1999). *Maverick! The success story behind the world's most unusual workplace*. Penguin Random House.

16. Laloux, F. D. R. (2014). *Reinventing organizations: A guide to creating organizations inspired by the next stage of human consciousness* (1st ed., Vol. 18, p. 360).
17. Taylor, F. W. (1911). *The principles of scientific management*. Harper & Brothers.
18. Dietz, J. L. G., Hoogervorst, J. A. P., Albani, A., Aveiro, D., Babkin, E., Barjis, J., Caetano, A., Huysmans, P., Iijima, J., van Kervel, S., & Mulder, H. (2013). The discipline of enterprise engineering. *International Journal of Organisational Design and Engineering*, *3*, 28.

Chapter 10
Exercise: British Post Office

Abstract The British Post Office Horizon scandal is commonly qualified as a major miscarriage of justice in recent British history. The case reconstruction defines the scope of interest and reconstructs the progression of the failure across organisational and legal contexts. The Enterprise Engineering perspective uses DEMO to establish the essential model of the British Post Office. This model serves as the reference for distinguishing changes in organisational essence from changes in its realisation during the period under study. The analysis indicates a categorical confusion of fact types: system-recorded and system-derived representations (informational and documental) were treated as if they were original production facts. As a consequence, the coordination acts required for timely revocation and correction within the involved transaction instances became practically unavailable, and the correction of the relevant representations was systematically delayed.

10.1 Introduction

The British Post Office Horizon scandal (1999–2024) is regarded as one of the most extensive miscarriages of justice in recent British history. More than seven hundred subpostmasters were wrongfully convicted on the basis of data produced by Fujitsu's Horizon system. Over the course of decades, the Board of the British Post Office (BPO) and the responsible government departments continued to affirm the system's reliability, notwithstanding indications of defects, internal assessments, and public criticism. The persistent denial of these shortcomings resulted in a cumulative failure of both the organisation and the constitutional order.

Silke van Rooij, me@silkevanrooij.nl

J. L.G. Dietz and H. B. F. Mulder, *Enterprise Governance and Management*, The Enterprise Engineering Series, https://doi.org/10.1007/978-3-032-24318-8_10

10.2 Case Description

The origins of the BPO can be traced to the sixteenth century, when King Henry VIII appointed a Master of the Posts to organise the royal correspondence. This court service was transformed under Charles II in the seventeenth century into a public institution, thereby establishing the foundation of a national postal service and embedding it structurally within the public order. From this royal point of departure, the BPO developed into a nationwide communication network that sustained the logistical and administrative infrastructure of the United Kingdom. It operated as a structural channel for the exchange of information and value between citizens and the state.

From an organisational perspective, the BPO was centrally governed. The Board of Directors, operating from the London headquarters, set the policies, financial constraints, and operational instructions that defined the uniform organisational identity. Below this level of governance, the post offices functioned as executing units within a hierarchical governance arrangement. The Crown Offices, comprising roughly one per cent of the network, were managed directly by the central organisation, whereas the vast majority of branches were operated by independent subpostmasters under uniform contractual provisions. This design yielded a hybrid structure in which public coordination coincided with private execution. The underlying rationale was pragmatic: a fully state-operated network was financially untenable, while local entrepreneurship provided scalability and societal embeddedness. As a semi-public enterprise, the BPO remained state-owned while its operational functioning was organised with a degree of commercial autonomy. Within this institutional arrangement, the state delegated its public mandate to the BPO, which in turn contracted subpostmasters for local execution. This produced a governance structure in which formal responsibility remained public, while operational control and information flows were partly external to the state's administrative domain.

The BPO functioned as a public interface for transactions between citizens and the state. Within a single organisational framework, postal, financial, and administrative processes were integrated in ways that provided direct access to public services. These services comprised the handling of postal items, the disbursement of social benefits, the execution of public payments, and the verification of identity for official documents such as passports. Through its nationwide reach, including extensive presence in rural areas, the organisation constituted a structural infrastructure that safeguarded citizens' effective access to public services across the United Kingdom.

After the Second World War, the position of the BPO shifted from being primarily a logistical service provider to acting as a broader executor of public tasks. In a period marked by changing communication structures, in which telex and telephony increasingly displaced physical mail, the organisation sought ways to maintain both its societal relevance and its nationwide presence. The expansion into financial services constituted a strategic response to this challenge. The establishment of the Post Office Savings Bank, later the National Girobank, marked the BPO's development into a financial intermediary. These services were directed at the large proportion of adults without a bank account, at the time approximately seventy-five per cent of the population, and were executed locally by subpostmasters who processed the transactions. The disbursement of social benefits in the United Kingdom was largely carried out through paper-based payment instruments. Beneficiaries received an order book containing money orders, which were redeemed at the post office. The subpostmaster made the cash payment, collected the money order, and recorded the transaction in the local administration, which was subsequently reconciled with the Department of Social Security (DSS).

By 1980, approximately seventy per cent of all benefits in the United Kingdom were paid out through subpostmasters. Throughout the entire period of the order book system, fraud remained a structural problem. Parliamentary reports repeatedly highlighted the vulnerability of the system, which caused substantial financial losses each year. According to estimates by the National Audit Office, losses due to fraud and administrative errors exceeded £150 million annually in the early 1990s. This persistent vulnerability formed the immediate rationale for transitioning to a digital system in which control, verification, and traceability are organised in a centralised and systematically governed manner.

In 1994, the British government initiated a procurement process for the digitisation of the BPO and the reform of the benefit payment system. The assignment included the development of an electronic payment card (Benefit Payment Card) for beneficiaries and the creation of a digital administrative system to replace paper-based administration and money orders. The transition concerned approximately 890 million annual payments and required the full computerisation of roughly nineteen thousand post offices. Execution was awarded to ICL Pathway, which had been owned by Fujitsu since 1990. The contract had a duration of eight years and an estimated value of £1.48 billion. After limited pilot phases, in which a small number of benefits were processed via the payment card and ten post offices had been digitised, it became apparent by mid-1997 that Fujitsu could not meet the contractual requirements. Internal evaluations identified structural deficiencies, yet both the BPO and the government decided to continue the project. The pilots stalled due to technical errors, delays, and escalating costs. Simultaneously, the Benefits Agency developed an alternative system, the Customer Accounting and Payment System (CAPS), which recorded benefits centrally and transferred payments electronically. The requirement that beneficiaries possess a bank account removed the need for disbursement via the post office.

In 1999, the initiative was discontinued, which formally ended the cooperation between the Benefits Agency, the BPO, and Fujitsu. The payment card was abandoned, and the entire undertaking was subsequently dismantled. The termination of the Benefit Payment Card project in 1999 did not mark an end to the BPO's digitalisation ambitions; rather, it prompted a reassessment of the automation trajectory. The original procurement of 1996 concerned the digitalisation of the benefit payment system through a payment card. After the project's cancellation, a scaled-down configuration was adopted. The new agreement between the BPO and Fujitsu no longer focused on the disbursement of benefits, but on the digitalisation of the post office network. The programme aimed at digitising counter transactions, transaction registration, and administrative processes within the post offices. Following this change of direction, the contract with ICL Pathway was continued under the name Horizon. The House of Commons Trade and Industry Committee characterised this renegotiation as a political-economic compromise, motivated by the intention to preserve earlier investments and to compensate, at least partially, the £180 million written off by ICL.

Until the 1990s, the administrative infrastructure of the BPO relied on paper-based registrations. Subpostmasters recorded their weekly transactions on spreadsheets, which they signed and sent to the central administrative office. This constituted the formal mechanism of accountability and oversight, yet it required intensive manual processing and offered no possibility for direct control or real-time verification. Digitalisation was intended to remove these limitations. Horizon was to replace the paper-based administration with a uniform digital infrastructure that would allow data to be recorded in real time and managed centrally. The pilot phase of Horizon revealed significant deficiencies. During this testing period, Fujitsu staff documented numerous bugs, errors, and defects that produced incorrect financial data, including fictitious surpluses and deficits in branch accounts. These issues were recorded in incident reports; some were temporarily mitigated through workarounds and patches, but the structural causes persisted.

An internal analysis of August 1999 identified six critical system faults, including discrepancies between cash summaries and electronic records. Fujitsu was unable to account for their underlying causes. In September, an internal memorandum recorded that senior management had serious reservations about the system's reliability and therefore withheld approval for national rollout. Despite this, in October 1999, after limited corrective work, it was decided to proceed with implementation without convincing evidence that the identified faults had been resolved. The subsequent nationwide rollout marked the transition from paper-based administration to the digital Horizon system. All post offices were equipped with hardware and network connections enabling daily uploads to the central mainframe. By 2001, the national implementation had been completed.

From the introduction of Horizon onward, administrative irregularities emerged almost immediately: unexplained deficits, reconciliation errors, communication failures, unreliable corrections, and persistent problems in technical support. From 2000 onwards, the first consistent indications appeared that previously balanced accounts suddenly displayed negative balances, sometimes amounting to tens of thousands of pounds. Subpostmasters, including Alan Bates, repeatedly reported discrepancies in their cash records, yet the help desk consistently informed them that the system was reliable and that any discrepancies must be attributable to their own actions. The BPO maintained its position that Horizon was "robust" and attributed all irregularities to human error or local mismanagement.

At the end of the 1990s, the BPO found itself in a period of structural reorientation. The liberalisation of the postal market, the rise of digital communication technologies, and the increasing pressure to organise public services on commercial principles necessitated a reconsideration of its institutional configuration. The government sought a model in which public service provision and commercial efficiency could be combined within an operationally autonomous organisation. This direction received its statutory expression in the Postal Services Act 2000, which formalised the corporatisation of the BPO. The BPO remained responsible for carrying out public tasks, yet was simultaneously mandated to operate on an economic basis. Although the Act was intended to strengthen efficiency and administrative clarity, it resulted in practice in a weakening of public oversight and a reduction of the network's economic resilience after the legal separation from Royal Mail.

Following corporatisation, the proportion of government contracts in the organisation's turnover decreased substantially. The execution of public services, such as benefit disbursement and identity verification, had constituted a significant component of its income, but declined sharply after 2000. In the same year, the BPO recorded its first loss in twenty-four years. The contractual relationship between the BPO and the subpostmasters was defined in the Subpostmasters' Contract, which was formulated in a highly unilateral manner. The contracts granted the BPO extensive powers of control and sanction, while subpostmasters bore almost all financial and operational risks. In this way, a structural asymmetry in responsibility and liability was legally embedded. Section 12 required subpostmasters to maintain their accounts in the form prescribed by the BPO and rendered them liable for all losses. This liability remained in force even after termination of appointment. In addition, the contracts authorised the BPO to modify working conditions unilaterally and to suspend subpostmasters in cases of suspected irregularities, with remuneration withheld depending on the outcome of investigation. Taken together, these provisions created a regime in which the BPO held full authority over execution, oversight and sanction, while subpostmasters carried virtually unlimited liability.

From the implementation of Horizon onwards, subpostmasters were confronted with deficits they could not explain. Under the contractual provisions, they bore full responsibility for the accuracy of their accounts and for covering any detected shortfalls, irrespective of cause. When discrepancies were identified, the helpdesk advised subpostmasters to "balance the books", effectively attributing deficits to them as personal liability. Subpostmasters had no access to the log files or system reports required to determine the source of discrepancies. Technical audits could be carried out only by Fujitsu, which meant that independent verification was effectively impossible. The audits that were conducted did not yield conclusive evidence of system faults. It later emerged, however, that Fujitsu staff could access the system through remote pathways that enabled alterations to transaction data without users' knowledge. BPO management interpreted the reported deficits as isolated cases of human error or fraud and continued to assert that Horizon operated reliably. Since the nineteenth century, the BPO maintained an internal investigation department tasked with addressing fraud and the theft of mail and funds. With the establishment of the Post Office Savings Bank in 1861 and the later introduction of giro services, the need to protect the financial integrity of transactions became institutionalised.

From the early 1990s onwards, the BPO strengthened its reliance on liability clauses in its relationship with subpostmasters. What had originally been conceived as an administrative mechanism to recover losses caused by theft of public funds evolved, under Horizon, into an instrument through which the BPO converted routine accounting discrepancies into personal liability for subpostmasters. In this transformation, the clause ceased to function as a control mechanism and instead became a financial compensation device for losses within the network. During the Horizon period, this department assumed a central role in the evidentiary process against subpostmasters. Internal investigators compiled case files, gathered evidence, and conducted interviews without external scrutiny by police or independent authorities. Consequently, the BPO simultaneously fulfilled the roles of injured party, investigator, and prosecutor, a structural conflict of interest. Within this structure, the presumed reliability of Horizon was no longer critically examined. Journalistic reconstructions indicate that internal investigators and auditors compiled reports and witness statements aligned with a narrative of fraud, while alternative explanations were intentionally excluded.

The United Kingdom's criminal justice system permits not only public but also private prosecutions. The BPO possessed this right of private prosecution, enabling it to bring criminal cases directly against individuals suspected of fraud or irregularities within its network. The BPO exercised this power while also maintaining an internal investigations unit that conducted independent inquiries, gathered evidence, and compiled prosecution files. This allowed the organisation to put cases before the court without prior assessment by the police or the Crown Prosecution Service (CPS). The direct access to criminal proceedings provided the BPO with a powerful instrument to enforce liability and maintain disciplinary control within the network. This created a pronounced power asymmetry between the organisation and individual subpostmasters. Under the threat of lengthy imprisonment and reputational damage, many consented to settlements or admissions in exchange for reduced sentences, even when they could not explain the alleged deficits.

In the United Kingdom, evidentiary standards for computer-generated material underwent a significant shift at the end of the twentieth century. Until 1999, Section 69 of the Police and Criminal Evidence Act 1984 (PACE) required that computer-generated evidence be admissible only if the prosecuting party could demonstrate that the system functioned reliably and had been correctly operated. This provision acknowledged the possibility of technical faults and placed the burden of proof on the prosecution. On the recommendation of the Law Commission, Section 69 was repealed by the Youth Justice and Criminal Evidence Act 1999, with no replacement safeguards. As a result, English evidentiary law adopted a common-law presumption that digital data are reliable unless proven otherwise. This change had profound effects. Computer output was henceforth treated as prima facie evidence. In the Horizon cases, this meant that accounting data derived from the system were accepted as factual evidence. Subpostmasters, who were contractually liable for all recorded deficits, thus found themselves in a dual evidentiary position: civilly as debtor and criminally as offender, without access to source code, logfiles, or independent expertise to challenge the data.

Courts accepted the Horizon-generated records as reliable, even in cases where the defence pointed to unexplained system anomalies. Convictions for false accounting followed when subpostmasters entered or confirmed Horizon-generated figures merely to close their administrative period; actions which the BPO subsequently interpreted as deliberate misstatements and presented as proof of fraud. In several cases, subpostmasters were encouraged or pressured to sign statements affirming the correct functioning of Horizon. These statements, often made in the context of settlements or as conditions for sentence reduction, strengthened the prosecution's evidentiary position and legitimised the assumed reliability of the system. Between 2000 and 2015, more than seven hundred subpostmasters were convicted on the basis of data generated by Horizon. The charges typically concerned theft, false accounting, or fraud, with administrative discrepancies treated as conclusive proof. The first indications of structural faults in the Horizon system did not originate from internal investigations, but from journalistic disclosures. In May 2009, Computer Weekly, under the editorship of Rebecca Thomson, published an article [1] in which seven subpostmasters independently reported unexplained deficits, ranging from several thousand to tens of thousands of pounds. The organisation responded defensively. A spokesperson stated that "Horizon is an extremely robust system" and that there was "no evidence" of technical defects. This narrative remained dominant in internal memoranda and public communications for the following decade, until the judicial reconsideration in 2019.

From 2010 onwards, investigative journalists such as Nick Wallis [2] expanded the reporting and connected the individual accounts into a structural pattern. This phase marked a turning point: whereas formal institutions treated system data as objective truth, the press reconstructed the factual reality of transactions and errors. The Post Office Horizon IT Inquiry [3] identifies this moment as the point at which institutional denial began to fracture.

In 2009, Alan Bates, former subpostmaster who had lost his branch following an unjustified Horizon-based procedure, founded the Justice for Subpostmasters Alliance (JFSA). The organisation emerged from a network of affected individuals who, after years of rejected complaints and unsuccessful individual litigation, joined forces to obtain recognition of the systemic faults in Horizon. The JFSA documented hundreds of cases of unexplained deficits and wrongful prosecutions, collected testimonies, and coordinated legal support.

Between 2009 and 2011, the JFSA repeatedly approached the Department for Business and the BPO's leadership with requests for independent technical review. The responses were formal and dismissive: both the state and the organisation maintained the presumed "robustness" of the system and denied structural defects.

From 2011 onwards, the dynamics surrounding Horizon shifted from operational incident management to legal and political arenas. Multiple subpostmasters initiated civil proceedings against the BPO, often coordinated by the JFSA. Under growing public and parliamentary pressure, the BPO agreed in 2012 to an independent investigation by the forensic accountancy firm Second Sight. The interim report of 2013 identified severe deficiencies in Horizon's operation, including instability, deficient data integrity, and inadequate internal control mechanisms. According to the investigators, software faults could generate unexplained discrepancies at branch level without being locally visible or correctable. The BPO responded defensively.

Shortly after publication, it terminated the investigation, closed the planned mediation scheme, and refused further cooperation with Second Sight. At the same time, the first parliamentary questions emerged in the House of Commons, particularly from James Arbuthnot, who highlighted the disproportionality of the legal responses and the absence of independent oversight. Following the termination of the Second Sight investigation in 2015, the Horizon affair became a recurring item on the parliamentary agenda and entered the realm of political scrutiny and accountability.

In 2017, Alan Bates, on behalf of the JFSA, initiated a civil group action against the BPO, culminating in the 2019 judgement Bates v Post Office. The High Court concluded that Horizon was "riddled with bugs, errors, and defects" and that the digital records used as the basis for prosecutions could not be regarded as reliable. The Court further held that the BPO had breached its duty of care towards subpostmasters and had systematically failed in fair contract management and in the disclosure of relevant information. This judgement marked the legal turning point. Drawing upon the High Court's findings, the Court of Appeal (Criminal Division) ruled in April 2021 that the earlier convictions constituted "an affront to the public conscience." The first 39 convictions were quashed, with further reversals following in subsequent years. In 2024, Parliament enacted the Post Office (Horizon System) Offences Act, which provided for the collective quashing of hundreds of wrongful convictions. In parallel, redress and compensation schemes were introduced, including the Horizon Shortfall Scheme (2020), the Group Litigation Order Scheme (2021), and the Overturned Convictions Scheme (2022). The legal resolution proceeds under the oversight of the ongoing Post Office Horizon IT Inquiry (2021–2025), chaired by Sir Wyn Williams.

The Post Office Horizon IT Inquiry documents extensive harm at both individual and institutional levels. For affected subpostmasters, the combination of Horizon-generated deficits, contractual liability, and criminal prosecution produced serious disruption of health, livelihood, and social relations. Many experienced long-term psychological distress and financial collapse, and the cumulative consequences rendered economic recovery in most cases unattainable. These outcomes were not incidental, but followed directly from the organisational design in which operational actors bore full responsibility without the means to verify or contest the system's records. The criminal prosecutions constituted the most severe form of direct harm. More than seven hundred individuals were convicted on the basis of system-generated data later shown to be unreliable. The resulting criminal records produced long-term exclusion from professional domains and a profound erosion of future prospects, demonstrating how deficiencies in governance can cascade through the legal system and materialise as large-scale personal damage. Several individuals died by suicide in the aftermath of their prosecution.

The scandal also generated far-reaching institutional harm. Public trust in the BPO, historically regarded as a dependable public institution, declined, and the financial burden of legal proceedings, redress schemes, and compensation now rests with society as a whole. Most significantly, the wrongful convictions undermined confidence in the rule of law by exposing weaknesses in evidentiary safeguards and procedural accountability. The inquiry characterises the totality of these effects as a collapse of trust, truth, and accountability. The harm therefore exceeds individual tragedy: it signifies a systemic breakdown in which organisational, legal, and moral checks failed simultaneously. In governance terms, the Horizon affair demonstrates how the absence of effective feedback, revocation mechanisms, and transparent authority structures can lead to the progressive erosion of a system's normative foundations.

In line with the human-centred orientation of Enterprise Engineering, the analysis focuses on the organisation's capacity to operate as a community of actors that can enter into, execute, and complete commitments in a reliable manner. This focus establishes the basis for the reconstruction of the essential model and for the assessment of the consequent degradation of the organisation's transactional capacity.

10.3 Reconstruction of the Essential Model

Within ALPHA theory, the organisation of an enterprise can be analysed in terms of four ontological layers (O, I, D, and M), distinguished by the kind of production acts performed. In this stratification, only original production acts create new facts in the enterprise's lifeworld and therefore require authorised human actors. Informational and documental acts may support original acts; their products can be generated and processed by artefacts, yet they do not in themselves constitute original facts (Table 10.1).

In the pre-Horizon configuration, the operational practice of the BPO can be interpreted as largely consistent with this stratification. Subpostmasters performed original acts that resulted in O-facts, such as declaring an end-of-day position and taking responsibility for observed discrepancies. These outcomes depended on human judgement under an allocated mandate, with responsibility and authority located in identifiable actor roles. Informational and documental layers supported this practice by recording, summarising, and transmitting data, while the corresponding products remained supportive to the original acts.

Horizon did not introduce new actor roles or transaction kinds to the essential configuration shown in Fig. 10.1. It functioned as an ICT artefact that supported the execution of existing roles; the post-Horizon situation is therefore analysed textually rather than modelled as a separate essential configuration. With the introduction of Horizon, the practical boundary between original acts and their informational/documental support became less clear. Computational and documentary outputs produced by the system—ontologically belonging to the I- and D-layers—were used in operational and evidential contexts as if they were original facts. In particular, system-generated statements of the period-end (often day-end) position functioned as authoritative bases for assessing the branch's financial state. As a consequence, the practical space for subpostmasters to independently establish, validate, or contest the relevant lifeworld facts through their own original acts diminished, while their formal responsibility for the outcomes remained in place.

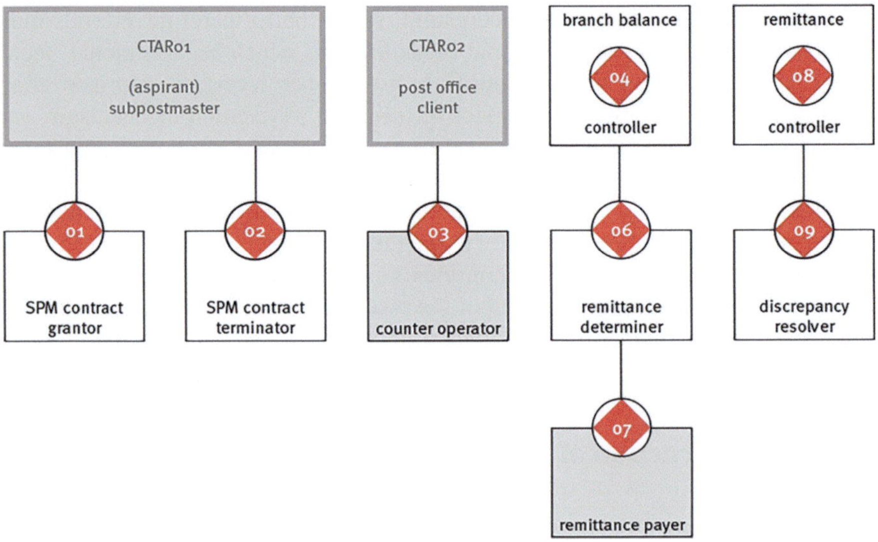

Fig. 10.1 CSD of the pre-Horizon British Post Office

The result is an ontological misalignment: artefactual outputs were accorded fact-like status in organisational and legal settings, whereas the human actors held responsible were, in practice, constrained in their capacity to validate those outputs at the level required for accountable original action. The essential model thus appears to have been altered in its practical operation without an explicit, conceptually grounded reallocation of authority and responsibility. This misalignment plausibly contributed to the evidential and judicial difficulties observed in the Horizon cases, in which system-generated data were often treated as decisive while mechanisms for human contestation and validation proved insufficient.

10.4 Governance Reconfiguration Through SIGMA

Within the SIGMA theory, operational disturbances fall under Enterprise Management (EM), whereas alteration of the essential model requires the authority of Enterprise Governors (EGs). The initial impetus for the Horizon trajectory originated outside the enterprise: the government sought to modernise benefit administration and reduce fraud vulnerabilities. This external requirement triggered a formal procurement process and the selection of ICL Pathway. Such a decision constitutes an act of enterprise governance, as it determines the technological and organisational conditions under which the essential model must operate. The pre-Horizon essential configuration is captured in Fig. 10.1 as a set of actor roles and transaction kinds that jointly produce and control the branch's financial position. In particular, branch balance control (TK04, executed by AR04) and remittance-related transactions (TK06–TK09, executed by AR06–AR09) constitute the operational accountability cycle in which O-facts are established and validated.

What followed, however, did not remain within the scope of governance. Once the procurement was completed, the development and introduction of Horizon proceeded as if it were a disturbance-handling initiative within the remit of EMs. The system was extended incrementally to counter operational failures and fraud risks, yet these extensions gradually assigned new organisational functions to the artefact—functions that affected the creation and validation of original facts in the O-organisation. These reallocations crossed the SIGMA boundary: EMs stabilise operations within the model; the authority to change the essential model lies with the Enterprise Governors (EGs).

Because this boundary remained unrecognised, Horizon evolved from an informational support artefact into a mechanism that produced outputs that, in practice, were treated as if they were O-facts. This transformation altered the essential model in its practical operation without deliberate governance. Enterprise Managers, lacking the mandate to redesign the O-organisation, continued to work under the assumption that they were handling local disturbances. Enterprise Governors, who held the authority to authorise such structural changes, were not engaged in this process.

The resulting displacement can be explained by considering the periodic accountability cycle represented in Fig. 10.1. Branch balance control (TK04) presupposes that a human actor (AR04) can establish and validate the relevant O-facts for a given period. In practice, Horizon-generated balance outcomes came to function as authoritative declarations within that cycle. Enterprise Managers were left to manage the consequences of these outcomes, while Enterprise Governors had not explicitly authorised the implied reallocation of production responsibility. Governance was therefore absent at the critical point where an operational measure effectively became a structural transformation of the enterprise's essential model.

10.5 Role Assignment, Delegation, and Systemic Drift

Within the KAPPA theory, assigning an actor role presupposes that the role-filler possesses the competences required for the associated production and coordination acts. In the pre-Horizon configuration, subpostmasters exercised these competences by establishing relevant preconditions, issuing declarations, and validating their correctness. After the introduction of Horizon, the formal actor roles remained in place, yet the execution and validation of decisive acts became operationally dependent on the artefact. Responsibility persisted while executability diminished, leaving roles formally assigned but substantively difficult to perform.

The GAMMA theory highlights the ontological problem of this shift. Artefacts can compute and record, but they lack social agency and therefore cannot perform commitment-creating acts such as deciding, accepting, or committing. Nevertheless, Horizon outputs were treated in practice as if they carried such performative meaning. Subpostmasters were held accountable for outcomes they neither produced independently nor could revoke, resulting in pseudo-delegation: decisional authority was effectively attributed to the artefact while accountability remained with human actors.

The tension becomes visible when relating formal role assignment to the accountability cycle reconstructed in Fig. 10.1 (TK04 and TK06–TK09). These transactions presuppose that actors can establish, validate, and, where necessary, contest the production facts for which they remain responsible. In the post-Horizon situation, validation and contestation increasingly depended on system-generated outputs and system-access privileges. Where verification, exception handling, and revocation are not architected at the level of human action, documentary products may acquire an evidential status that exceeds their ontological scope.

This drift gained an institutional dimension through the BPO's statutory power to initiate private prosecutions. As prosecuting body, the BPO treated system outputs as decisive facts in criminal proceedings while simultaneously acting as their evaluator, creating a closed evidentiary loop. Subpostmasters lacked access to underlying logs and therefore lacked practical means of contestation, whereas technical staff with privileged access could alter records beyond their knowledge.

In effect, Horizon shifted the effective point of business-level fact production towards a computational artefact while legal liability remained with human actors deprived of authority and competence. This configuration structurally weakened the possibilities for contestation and revocation that are constitutive for reliable coordination.

10.6 The Collapse of Social Interaction

The PSI theory clarifies that the integrity of organisational interaction depends on the complete execution of the Complete Transaction Pattern (CTP): request, promise, declare, and accept. The CTP also presupposes practical possibilities for revocation and recovery when assumptions prove incorrect or discrepancies arise. These possibilities enable symmetrical interaction and allow actors to assess the validity claims embedded in coordination acts.

After the introduction of Horizon, the practical attainability of these coordination states became constrained. The promise–declare–accept cycle was operationally compressed into a computational sequence, reducing the space in which actors can assess the factual and normative basis of commitments. What had previously been determined through interaction and control increasingly became determined through system output. System-generated outputs functioned as authoritative reference points, weakening the link between coordination acts and the evidential grounds required to perform them responsibly. Revocation and contestation became difficult in practice, as actors lacked authority, information, and evidential access to challenge system-generated states.

Table 10.1 TPT of the pre-Horizon British Post Office

Transaction kind	Product kind	Executor role
TK01 SPM contract granting	PK01 [SPM contract] is granted	AR01 SPM contract grantor
TK02 SPM contract termination	PK02 [SPM contract] is terminated	AR02 SPM contract terminator
TK03 counter service delivery	PK03 [counter service] is delivered	AR03 counter operator
TK04 branch balance controlling	PK04 [branch balance] for [period] is controlled	AR04 branch balance controller
TK06 remittance determination	PK06 [remittance] for [period] is determined	AR06 remittance determiner
TK07 remittance payment	PK07 [remittance] is paid	AR07 remittance payer
TK08 remittance controlling	PK08 [remittance] for [period] is controlled	AR08 remittance controller
TK09 remittance discrepancy resolution	PK09 [remittance discrepancy] for [period] is resolved	AR09 discrepancy resolver

The BPO's statutory power to initiate private prosecutions intensified this deformation. The prospect of criminal escalation could compromise the assessment of validity claims of coordination acts, because attempts to decline, question, or revoke system-generated states risked being interpreted as wrongdoing. As a result, the discursive space required for counterclaims and clarification narrowed.

Period-end accountability (TK04 and TK06–TK08) makes the consequences concrete. In the pre-Horizon configuration, the branch's financial position and the corresponding remittance for a given period were established through interaction between determination, payment, and verification, with practical room for clarification and correction when outcomes diverged from expectations. After the introduction of Horizon, these interaction possibilities became constrained, because system outputs functioned as de facto declarations while the actor's capacity to validate, contest, or revoke them was curtailed.

The assess phase of DEMO's Action Model (cf. Chap. 9) makes the mechanism explicit: limited evidential access constrains truth assessment; computational opacity constrains rightness assessment; and sincerity may be compromised where defects or privileged interventions are not transparently disclosed. Under such conditions, validity assessment cannot be performed reliably. The CTP therefore becomes difficult to realise as a genuine transaction pattern, and coordination risks degrading into compliance.

References

1. Thomson, R. (2009, May 11). *Bankruptcy, prosecution and disrupted livelihoods—Postmasters tell their story. Computer Weekly.* https://www.computerweekly.com/news/2240089230/Bankruptcy-prosecution-and-disrupted-livelihoods-Postmasters-tell-their-story
2. Wallis, N. (2021). *The great Post Office scandal.* Bath Publishing.
3. Post Office Horizon IT Inquiry. (2025). *Final report.* UK Government.

Chapter 11
Exercises: Semco and Netflix

[A leader] is coach and counsel, not a judge.
W. Edwards Deming

Abstract This chapter analyses two contrasting cases: Semco and Netflix. The case material is interpreted through complementary interpretive anchors (Deming, Drucker, Covey) that sharpen attention to aim-guided learning, responsible autonomy, and the normative conditions for truthful transparency. Across both cases, the chapter identifies a decisive governance variable: alignment between commitment authority, responsibility attribution, and inspectable information in the coordination layer. The chapter concludes with design implications for governing knowledge-intensive and digitally mediated enterprises while preserving responsible autonomy.

11.1 Exercise I—Semco

Semco's transformation, as described by Ricardo Semler in Maverick [1], is often summarised as "democracy at work" or "self-management." Such characterisations, however, leave unspecified why Semco is analytically relevant for Enterprise Engineering. Semco is a Brazilian firm that originated in the 1950s as an industrial manufacturing enterprise and later developed into a diversified engineering and services organisation [1]. The transformation unfolds against the background of a generational transfer of leadership: Semler assumes responsibility for an enterprise that had been built and scaled under the prevailing industrial governance logic of its period, characterised by centralised authority and supervisory control [1].

Semler inherited an enterprise whose governance model had been viable under conditions of predictable production and hierarchical coordination. The descriptive relevance of the case lies in the subsequent sequence of interventions. Semco does not present a single replacement blueprint; it presents a trajectory in which the limits of

Silke van Rooij, me@silkevanrooij.nl

J. L.G. Dietz and H. B. F. Mulder, *Enterprise Governance and Management*, The Enterprise Engineering Series, https://doi.org/10.1007/978-3-032-24318-8_11

hierarchical control are progressively recognised and responsibility and judgement are redistributed in response to changing organisational and environmental conditions [1]. Within that trajectory, Semler's contribution is described as providing an explicit direction for change and a legitimising frame for redesign, repeatedly emphasising trust, transparency, and responsibility as operating premises [1].

11.1.1 From Paternal Control to Governance by Design

Semco was built by Ricardo Semler's father as a traditional industrial enterprise, organised according to the governance logic of mass production. When Semler "took over Semco from his father," he characterises it as "a traditional company in every respect," marked by a pyramidal structure and extensive rules intended to anticipate contingencies ([1], p. 1). Authority was concentrated at the top, supervision was layered, and decision-making followed hierarchical escalation. In Semler's account, this control-oriented arrangement had been compatible with an earlier period in which production could be planned and standardised with relatively stable premises.

By 1980, when Ricardo Semler took leadership, Brazil's economic conditions had become quite volatile. The existing governance model increasingly produced bureaucratic distance, delayed and distorted information flows, and decision-making was detached from operational reality. Semler's initial significant interventions were presented as measures to improve the organisation's capacity for timely and reliable decision-making. One concrete intervention was the dismissal of "60 percent of Semco's top management" during the initial transition ([1], p. 22). He frames this decision as a break with existing authority patterns and links it to a reduction in dependence on hierarchically filtered information.

A key diagnostic episode concerns the introduction of time-and-motion specialists. Semler recounts that these experts were hired to increase productivity, yet workers quickly learned to manipulate the measurement process, rendering the study ineffective ([1], p. 75). He concluded that supervision-based governance amplified risk rather than mitigating it, and he began to explore governance arrangements that restored judgement, responsibility, and reliable feedback at the level where work was performed.

11.1.2 Early Institutional Prototypes: Committees and Recurring Decision Forums

Semler's first structural countermeasure focused on the interface between management and the production units. In each of four business units, employees from the shop floor and other producing departments formed factory committees composed of operational representatives, explicitly excluding management. These committees met regularly with senior managers, were given paid time and a clear mandate to articulate operational concerns and included union representation to ensure institutional legitimacy [1].

The analytical relevance of these committees lies not in participation as such, but in their function as governance instruments. They created a recurring arena in which tensions from operational practice could be articulated before being filtered, delayed, or suppressed by hierarchy. Semler explicitly notes that these arrangements did not function smoothly from the outset. Participation proved socially demanding, revealing that voice does not emerge automatically from formal structures. In parallel, Semler introduced routine decision forums to replace approval chains. In the food-service equipment unit, hierarchical escalation was substituted by weekly meetings in which proposals were presented, debated, and decided collectively when consensus failed.

11.1.3 Redesigning Structure: "Rounding the Pyramid" as a Governance Mechanism

Semler's most explicit structural redesign is his replacement of the classic pyramid with a fluid circle-based scheme: three circles and four job categories, supported by a small number of recurring meetings. He motivates this redesign by pointing to how pyramids constrain mobility, enforce "up, down, or out," prevent direct communication across levels, and tie pay progression to hierarchy rather than skill or contribution. The circle model is not presented as aesthetic. It is meant to remove governance pathologies that arise from fixed rank ([1], pp. 190–191).

Semler describes the roles and their intended functions: a small inner circle of "Counsellors" coordinates general policies and strategies; a second circle of "Partners" runs the business units; a large circle contains "Associates"; "Coordinators" appear as triangles floating around the large circle, marking a limited set of essential leadership roles. Importantly, the design enforces flattening constraints: one Coordinator cannot report to another Coordinator; one Associate cannot report to another Associate. It also limits the number of Coordinators, intentionally shifting the ratio of "Indians to chiefs" ([1], pp. 191–193).

Two further design choices are described by Semler as integral to making the circle scheme operative in practice.

- First, Semler eliminates formal job descriptions and redistributes tasks without re-codifying them. When a supervisor role disappears, the response is not "write a new structure." The response is: "This person isn't here anymore," then the people involved figure out how to absorb the work. This is governance by enabling local coordination rather than governance by blueprint ([1], p. 195).
- Second, Semler refuses the organisational chart as a governing instrument. Consultants who ask for an org chart are told there is none, and Semco does not intend to reintroduce one after many years without one. Semler argues that

formal charts misrepresent actual competence and decision power, suggesting a "parallel organisational chart" based on perceived competence would diverge significantly from the official one ([1], pp. 195–196). This position is reiterated in the internal booklet excerpts he includes, which state that Semco does not have an organisation chart and that any necessary sketch is treated as temporary ([1], p. 300).

This structural redesign, taken seriously, is not "absence of structure." It is a replacement of rank-based coordination by competence- and forum-based coordination: issues move to weekly unit meetings and to a cross-unit Tuesday meeting for decisions affecting multiple units or large investments. The enterprise thus shifts from permission chains to repeated, reality-facing deliberation cycles [1].

11.1.4 Radical Transparency as an Operating Condition

Semler presents transparency as a designed operating condition rather than a supplementary policy. He states that "virtually all corporate information" at Semco is open, and he specifies that this includes matters that are commonly treated as confidential in other firms, such as financial results, strategic and operational information, and pay ([1], p. 335). He also describes transparency as inseparable from capability building: employees are taught how to interpret the financial representations that are made available, including the reading of financial statements.

Within this arrangement, transparency directly supports upward communication and contestation. Semler explicitly links access to information to employees' ability to speak openly, including towards superiors. This principle is institutionalised in Semco's manager evaluation system, where employees periodically assess their managers through anonymous questionnaires. The resulting evaluations are aggregated into scores that are made public, enabling comparison and creating visible accountability. Scores below an agreed threshold trigger structured follow-up conversations between managers and employees [1].

11.1.5 Commitments Beyond Rules, Without Pretending Rules Disappear

Semco deliberately reduces formal rule density and managerial micromanagement, without dissolving governance into organisational indeterminacy. Formal controls are replaced by designed commitment structures based on transparency, peer visibility, and recurring deliberation [1]. Fixed organisational charts and standardised hierarchical titles are absent, leadership roles are reversible, and responsibilities are adjusted in practice rather than continuously formalised.

This arrangement presupposes a covenant-like governance condition: local autonomy is legitimate only insofar as it remains bounded by enterprise reality and peer accountability. Semco reinforces this condition by making commitments and their consequences visible. Managerial performance is publicly evaluated and discussed, while unit-level decisions are debated in recurring forums and resolved collectively when necessary.

The practice of self-set pay further illustrates this logic. Introduced after transparency and bureaucratic reduction were established, it relies on staged participation and social accountability rather than additional control mechanisms. Discretion over-compensation is bounded by visibility and peer judgement, preserving coherence without reintroducing hierarchical policing.

11.1.6 Designed Conditions that Make Autonomy Non-Naïve

Semco's autonomy practices depend on a deliberately constructed social infrastructure. Semler lists several elements that function as enabling conditions: transparency (open information and financial education), training driven by employee requests with expenses approved in weekly unit meetings, working at home for those who can, and the removal of support-staff roles so that "everyone does their own" administrative tasks. Two further infrastructural designs are particularly relevant.

- The first is unit size as an explicit governance constraint. Semler argues that large, centralised organisations tend to produce alienation and weakened mutual responsibility. He therefore states an operational principle: people can realise their potential when they know most of their coworkers—often around 150—and he reports that Semco splits units when they grow beyond that scale ([1], pp. 278–279). In his account, limiting unit size is a structural measure intended to keep accountability socially viable by preventing relationships from becoming anonymous.
- The second is what Semler calls the "Satellite Program." He describes how Semco supported employees in establishing their own small businesses, including leasing production machines on favourable terms and offering advice on pricing, quality, and taxes. He also notes that these firms were not restricted to Semco as a single client and could sell to competitors ([1], pp. 262–265). In Semler's framing, the programme is meant to change the dependency relation between the enterprise and the worker by relocating part of the responsibility for outcomes to an explicitly market-facing position.

Taken together, these elements show that "autonomy" at Semco is not narrated as an absence of coordination. It is narrated as an outcome of designed conditions that support interpretation and responsible action: financial literacy under informational openness ([1], p. 20), routine arenas for discussion and decision ([1], pp. 192–193), visible accountability through published managerial grades ([1], pp. 39–40), and organisational scale constraints that keep mutual monitoring and trust socially manageable ([1], pp. 278–279).

11.2 Exercise II—Netflix

Netflix's trajectory is best understood as a coupled redesign of strategy, technology, and culture. In this case, culture does not operate as a "soft" overlay, but as an enabling condition for fast decision-making, rapid learning, and scalable coordination under persistent uncertainty. Netflix built this operating model through explicit membership governance (talent density), systematic context sharing (radical transparency), a normative decision rule ("act in Netflix's best interest"), institutionalised feedback and learning loops (candour, sunshining, and experimentation infrastructure) [2, 3]. Where Semco stabilises autonomy through community-scale covenanting, Netflix stabilises it through capability thresholds and traceable accountability.

11.2.1 Startup Origins and a Disruption Ethos

Netflix emerged in the late 1990s, a period in which Silicon Valley start-ups explored newly accessible digital markets and online transactions became socially and economically plausible. Hastings [2] and Randolph [4] developed the venture in that environment, shaped by entrepreneurial iteration and a willingness to test ideas quickly rather than perfect them in advance [4]. In their early formation story, the culture was not presented as ideology. It functioned as a practical response to uncertainty: the market moved fast, so the organisation had to move fast.

11.2.2 Market Sensing: DVD as Enabling Technology, Streaming as Horizon

The decisive enabling condition was the DVD. Earlier "movies by mail" ideas had been constrained by the logistics of VHS. The DVD's compact format made postal distribution economically feasible, allowing Netflix to launch Netflix.com in 1998 as an online rental platform supported by digital ordering, fulfilment, and returns [4]. Even in that phase, Netflix experimented with recommendation mechanisms, indicating an early orientation towards product learning rather than pure logistics [4]. The company name itself reflected a larger horizon: streaming was not yet technically viable at scale, yet the founders anticipated that internet infrastructure would become the long-run distribution channel for media [4, 5].

11.2.3 The Rulebook Lesson: Bureaucracy Grows Around Exceptions

In its early DVD era, Netflix initially resembled other start-ups of the time: a relatively hierarchical structure, sharply defined roles, and formalised processes, partly because physical distribution punishes operational variance [4]. The deeper cultural shift came less from the DVD operation itself and more from Hastings' prior experience at Pure Software. Hastings describes how rapid growth was accompanied by the accumulation of rules, handbooks, and approval processes intended to control errors and standardise execution—yet those instruments began to constrain precisely the professional judgement that complex work requires [2]. The lesson that later reappears at Netflix is specific: organisations often design governance for the one person who does not perform, and the cost is paid by everyone else through approvals, permission chains, and procedural compliance [2, 3]. This becomes a design driver: do not build the enterprise around the lowest capability threshold; raise the threshold.

11.2.4 Crisis, Downsizing, and the Discovery of Talent Density

The dotcom crisis forced Netflix into a survival posture around 2000–2001. After failed acquisition or partnership scenarios, the company had to continue independently and became constrained by capital and time [4]. The 2001 restructuring did more than cut costs. It produced an organisational observation that later became a governance principle: a smaller team of strong performers could generate more focus, energy, and quality than a larger team with average capability spread [2, 3]. Netflix named this "talent density" and treated it as a condition for agility. The "rockstar" logic—paying at the top of personal market value to attract exceptional contributors—was not framed as generosity. It was framed as a bet that high capability reduces the need for controls, because mature professionals can exercise judgement without constant authorisation [2, 3].

Over time, this membership logic hardened into explicit practices such as the keeper test: leaders continuously ask whether they would fight to keep a given employee, and if not, the organisation prefers an honourable exit over retaining a poor fit [2, 3].

11.2.5 "Act in Netflix's Best Interest": Autonomy Anchored in Adult Judgement and Context

Netflix's next move was to test whether adult responsibility could replace procedural controls. Early experiments used a simple norm—spend money as if it were your own—especially for travel and expenses. When that worked, Netflix replaced approval systems with a broader behavioural rule: "Act in Netflix's best interest" [2, 3]. That phrase matters because it is not permissive. It pushes decision-making down while preserving a clear evaluative standard: actions are judged against enterprise interest, not personal convenience.

This autonomy norm required a complementary infrastructure: radical transparency and context sharing. Netflix's logic is direct: if employees are expected to decide like leaders, they need access to leader-level information and trade-offs [2]. Autonomy without context would drift towards arbitrariness. Context without capable actors would drift towards noise. Netflix attempted to couple the two: keep the team strong, share the "why" and the constraints, then remove many controls [2, 3].

11.2.6 Candour and Sunshining: Making Mistakes Visible Enough to Learn

A freedom-based model faces a predictable failure mode: errors can remain private, and learning can be lost. Netflix responded by normalising direct feedback and creating social permission to surface problems early. Hastings and Meyer describe candour routines as core to "freedom and responsibility," because weak feedback loops allow poor decisions to repeat [2]. Song's resilience study describes related practices in which problems are "sunshined", meaning they are brought into the open rather than contained in quiet channels [6]). The analytical point is not that Netflix celebrates failure. The point is that Netflix tries to make failure legible: visible enough to analyse, discuss, and turn into a better decision standard.

The case narrative contains concrete episodes that illustrate this learning posture. Netflix's withdrawal from a planned UK move in 2004, for example, can be read as a decision reversal treated as learning rather than a reputational disaster [4]. The more public example is Qwikster in 2011: the attempt to separate DVD and streaming into distinct services with separate customer experiences triggered strong negative reaction, rapid subscriber loss, and a sharp correction. Netflix reversed the plan quickly and acknowledged the misjudgement [2].

A similar pattern appears in the internal debate about offline downloading. Hastings reportedly held a strong conviction that streaming would be sufficiently available, delaying a download feature even as internal voices noted practical user needs in less reliable connectivity contexts. When external constraints persisted, Netflix adjusted [2]. The governance relevance lies in the willingness to revise a strong thesis when the operational case changes, without rewriting the entire operating model into a compliance regime.

11.2.7 Product Focus Over Hardware: Platform Choices as Organisational Design

As Netflix moved towards streaming, it faced a choice: control the end-to-end hardware experience or focus on product and distribution through partners. The company abandoned a dedicated hardware device path in favour of an open integration strategy, enabling Netflix to be built into TVs, consoles, and media boxes via platform integration rather than proprietary devices [4, 5]. This is a governance-relevant design choice: it avoids tying agility to hardware cycles and expands the organisation's effective reach through an ecosystem.

Technical infrastructure decisions reinforced the same direction. Streaming stressed Netflix's on-premise data centres, and a major incident made scaling and resilience constraints concrete. Netflix decided to migrate core streaming infrastructure to Amazon Web Services, trading ownership of hardware for the ability to scale rapidly and reduce infrastructure bottlenecks [5]. The organisational implication is subtle but important: cloud infrastructure tends to support smaller, more autonomous delivery teams because provisioning and deployment can be standardised and accelerated. In that way, architecture supports culture: speed and autonomy become easier to sustain when teams are not blocked by centralised infrastructure gatekeeping.

11.2.8 Experimentation as a Discipline: Learning at Product Velocity

As streaming scaled, Netflix gained richer behavioural data: viewing starts, pauses, drop-offs, returns, and device contexts. Those signals increased the value of controlled testing and accelerated the move from ad hoc A/B tests to a systematic experimentation discipline. Diamantopoulos et al. describe Netflix's experimentation platform as science-centric infrastructure designed to run large-scale, continuous tests, and produce fast evidence about effect sizes under real conditions [7]. This is not merely a data story. It is a governance mechanism: experimentation reduces reliance on opinion battles and refreshes "the case" with empirical feedback.

At the same time, the literature supports a non-technocratic reading. Van Es frames Netflix's data practices as strategically ambivalent: data infrastructures shape choices, yet interpretive work remains human, cultural, and strategic [8]. Netflix's own narrative similarly treats data as an input to judgement rather than a substitute for it [2]. This balance is visible when evidence informs a choice, while leadership still commits under uncertainty.

11.2.9 From Distributor to Studio: Content Creation and Leadership Alignment

The step into original content production marks a further coupling of technology and judgement. The "House of Cards" decision illustrates the hybrid logic: data supported the hypothesis of demand and fit, while the commitment—ordering full seasons and taking creative risk—required human conviction about quality and strategic differentiation [5, 8]. As Netflix scaled content production globally, the enterprise increasingly operated as a dual system: a technology platform that must run reliably and evolve continuously, and a studio operation that must manage creative processes and market-specific differences.

11.3 Cross-Case Analysis Through EE Criteria and Interpretive Anchors

This section compares Semco and Netflix against the three generic Enterprise Engineering goals—*intellectual manageability, organisational concinnity, and social dedication*—as the chapter's explicit criteria for disciplined observation and evaluation. The comparison is conducted using the management-philosophical lineage introduced earlier—Deming, Drucker, and Covey—as interpretive anchors: they sharpen what is observed and how it is articulated, without replacing the EE framing.

11.3.1 Intellectual Manageability (Deming: Aim, Variation, and Inspectable Learning)

In this exercise, intellectual manageability is understood as the condition that the enterprise can be understood and discussed in terms of essential commitments, responsibilities, and governing premises, enabling competent actors to reason about change without reliance on hidden assumptions. Deming [9] sharpens this perspective by focusing attention on whether decisions are aim-guided, whether inspection is informed by variation, and whether learning loops are institutionalised as disciplined routines rather than rhetoric.

- Semco increases manageability by making previously implicit premises explicit and inspectable, foremost through radical transparency. Semler states that "virtually all corporate information" is open, including financial results and pay, and he couples openness to capability building by teaching employees to interpret the financial representations made available. This transforms "knowing" from a managerial privilege into a distributed capacity. In Deming's terms, the governance gain is not openness for its own sake, but the creation of conditions

under which operational observations can be surfaced, inspected, and discussed in relation to enterprise purpose and performance variation.
- Netflix increases manageability by replacing implicit managerial discretion with a concise normative decision premise—"Act in Netflix's best interest"—and then supplying the informational conditions required for actors to apply that premise in practice. The explicit rule reduces ambiguity about evaluative direction, while radical transparency and context sharing reduce ambiguity about constraints and trade-offs. In Deming's terms, candour and "sunshining" function as mechanisms that prevent error from remaining private and therefore non-learnable; they make outcomes legible enough to be studied and turned into improved decision standards.

11.3.2 Organisational Concinnity (Drucker: Clarity of Task, Autonomy, and Assessable Contribution)

Concinnity is used here as the condition under which local choices remain mutually consistent and aligned with enterprise-wide intent, despite distributed decision-making. Drucker [10] sharpens this criterion by forcing the question "what is the task?" and by linking autonomy to responsibility for results and to accountability that makes contribution assessable.

- Semco preserves coherence by redesigning coordination away from permission chains towards repeated, reality-facing deliberation cycles. The early factory committees and decision forums are analytically relevant because they create recurring arenas in which tensions from operational practice can be articulated before being filtered or delayed by hierarchy. Later, the circle-based structure and the refusal of the organisational chart are not "absence of structure" but a shift towards competence- and forum-based coordination: issues move to weekly unit meetings and cross-unit meetings for decisions that exceed local scope. In Drucker's terms, this pattern keeps autonomy from dissolving into individual preference because decisions remain tied to the concrete task and to collective assessment in institutionalised forums.
- Netflix preserves coherence under scale by coupling high autonomy to a strong evaluative premise and to systematic context sharing. The case explicitly frames the design logic: autonomy without context drifts towards arbitrariness; context without capable actors drifts towards noise. Netflix therefore treats membership governance ("talent density," keeper test) as a coherence condition, because high capability reduces the need for procedural control while keeping judgement accountable. Drucker's lens clarifies the governance move: the organisation does not merely "trust"; it designs a setting in which professional judgement can be exercised and evaluated as contribution to the enterprise task.

11.3.3 Social Dedication (Covey: Whole-Person Engagement and Enabling Leadership)

Dietz, Hoogervorst et al. [11] link social devotion to empowerment and knowledgeable governance. In this chapter, social devotion is understood as the condition that professional responsibility is practicable: authority is transparent, information is accessible, and accountability arrangements match role capacity. Its governance grounding is given by Fundamentals 5–7: distributed operational responsibility, distributed governance responsibility, and human-centred, knowledgeable management. Covey [12] sharpens this dimension by emphasising the normative and motivational conditions that sustain autonomy and learning: trust, meaning, and enabling leadership.

- Semco illustrates Fundamentals 5–7 in [11] through designed social infrastructure that makes autonomy non-naïve. Transparency supports voice and contestation, and accountability becomes visible through publicly aggregated managerial evaluations with structured follow-up when thresholds are not met. Authority is therefore not merely "delegated"; it is placed in a setting where consequences remain socially inspectable. Semco also uses structural constraints to keep accountability human-scale: unit size is treated as a governance constraint intended to prevent anonymity and preserve mutual monitoring and trust as practicable social relations. In Covey's terms, this is an attempt to stabilise discipline through explicit expectations and visibility rather than surveillance and sanctions, while recognising that participation is socially demanding and does not arise automatically.
- Netflix illustrates Fundamentals 5–7 in [11] through a different stabilisation mechanism: capability thresholds, context density, and fast feedback. The organisation explicitly replaces procedural controls with professional judgement ("Act in Netflix's best interest"), while treating radical transparency and context sharing as necessary conditions for responsible autonomy. Candour and sunshining operate as social mechanisms that keep responsibility coupled to learning: errors are surfaced early so they can be analysed and corrected without reverting to bureaucratic control regimes. In Covey's terms, this is a trust-based discipline that requires role clarity and truthful reporting; transparency is not assumed to work automatically, because transparency without trust can suppress truth, while trust without inspectability weakens accountability.

11.4 Conclusion

Autonomy is not a personal privilege; it is a governance property of the enterprise. The decisive design variable is the alignment between authority, responsibility, and inspectable information in the coordination layer: authority to create or revoke commitments, responsibility for their consequences, and the availability of representations that allow actors to assess fulfilment and justify revision [13].

This chapter operationalises this variable by using the cases as observation material. The Semco case illustrates a governance configuration in which broad decision latitude is stabilised by provisions that keep commitment-making transparent and accountability attributable at the scale at which coordination remains socially inspectable. The Netflix case illustrates a different configuration: autonomy is coupled to explicit context-sharing and structured learning loops, so that professional judgement remains corrigible through continuous feedback and systematic revision of assumptions. In both cases, autonomy works only insofar as commitment authority, accountability attribution, and informational inspectability form a coherent control pattern.

This alignment directly supports the three generic Enterprise Engineering goals. It increases intellectual manageability because decision rights and accountability relations become structurally knowable rather than interpretative. It sustains concinnity because local variation is bounded by enterprise-wide conditions for valid commitments and their assessment. It strengthens social dedication because actors can understand, contest, and correct accountability assignments on the basis of inspectable grounds, instead of informal power. Accordingly, the governance question is not whether autonomy should be "allowed", but how enterprise organises commitment authority, accountability, and inspectability as an integrated control pattern.

References

1. Semler, R. (1999). *Maverick! The success story behind the world's most unusual workplace.* Penguin Random House.
2. Hastings, R., & Meyer, E. (2020). *No rules rules: Netflix and the culture of reinvention.* Penguin Press.
3. McCord, P. (2014). How Netflix reinvented HR. *Harvard Business Review, 19*(1/2), 70–76.
4. Randolph, M. (2019). *That will never work: the birth of Netflix and the amazing life of an idea.* Little Brown and Company.
5. Mier, J., & Kohli, A. K. (2021). Netflix: Reinvention across multiple time periods—Reflections and directions for future research. *AMS Review, 11*(1), 194–205.
6. Song, M. (2022). A study on the organisational resilience of Netflix. *International Journal of Internet, Broadcasting and Communication, 14*(3), 40–50.
7. Diamantopoulos, N. E. A. (2019). *Engineering for a science-centric experimentation platform.*
8. Es, K.V. (2023). *Netflix & big data: The strategic ambivalence of an entertainment company. Television & New Media, 24*(6), 656–672.
9. Deming, W. E. (2018). *The new economics for industry, government, education* (3rd ed.). MIT Press.
10. Drucker, P. (1999). *The new economics for industry, government, education* (3rd ed.). MIT Press.
11. Dietz, J. L. G., Hoogervorst, J. A. P., Albani, A., Aveiro, D., Babkin, E., Barjis, J., Caetano, A., Huysmans, P., Iijima, J., van Kervel, S., & Mulder, H. (2013). The discipline of enterprise engineering. *International Journal of Organisational Design and Engineering, 3*, 28.
12. Covey, S. R. (2004). *The 8th habit: From effectiveness to greatness.* Free Press.

13. Dietz, J. L. G., & Mulder, H. B. F. (2024). *Enterprise Ontology—A human-centric approach to understanding the essence of organisation* (2nd ed., p. 475). The Enterprise Engineering Series. Springer Nature.

Chapter 12
Real-Life Applications of DEMO

12.1 Overview

In the next sections, five appealing real-life applications of DEMO are presented and discussed. These DEMO applications are reported on (between brackets the contributing authors):

Section 12.2: Cooperating Airlines (Dirk Gemke, Rob Mocking).
Section 12.3: Responsible Enterprise Governance Through Enterprise Ontology (Shakha Mirza).
Section 12.4: Rethinking Strategy Execution through Enterprise Engineering (Thabani Mudavanhu, Bruno Emwanu).
Section 12.5: Nationale Nederlanden (Yuri Bobbert).
Section 12.6: Resolving an Integration Stalemate with Enterprise Ontology (Edwin de Haan, Rikkert van Capelleveen).

All applications are reported in the STARR framework (Situation, Task, Approach, Result, Reflection):

The **Situation** in which the case is positioned. It includes, but is not limited to, the context of the case organisation (e.g. market, competition), the characteristics of the case organisation (facts & figures), its challenges and opportunities, important stakeholders, the reason why the project was initiated, a history of earlier attempts, etc.

The **Task** that has been conducted. It includes, but is not limited to, the goals and objectives of the project, its budget and timelines, special requirements, the roles of the various stakeholders, etc.

The **Approach** taken to conduct the task. It includes, but is not limited to, the method used, the various steps in this method, the paradigm or underlying philosophy of the approach/method, the products and deliverables, the way in which the project was planned and managed, the risk management approach and the tools used, etc.

J. L.G. Dietz and H. B. F. Mulder, *Enterprise Governance and Management*, The Enterprise Engineering Series, https://doi.org/10.1007/978-3-032-24318-8_12

The **Result** of the project. It includes, but is not limited to, the actual benefits for the case organisation and the stakeholders, a cost/benefit analysis, the extent to which the case organisation was actually transformed, etc.

A **Reflection** on the case. It includes, but is not limited to, a discussion about the faced challenges, the way in which the existing methods, frameworks, etc., aided in dealing with these challenges, omissions and limitations found, thoughts on how to 'fix' such omissions and limitations, etc.

12.2 Cooperating Airlines

Dirk-Vincent Gemke and Rob Mocking

12.2.1 Situation

The airline business is one of the most internationally oriented businesses in the world. Paradoxically this is the result of the value national governments attach to their national airline, and the associated limitations to mergers and acquisitions that would result in global companies and brands like we have Apple, Google, Microsoft, Amazon, Booking, Philips, and Shell.

To nevertheless create continental and global network reach for customers, without having to operate flights themselves, airlines started to cooperate in 1947 based on so-called interline agreements. This was still the age of hand-written paper tickets. The next and deeper level of cooperation started during the migration to electronic tickets and emergence of Global Distribution Systems: these pioneers of the so-called code sharing were Qantas and American Airlines in 1987. Unsurprisingly, airlines with a smaller home market, like KLM, SAS, Sabena and Swissair, were pioneering the most, based on new air-political agreements, and by creating as many interline and code share agreements as possible to anchor their vulnerable market position.

Around 2000 further clustering of cooperating airlines took place to create alliances: STAR, Oneworld and SkyTeam were born. SkyTeam is an alliance of airlines (a cooperative of members, incorporated in The Netherlands) founded by Aeromexico, Air France, Delta Air Lines and Korean Air in New York City on June 22, 2000. In 2005 KLM Royal Dutch Airlines joined the alliance, which grew to its current 19 members, including SAS that switched in 2025 from STAR to SkyTeam. Two airlines joined but also left SkyTeam: China Southern Airlines and Czech Airlines.

Some members only cooperate on the level of code sharing while others further deepened their cooperation to the level of Joint Ventures with Anti-trust Immunity to coordinate networks and schedules, prices, and share revenues. Membership involves implementing a series of membership requirements that enable day-to-day interoperability between members to ensure SkyTeam members fulfil their agreed mission: "SkyTeam is dedicated to powering the most seamless customer journey of any global alliance. Our members work together to connect millions of passengers across an extensive global network. SkyTeam offers the most comprehensive priority services of any alliance, easy and efficient transfers, and the opportunity to earn and redeem miles across all member airlines."

The common goals of all these efforts, whether with 1 partner or in an alliance-context with many, are reaching seamlessness for the customer, followed by flexibility and scalability for future changes, at the lowest possible cost and shortest time.

Seamlessness means that customers search for, select, order, pay, claim loyalty awards and check-in with the airline of their choice, and receive tickets, seats, flight statuses, and awards for their entire journey even it this involves other airlines.

12.2.2 Task

Until around 2008 the projects dealing with creating partnerships followed IATA and GDS standards as much as possible but were mostly undertaken as one-offs, every time again. And since each airline is organised differently with different silo's leading to the same effort, this resulted in tightly coupled solutions with low flexibility and scalability. Some elements of the desired seamlessness were achieved, for example ticket issuance, while mobile check-in for the full journey remained impossible and loyalty credits could not always be awarded. So, while outcomes for customers were the same (a ticket plus ancillary services, a seat number with a boarding pass, a checked bag and awarded loyalty credits) different IT implementations resulted in seams and increasing complexity and cost to close them.

After being actively involved in the post-merger projects to connect Air France and KLM, enterprise architects also became involved in new partnership and alliance projects, to help steer towards more flexible and scalable solutions.

In 2008, KLM's CIO Office team of enterprise architects and the alliance liaison to the business side of Air France and KLM discovered Design and Engineering Methodology of Organisations, became DEMO professionals, and never looked back. The team was encouraged to experiment with DEMO in actual projects to find faster and more scalable value than before.

12.2.3 Approach

The first application of DEMO was Air France and KLM Cargo Post Merger Decision Making. The next was the so-called Lounge Access service for verifying eligibility of customers for the comforts of various SkyTeam member lounges across the world.

Learning from such explicit as well as more covert use of DEMO resulted in the creation of a 'praatplaat' (visual for discussion) of the CM for network airlines. Such a 'praatplaat' enabled focusing on different perspectives of airlines: the need to find and work with actors instead of hierarchical departments, separation of concerns, and working with source transaction) data instead of creating yet another copy of data.

The CM reconciles all different actors and transactions independent of hierarchical organisations in a consistent, coherent, and complete way. As a result, the airline CM is also an airline alliance CM. The praatplaat was shared and discussed with the Enterprise Architects of all 19 SkyTeam members in the bi-annual Architects meeting of 2015 in Nairobi, Kenya.

12.2.4 Result

The only full IT implementation following Enterprise Engineering and service-oriented thinking is the lounge access service of SkyTeam. Traditionally the eligibility checks required lounge agents to apply the rules of the customer's airline or loyalty program and, on behalf of them, to allow the customer in, or not. Changes to the rules involved distributing new rules booklets to all lounges in the world. And settlement of the cost required lounges sending an excel sheet with all the lounge visits to the relevant airlines and loyalty programs and await the settlement, often involving controllers (Fig. 12.1 and Table 12.1).

Using DEMO changed the entire process and service to having the customer's boarding pass or loyalty card scanned, after which a real-time request is made to the

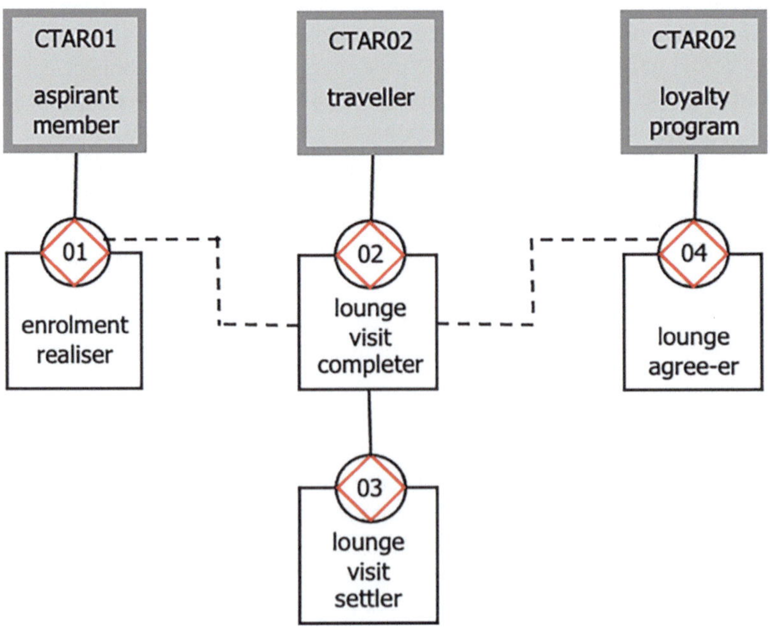

Fig. 12.1 CSD of the lounge access service

Table 12.1 TPT of the lounge access service

Transaction kind	Product kind	Executor role
TK01 enrolment realising	PK01 [enrolment] **is** realised	AR01 enrolment realiser
TK02 lounge visit completing	PK02 [lounge visit] **is** completed	AR02 lounge visit completer
TK03 lounge visit settling	PK03 [lounge visit] **is** settled	AR03 lounge visit settler
TK04 lounge agreeing	PK04 [lounge] **is** agreed to program	AR04 lounge agree-er

loyalty program and airline to let the customer in, or not. And if yes, to send an invoice number to the lounge for settlement of the cost. The result was a dramatic reduction of complexity of changes to the eligibility rules, and the process of settlement became beyond dispute. The service pattern can be applied infinitely for any type of eligibility check, including boarding of a flight.

Elsewhere, the CM served as reference to *nudge* traditional approaches, and each airline's own implementation, in the direction of the reference. However, often new off-reference implementations were preferred to save project time and cost: short-term cost over long-term value. *Nudging* was applied for the review of SkyTeam Membership requirements, Air France-KLM application rationalisation and 2 major business transformation programmes.

More recently, IATA's Modern Airline Retailing program was subjected to DEMO and the airline CM. In essence (pun intended), this program aims to modernise and replace (a.k.a. renovate and innovate) the business actors and standards, and IT standards from the very beginning of digitisation of the airlines in the 1960s: marketing and operating carrier, tickets, passenger name records, electronic miscellaneous documents, boarding passes, and all interoperability needed to produce them within and across airlines. In its turn will this enable airlines to broaden the scope of their products and services beyond the capabilities of tickets, PNRs and EMD's and hence create more value. Unsurprisingly IATA also had to resort to *actors* instead of traditional hierarchical departments names that are different in name and scope across airlines, and to outcomes for these actors instead of detailed legacy processes and system names.

We found that our airline CM can also be the model for IATA's Modern Airline Retailing vision and in support of airlines subscribing to the IATA programme; but also, for (blockchain-enabled) travel consortia like Chain4Travel that have a much broader scope than IATA. Key actors for IATA and our CM are Customer, Retailer and Supplier. The key ambiguity created and needing resolution by IATA, is the cross and duplicate use of *organisations* and *actors*. The resulting key discussion is if the split between the Retailer role and the Supplier role should not only apply between airlines but also within airlines. Test questions for any proposal not based on the CM: does it also work when the Retailer is not an actor in an airline, and does it work when the Supplier is not an airline? Also, who recovers disrupted orders, with all legal consequences: the retailer or the supplier?

12.2.5 Reflection

Johan Cruijff's quote "You'll only see it when you understand it" applies to DEMO to use it to maximum effect with uninitiated colleagues. Helping them take the perspective of an engineer is key but may not always be achieved: hierarchical perspectives are extremely difficult to eradicate. Sometimes, explaining the difference between the black-box and white-box model helped. What may also help is Hans Mulder's storytelling on page 95 in [1].

Irrespective of the use of DEMO, having a *champion* in a company's leadership team is all-important for success: one who can think out of the usual boxes ands silo's, can helicopter up and down between actors and who deeply understands a need for true transformation.

In the case of each airline's internal implementation of IATA's Modern Airline Retailing, the biggest risk is that without a strong reference architecture team, reporting to overall (business) steering group, the new concepts and standards will be implemented in old organisations: the value destruction will be unsurpassed, and the potential reduction of complexity and cost will not be captured. DEMO can help to prevent this.

In terms of *governance* (metaphorically: setting the direction of the ship) the decision of an airline to need and look for partnerships to ensure long-term success paves the way for designing, prioritising, funding, and implementing the required interoperability with these partners. These are decisions of the Board of Directors of an airline.

For many outcomes produced by, for example, *interline ticketing* and *through check-in* airlines take part in the development, and rely on the standards developed by organisations like IATA; these are standards for business agreements and the underlying IT implementations. It is worth noting that many of these agreements and standards were developed more than 35 years ago when technological capabilities were infinitely more limited than today. Their worldwide implementation is, paradoxically, the main reason for today's extreme low speed-of-change to capitalise on new organisational and technological insights and opportunities.

For other outcomes, such as lounge access and priority baggage check-in and priority boarding, airlines first created their own 'standards' and later adjusted to any new standards associated with signing up for alliance membership. Such signing up for an alliance (and to take part in providing a seamless customer experience across all members) is also a decision of the Board of Directors of an airline once all incumbent alliance members agreed to the new one.

Design decisions also fit here, under *governance,* but some clear differences can be observed. In a traditional hierarchy and silo organisation design decisions are mostly prepared and proposed by business- and IT-architects from within the silo that claims ownership of and funds the change. Design proposals are often subject to 'faster, please, and cheaper', and are subsequently not necessarily well-fitted in the overall architecture. Enterprise architects influence and steer the creation of proposals but have no formal power. Metaphorically, this type of *navigation* and steering of an enterprise can be compared with using the very first (sixteenth century) Mercator map projections and hand-held sextants on an ultramodern Panamax container vessel.

At a much higher maturity level, an enterprise can be steered by the executive leadership, and design decisions based on a CM reflecting the essence of an enterprise. The lounge access service of SkyTeam was conceived, designed and implemented on the basis of the CM of cooperating airlines, and recommended to executive leaders based on its ease to implement changes in eligibility and alliance members over the years. Associated with this design is that there is no differentiation between internal and external actors. Metaphorically, this type of navigation and steering can be compared with using Digital Charts and Global Positioning Systems.

In terms of *management* (metaphorically: keeping the ship on a set route) airlines obviously regularly check their dashboards if their own customer experience, revenues, operational excellence, and cost are still on track. If adjustments need funding such *business case* decisions may need Board approval but may also be approved on lower levels in the organisation. From experience with more than 20 airlines, it follows that more often than not such decisions are made in the various organisational silos, without due attention to enterprise-wide checks and adjustments. These airline internal business cases obviously have the highest funding and resourcing priority.

While governance decisions to join and participate in an alliance are always taken on Board of Director level, the actual funding and resourcing for compliance with the membership requirements is mostly delegated to lower levels in the organisation of airlines. Proper communication of executive decisions is essential, as one of the most common frustrations within an alliance member (e.g. KLM) and in the alliance organisation (SkyTeam Office) was to hear that certain alliance wide projects were approved by the joint CEO's, but no communication of such reached the lower levels of the airline organisations, and no priority was given in the *portfolio management* processes to execute these decisions.

Finally, a note on *timing*. Under pressure of time-to-market and costs, many a change is chosen without proper engineering and architectural scrutiny and hence less future-proof. Incidents and accidents associated with Boeing's upgrade of its 737 to 737Max come to mind. The short-term benefits are then offset by increasing risk, cost of complexity, and longer time-to-market for every new change.

Enterprises with a high maturity level of governance invest time and energy in creating their CM and having executive leadership and management mutually understand its relevance and usability. Together with an equally mature portfolio management process for business process and technology changes will then enable faster time-to-market, future-fitness, and lower cost of complexity. Airlines undertaking the transformation from PNRs, Tickets and EMDs to Offers and Orders would significantly benefit from such maturity.

12.3 Responsible Enterprise Governance Through Enterprise Ontology

Shakhawan Mirza

12.3.1 Situation

The Dutch childcare allowance scandal (2013–2019) is a paradigmatic case showing how institutional design choices determine whether a welfare system protects or erodes citizens' rights. Families were frequently forced to repay benefits on the basis of trivial administrative discrepancies and discriminatory profiling, a pattern documented by the National Ombudsman [2], Amnesty International [3], and the Dutch Data Protection Authority [4]: a €190 slip could trigger debts of many thousands.

By September 2025, 43,221 parents had been formally recognised as victims, confirming the scale of the failure [5]. The Children's Ombudsman [6] reports that roughly 70,000 children were affected, and more than 2000 people lost custody through cascading effects. At the core lies a recovery problem of exceptional magnitude: the Donner Commission [7] calculated that 1.2 million people faced €4.3 billion in recoveries over fifteen years, with over 90,000 individuals each repaying more than €10,000, largely through automated processes that removed professional discretion and proportional assessment.

12.3.2 Task

It was our task to analyse the causes of the childcare allowance scandal and to suggest changes in the organisation and/or in its governance and management. Concerning the way in which the allowance was organised, after-the-fact checks created uncertainty and room for abuse. The Data Protection Authority found that between March 2016 and October 2018 nationality was used unlawfully in the process [8].

Judicially, case law entrenched an all-or-nothing recovery line until late 2019, when the Administrative Jurisdiction Division of the Council of State reversed course.

Within this setting, ministers faced a design choice. In April 2018, the State Secretary for Social Affairs and Employment rejected DUO's direct-financing option and pursued improvements within the existing system. The subsequent shift to proportional establishment acknowledged safeguards [8].

12.3.3 Approach

We produced the CM of Childcare Allowance processes, expressed in the Transactor Product Table (TPT) in Table 12.2 and the Coordination Structure Diagram (CSD) in Fig. 12.2. The TPT lists the eight transaction kinds with their product kinds and the responsible executor roles. The CSD shows the coordination structure, thus the initiator and executor roles, and the inspected information sources. The parents fill the composite transactor role CTAR01 as well as AR06 (the CA payer). The facts they have to provide when applying for a childcare allowance are contained in the (external) multiple transaction bank MTB09.

Table 12.2 TPT of childcare allowance

Transaction kind	Product kind	Executer role
TK01 CA granting	PK01 [CA] **is** granted	AR01 CA granter
TK02 CA eligibility assessing	PK02 **the** eligibility **of** [CA] **is** assessed	AR02 CA eligibility assessor
TK03 CA amount determining	PK03 **the** monthly amount **of** [CA] **is** determined	AR03 CA amount determiner
TK04 CA duration determining	PK04 **the** duration **of** [CA] **is** determined	AR04 CA duration determiner
TK05 monthly controlling	PK05 monthly controlling **for** [month] **is** done	AR05 monthly controller
TK06 CA paying	PK06 **the** paying **of** [CA] **in** [month] **is** done	AR06 CA payer
TK07 annual controlling	PK07 annual controlling **for** [year] **is** done	AR07 annual controller
TK08 CA final settling	PK08 **the** final settling for [CA] **in** [year] is done	AR08 CA final settler

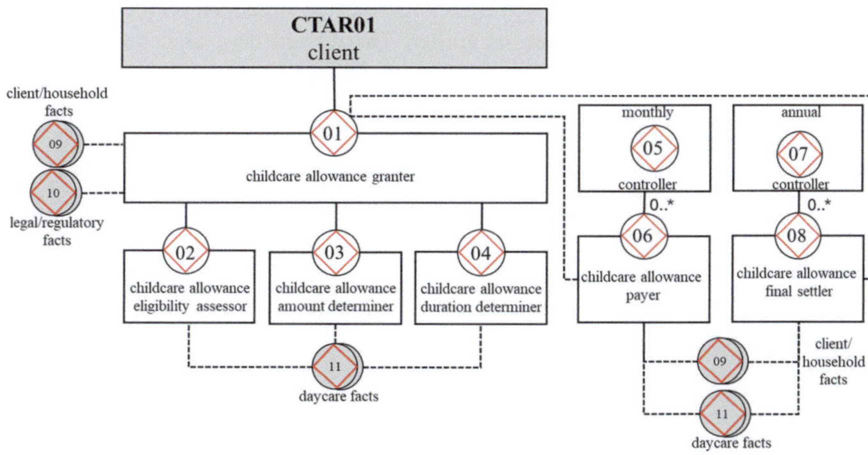

Fig. 12.2 CSD of childcare allowance

Contrary to what the CTP (cf. Fig. 4.11) allows, the discussion states (dc) and (rj) were unreachable in practice. Consequently, revocations such as [rv-dc] and [rv-rj] could not be performed. This is consistent with the parliamentary record of a mass, "all-or-nothing" execution style that bound frontline staff to scripts and left little scope for judgement, with caseworkers describing themselves as robots reading scripts. The Ombudsman documented how minor errors escalated into debts of tens of thousands, while final settlements became punitive instruments rather than corrective reconciliations.

The CSD in Fig. 12.2 exposes the role-task misalignment that drove this pattern. Parents became de facto executors for evidence gathering and document validation, while professionals lacked a mandate to adjust promises or revoke declarations when new facts emerged. At the same time, opaque selection tools amplified the one-way flow: the Data Protection Authority found that nationality was unlawfully processed as a risk factor in the classification model, and the Fraud Signalling Facility accumulated hundreds of thousands of flags, later sanctioned with €3.7 million in fines. Design choices disabled routine revocation moves across the pattern. Parents could not withdraw requests [rv-rq]; officials could not revoke promises [rv-pm] or declarations [rv-da]. Attempts to retract acceptance triggered suspicion rather than revokes of an acceptance [rv-ac]; also, revoke decline [rv-dc] and revoke reject [rv-rj] were not used to reopen decisions proportionately.

Applied to DUO's direct-financing design, the childcare provider becomes a formal actor rather than a passive payee: providers submit verified attendance and fee declarations, receive monthly advances, and reconcile mismatches with DUO on a fixed cadence [9]. This shifts validation from parents to professionals who hold registers and issue invoices, reducing families' exposure to retrospective corrections [8].

DUO's direct-financing approach trades more cross-organisational coordination and programme effort for greater reliability. The design depended on joint work with sector partners, a formal governance set-up, agile delivery in four-week sprints, and tight integration with childcare providers and their software so that contract and invoice data could be supplied and tested end-to-end before live use. In return, the model aimed to give parents earlier and more reliable certainty about their own contribution, validate information at the source, and settle on regular billing cycles to prevent large retrospective debts [9].

12.3.4 Result

Comparing DUO's direct financing with the Tax Authority's allowances system reveals opposite designs for preserving trust. DUO's model routed public payments directly to childcare providers and reconciled monthly, thereby reducing families' exposure to large retrospective corrections that stem from an advance-payment approach (and was prepared and tested between 2015 and 2018). This option was explicitly before ministers and senior officials, who recognised its policy rationale, preventing large back-claims created by annual reconciliation, while also noting the accompanying ICT and coordination risks. The result is a design whose short monthly cycles keep proportionate correction structurally available during processing rather than after harm has accumulated [8, 10].

By contrast, the Tax Authority's configuration embedded a mechanistic operating philosophy: because of the high volumes, "it must work like a machine," and "exceptions" were seen as "sand in the gears". That institutional stance translated into group handling and an "all-or-nothing" recovery line that displaced proportional judgement in day-to-day operations [8]. Amnesty International [3] independently documented how opaque, risk-classification practices and long, frustrating procedures created severe and lasting consequences for families, including family breakdowns.

The Dutch Data Protection Authority's investigation substantiated unlawful use of nationality data in both assessment and risk classification, identifying structural breaches in collection, storage and use-practices that undermined procedural fairness and contributed to discriminatory outcomes. These findings align with the parliamentary record that frontline discretion was bound by rigid rules and scripts, making proportionate "in-flight" corrections practically unreachable in ordinary handling [8].

Against this, the Donner review called for a restoration of the "human scale" in execution and a re-balancing of enforcement with service, so that proportionality is designed into processes and not left to ex post repair [7]. DUO's direct-financing prototype embodies that shift at the design level: provider mediation moves validation to professionals with the registers and invoices; monthly reconciliation keeps governed rollback moves available as routine operations; and parents interact mainly to choose a provider and pay their predictable contribution, rather than acting as de facto case managers and evidence verifiers[10].

Taken together, these findings show that the decisive variable is Enterprise Governance. A design that places validation with professionals and reconciles monthly keeps discussion states and governed reversals available during processing, so errors are corrected before they harden into harm. A design that centres mass processing and binary enforcement collapses those states, transfers residual risk to families, and turns settlement into recovery. The governance choice is therefore constitutional in effect: it determines whether the state can correct itself in time and whether citizens experience government as a reliable counterpart. DUO's model makes proportionality routine; the allowance model shows how its absence destroys trust.

12.3.5 Reflection

STARR analysis shows childcare-allowance breakdown was fundamentally a consequence of governance design choices rather than isolated operational errors. Situation revealed fragmentation displacing accountability. Task required financing regime preserving proportionality at scale. Action tested whether discussion and discourse layers including revocations were structurally available. Result showed

Tax Authority's pattern concentrated risk on households and removed built-in correction, while DUO's pattern preserved bilateral communication, distributed validation to professional actors, kept proportional repair available.

The governance lesson is that trust must be specified and engineered. Performative trust rests on credible promises and predictable fulfilment. Epistemic trust depends on intelligible facts and a shared understanding of what they mean. Procedural trust requires real access to proportionate correction during processing. The CTP provides a safeguard by tying authority to responsibility, maintaining bilateral communication across standard, discussion, and discourse layers, and embedding explicit one-step revocation paths.

Responsible and humane systems require three integrated design commitments. First, revocation capacity must be embedded so proportionate correction is possible while cases are in flight. The six governed reversals of the CTP should operate as routine safeguards, allowing a case to roll back exactly one step for timely repair rather than relying on retrospective fixes. Second, professional judgement must be preserved by keeping authorised people in control and accountable. Roles, information, and controls should be aligned so discretion can be exercised with reasons, context can be weighed, and families are not turned into de facto case managers. Third, protected learning loops must be installed through ex ante checks before deployment and continuous monitoring in operation, with transparency, early-warning indicators, and a real stop button that halts harm when signals arise.

The central lesson is clear. Automating governance without embedding accountability makes failure predictable. The Dutch experience shows that when human safeguards are stripped out, harm accumulates and trust collapses. The task for the digital state is to combine efficiency with the human measure, ensuring systems work for real people rather than against them. This is not leniency on fraud; it is the disciplined handling of human complexity with proportionality and care.

12.4 Rethinking Strategy Execution Through Enterprise Engineering

Thabani Mudavanhu and Bruno Emwanu

12.4.1 Situation

In both the academic and practitioner domains, the gap between strategic intent and strategy execution has been widely acknowledged. Despite the proliferation of frameworks, best practices, and management tools, strategy execution continues to suffer high failure rates. This is exacerbated by the limited theoretically grounded evidence on why companies are failing to deliver or execute strategic initiatives [11, 12]. To make matters worse, there is little investment in research (time and effort) to understand the challenges and the underlying reasons why strategy execution has a high failure rate [13, 14]. Where there is some progress in developing theory around strategy execution, it is largely discipline biased. Further to this, the current approaches are largely experienced and case-based implementation frameworks—aided by heuristics that are not theoretically grounded nor firmly backed by empirical evidence [11, 15, 16].

Extant literature has shown that traditional strategy implementation efforts often emphasise tactical dimensions such as KPIs, leadership alignment and change management without addressing the deeper structural causes embedded in the enterprise itself. This case focuses on the application of Enterprise Engineering (EE) and Enterprise Ontology (EO) to overcome this challenge by designing or re-engineering the enterprise from its ontological layer, the level at which commitments and transactions occur.

12.4.2 Task

The core task was to determine how principles of Enterprise Engineering, particularly those grounded in enterprise ontology can be applied to improve the success rate of strategy execution. The aim was twofold: 1) Identify the ontological construction flaws that typically impede execution, and 2) Develop a methodological approach to re-engineer the enterprise for execution readiness, prior to launching strategic initiatives.

12.4.3 Action

A three-phase methodology was deployed: Structured Literature Review, Delphi Study with experts, and Ontological Modelling.

Structured Literature Review: This phase identified conceptual and empirical gaps in current strategy execution literature. It revealed a predominant focus on surface-level implementation (e.g. process flows, KPIs) while neglecting the ontological construction of the enterprise.

Delphi Study with Experts: A two-round Delphi study was conducted with 31 and 25 experts, respectively, drawn from academia and various industries across 11 countries. Questions were organised to explore the relationship between enterprise design and execution, the recognition and experience with elementary construction flaws, and the feasibility and impact of re-engineering the enterprise based on EE principles.

Ontological Modelling: The basic transaction pattern (request–promise–produce-declare–accept) was used to diagnose and model enterprise cooperation structures. This modelling revealed key ECFs such as "Missing Executor", "Split Responsibility Executor", and "Missing Authority Initiator", which directly correlate to strategy breakdowns.

12.4.4 Result

Three aggregate dimensions were synthesised: Ontological Essentials, Basic Requirement, and Consequential Dimensions.

Ontological Essentials: These include the foundational enterprise components (e.g. purpose clarity, actor role clarity, core transactions and related agreements).

Basic Requirements: factors like communication infrastructure, leadership alignment, and information flows that enable execution.

Consequential Dimensions: Emergent cultural and behavioural attributes (e.g. performance culture, psychological ownership) that result from a well-structured enterprise.

Over 90% of the Delphi panel confirmed experiencing key construction flaws in their professional context. Moreover, 88% agreed that incorporating execution-aligned elements into ontological agreements (e.g. contracts, decision protocols) significantly reduces downstream failure during implementation. Almost all participants of this study highlighted the need for a performance culture to support SE, but at the same time lamented its complexity.

12.4.5 Reflection

This study extends existing knowledge about the influence of organisational design on strategy execution by presenting a novel theoretical lens that challenges the conventional view of organisations. The study confirms that many execution failures are not just due to poor strategic ideas or weak leadership but rather at its root, among other reasons—is an enterprise not ontologically prepared to carry out its strategy. Such ontological considerations include the 'people'. As a minimum, the workforce roles and responsibilities should be clearly defined so are the decision rights of their superiors and themselves [16, 17]. The Enterprise Engineering toolbox ensures that job descriptions are clear and not open to different interpretations [18]. A job description that evolves from the construction model of an enterprise will clearly list the essential actor roles for the specific job and the competencies required for the role as opposed to vague job descriptions [16] shift from managing symptoms to diagnosing root causes by treating the enterprise as a purposefully constructed system of social cooperation. Like any purposely constructed system, enterprises are susceptible to design errors. It follows that revealing the wiring diagram or construction model at the ontological layer will, for example, assist in locating communication-related errors that are constrain strategy execution. Further, while recognising that there are various dimensions of effective communication, our study shows information flow and clarity of communication as critical contributors to successful strategy execution.

The ability to view strategy execution from an enterprise engineer's perspective requires understanding the inner workings of the organisation ("white box" perspective) so as to expose elements that influence strategy implementation. For illustration,

Fig. 12.3, taken from [19], compares two different perspectives regarding an analysis of the underlying drivers of the dominant SE themes, one perspective held by a traditional observer and the other by an enterprise engineer.

The argument made here is that if an organisation engages the "right" people (i.e. competent and accountable people that are the right match for the role/s), their responsibilities clearly laid out, with the related support systems in place (for example, real-time information banks), the "right" transactions (the agreements and commitments) related to the strategic intent correctly structured and finalised, and infused with the right leadership, an execution culture naturally evolves, all other things being equal [19].

In conclusion, this case demonstrates that purpose clarity, clarity of actor roles, clarity of transactions and the related transaction boundaries, and real-time information availability can be modelled, validated, and restructured at the ontological level before executing a strategy. Enterprise ontology thus provides a rigorous lens and actionable toolbox for leaders seeking to bridge the perennial strategy-execution divide. Consequently, this study supports its overarching proposition that in any enterprise setting, there exist fundamental elements that drive execution and there is a relationship between *enterprise design* and *strategy execution.*

12.5 Nationale Nederlanden

Yuri Bobbert

12.5.1 Situation

NN Group (Nationale Nederlanden) is a multinational financial services organisation active in insurance, banking, and asset management. Headquartered in the Netherlands, NN Group operates in a highly regulated environment and is supervised by, among others, De Nederlandsche Bank (DNB). In addition to the General Data Protection Regulation (GDPR), the organisation must respond to a growing set of European regulatory regimes such as NIS2 and DORA, while anticipating the governance and compliance implications of the forthcoming EU AI Act.

The scale of NN Group, combined with a heterogeneous application landscape and stringent supervisory expectations, makes it a relevant empirical setting to study how governance can be operationalised at enterprise scale. In particular, the case illustrates how Enterprise Engineering (EE) principles can be used to translate governance intent into operational commitments, while preserving accountability and producing audit-ready evidence. This becomes especially relevant for AI governance, where decision-making is increasingly distributed across teams, models evolve iteratively, and risk exposure can shift rapidly over time.

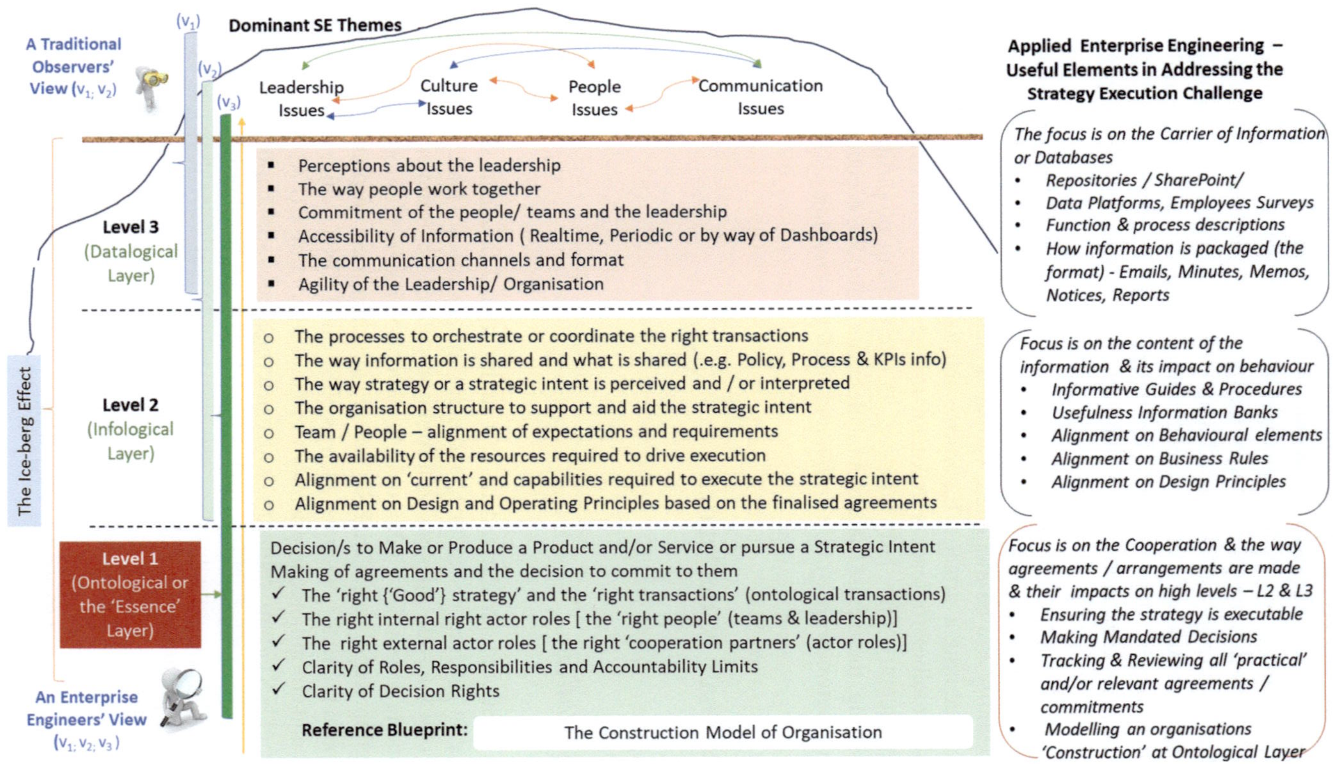

Fig. 12.3 Mapping of the dominant themes against the cooperation levels in an organisation—enterprise engineers perspective

This STARR case analysis examines NN Group's GDPR implementation through SECA (security and compliance automation technology) and its LockChain instantiation. The case is treated as an empirical precursor for EU AI Act implementation scenarios, and is based on empirical findings resulting from the application of the AnoveAI artefact.[1] While GDPR and the EU AI Act differ in scope and legal constructs, both require organisations to demonstrate that governance is not merely documented, but enacted through explicit responsibilities, enforceable controls, and traceable evidence.

Enterprises are increasingly confronted with regulatory inflation: multiple frameworks evolve simultaneously, overlap partially, and demand comparable forms of organisational proof. In parallel, AI adoption accelerates through decentralised experimentation and local optimisation. This shift changes the governance problem materially. Traditional governance structures assume stable processes, clear system boundaries, and centralised oversight. In contrast, AI-enabled practices introduce dynamic models, fast-changing dependencies, and new forms of operational risk, including "shadow AI": AI usage that is not formally registered, assessed, or governed through established compliance channels.

This combination creates a governance–operations gap. Formal accountability may be assigned at the top of the organisation, yet operational decisions occur at the edges of the enterprise where engineering teams build, deploy, and iterate. In many organisations, delegation of responsibilities remains implicit or fragmented. Control ownership is often documented in spreadsheets or dispersed across tools that do not provide traceability. As a consequence, governance becomes difficult to enforce consistently, and assurance becomes difficult to demonstrate credibly. From a supervisory perspective, this weakens regulatory confidence: organisations may claim compliance, but struggle to show who decided what, on which basis, and which evidence supports that decision.

For AI governance, this gap is even more pronounced. AI risk management depends on explicit ownership of use cases, transparency of model purpose and limitations, and the ability to demonstrate that human judgment is applied where required. Without an explicit delegation and evidence model, AI governance risks remaining aspirational rather than operational.

12.5.2 Task

The task in this case was to engineer an enterprise-wide delegation model that strengthens governance by making accountability explicit and enforceable, while allowing execution to scale through automation. The objective was not to automate governance itself, but to ensure that governance decisions translate into operational behaviour and measurable proof.

[1] https://www.anove.ai/en/ai-management.

This required translating legal obligations into an aligned structure across governance, management, and operations. It also required making accountability explicit through concrete artefacts, including the AnoveAI application and its AI Use Case Register, which functions as governance instruments rather than administrative repositories. Finally, it required applying Enterprise Engineering principles—specifically DEMO-based modelling—to represent actor roles, transactions, commitments, and the evidence obligations that follow from those commitments.

Methodologically, the work was conducted within a Design Science Research (DSR) paradigm. DSR was used to design, refine, and validate RegTech artefacts, including Securimeter, SECA/LockChain, and AnoveAI. The methodological foundation for Securimeter is detailed in [20, 21]. The design and engineering of SECA and its LockChain instantiation are described in [22, 23]. Validation approaches using Group Support Systems (GSS), consistent with earlier empirical work on security artefact validation, are described in [21].

12.5.3 Action

The intervention began with enterprise modelling. Core business processes were analysed using DEMO, not merely to document process steps, but to expose the governance logic embedded in commitments and coordination acts. By explicitly modelling transactions, actor roles, and production results, the organisation could clarify who commits to which obligations, under which conditions, and with which evidence expectations. This made delegation chains visible, discussable, and governable, particularly for risk treatment decisions, compensating controls, and assurance responsibilities.

At NN Group, SECA was deployed across central business units to operationalise these delegation structures. In practice, SECA supported the assignment of tasks to accountable roles, the tracking of approvals and responsibilities, and the structured collection of evidence relevant to GDPR obligations. This matters for governance because it creates a reliable mechanism through which governance decisions become executable obligations. Instead of relying on policy statements alone, the organisation can operationalise governance as a system of delegated commitments with traceable outcomes.

For AnoveAI, the same approach is extended to AI governance, where governance requirements must be embedded into the lifecycle of AI use cases rather than handled as a periodic audit exercise. This includes delegative tasks that deliberately trigger Human-in-the-Loop (HITL) interventions where judgement is required, and cross-organisational transaction flows that address third-party risk, subcontractor dependencies, and assurance requirements across supply chains. In AI governance terms, this means that accountability does not stop at registration of a model or use case; it continues through decisions on risk classification, monitoring, and intervention.

To prevent governance from remaining purely strategic, the delegation model was operationalised across three interlocking layers. At the strategic layer, decision rights and ownership were clarified and aligned with risk appetite, including explicit mandates for HITL intervention in high-risk contexts. At the managerial layer, risk registers and model documentation practices were maintained, standards and regulatory mappings were consolidated, and reporting cycles were established to ensure evidence could be aggregated across regimes. At the operational layer, technical guardrails were implemented and evidence was collected continuously through telemetry, including signals from DLP, firewall events, and IAM logs. This operational layer also supported the detection of shadow AI usage and enabled coaching and escalation mechanisms under HITL oversight.

Validation was performed using DSR and GSS methods to ensure that the artefacts were not only technically plausible, but also organisationally usable. This evaluation logic is consistent with earlier empirical studies on security and privacy artefact validation [20, 21]. A conceptual representation of this governance mechanism is provided in Fig. 12.4. The figure illustrates how delegation theory functions as the connecting mechanism between governance intent, managerial control structures, and operational execution, while anchoring assurance in evidence rather than informal reporting. In this sense, the model positions delegation engineering as a governance instrument: it converts abstract obligations into explicit commitments, assigns accountable actors, and makes evidence production an inherent part of execution.

12.5.4 Result

The deployment of SECA/LockChain at NN Group resulted in measurable operational impact. Approximately 60% cost reduction was reported as a consequence of delegating security tasks to teams with clear and enforceable instructions, reducing the coordination burden and enabling more distributed execution. The onboarding capacity of the organisation increased substantially, with over 1200 applications onboarded in less than one year. User adoption also demonstrated that the approach was not confined to a small expert group: approximately 1100 users were supported, with around 100 daily active users managing and approving critical-asset security.

From a governance perspective, the results are significant because they show that governance can be scaled without dissolving accountability. Accountability became auditable rather than implicit, as delegation chains could be traced through roles, tasks, approvals, and evidence artefacts. Controls and evidence became more reusable across multiple regulations, supporting the principle of "test once, comply many." Most importantly, the organisation gained a practical pathway from governance mandates to operational proof, strengthening readiness for DNB supervision and GDPR-related IT risk assessments.

This governance value translates directly to AI governance readiness. AI governance requires that use cases are owned, risks are assessed, and controls are not

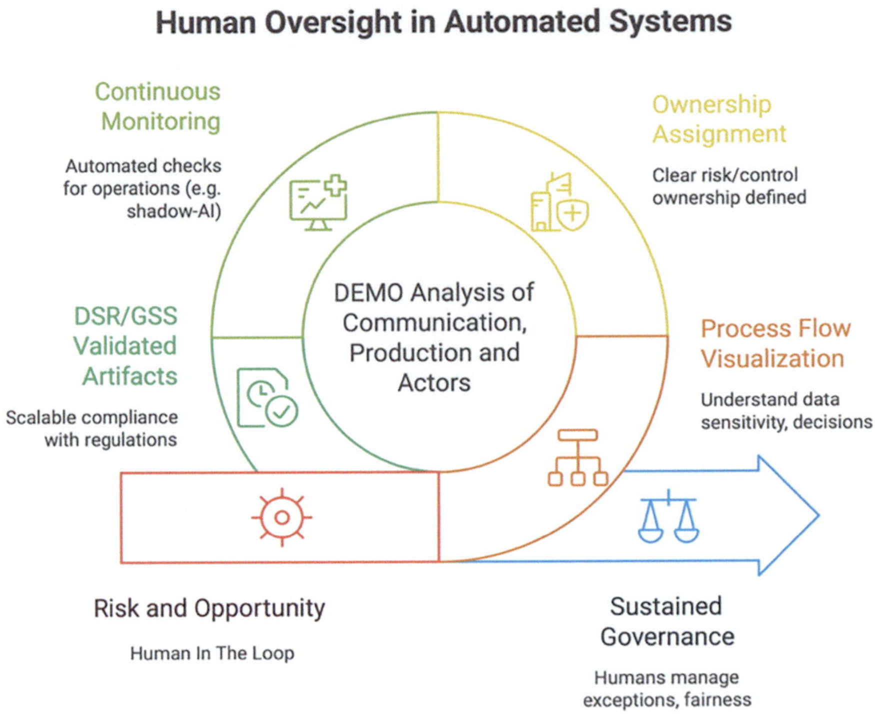

Fig. 12.4 Conceptual model of the delegation theory in artefact development and implementation

only designed but continuously enforced. The case demonstrates that a delegation-and-evidence approach can provide the operational backbone for these requirements, including the ability to detect deviations (such as shadow AI), escalate exceptions, and demonstrate that human judgment is applied where required. SECA remains in active use at NN Group today. Its continued use indicates that the approach supports ongoing governance rather than a one-off compliance project, particularly in domains where escalation and HITL decision-making remain essential.

12.5.5 *Reflection*

This case supports a core proposition from Enterprise Engineering delegation theory: automation can increase consistency and scale, but accountability remains inherently human and must be explicitly assigned. DEMO-based modelling proved valuable because it enabled the organisation to distinguish between transactions that can be automated and those that require human judgment. By analysing communication patterns, production outcomes, and actor roles, DEMO provided a shared language for managers and practitioners to reason about commitments, decision points, and evidence obligations.

For AI governance, this distinction is critical. AI governance cannot be reduced to technical controls alone, because it requires decision-making about acceptable risk, fairness trade-offs, model limitations, and escalation thresholds. Delegation engineering offers a way to embed these governance decisions into operational workflows while preserving traceability. In this sense, the approach does not merely “support compliance,” but strengthens governance as a capability: it ensures that governance intent is translated into enforceable commitments, and that assurance is continuously substantiated through evidence.

Sustained governance, however, is not achieved through tooling alone. It requires explicit ownership and risk appetite definition, and it depends on clear standards that translate regulatory expectations into operational behaviours. Delegation must be pushed as low as feasible in the organisation to ensure execution occurs where the work is performed, but this must be balanced with periodic verification and continuous evidence collection. In AI-enabled contexts, governance also requires transparency over subcontractors and LLM supply chains, and mechanisms to detect and address shadow AI behaviours. This combination enables a “machines check machines” paradigm, in which automated monitoring provides continuous assurance signals while human actors focus on exceptions, fairness, and high-impact decisions.

Enterprise Engineering delegation theory, grounded in DEMO and matured through DSR-validated artefacts, provides a principled and scalable approach to strengthening governance in regulated, AI-enabled enterprises. The NN Group case demonstrates that by explicitly modelling commitments and linking them to verifiable evidence, organisations can operationalise GDPR compliance and establish a credible pathway toward EU AI Act readiness.

The “test once, comply many” principle, implemented through artefacts such as Securimeter, SECA/LockChain, and AnoveAI, offers an empirically grounded governance mechanism to align strategy, management, and operations under expanding regulatory pressure. For AI governance in particular, the approach provides a structural solution to a recurring challenge: ensuring that accountability remains explicit and human, while execution and monitoring can scale through automation and continuous evidence.

12.6 Resolving an Integration Stalemate with Enterprise Ontology

Edwin de Haan and Rikkert van Capelleveen

12.6.1 Situation

Achmea, the largest cooperative financial service provider in the Netherlands, acquired Agis Zorgverzekeringen in 2008. This took place within the Dutch healthcare insurance market, which is characterised by mandatory universal acceptance, an obligation to provide access to healthcare providers, an annual sales cycle with a decisive switching window in December and a fierce price competition. Achmea's management board decided to integrate its Zilveren Kruis organisation with Agis, with the goal of achieving full operational integration by 2011, while preserving the unique brands and insurance propositions of both. A programme was launched to merge the two organisations into "one way of working", focussing on four key milestones: (1) unified financial control, (2) integrated sales and support, (3) unified processes and departments, and (4) a joint ICT system.

To be successful, the programme had to be completed before December 2011; missing this deadline would incur another year of high, duplicate operational costs. However, the programme stalled in its initial study phase. Managers were fundamentally divided on how to operationally serve distinct propositions. They were debating over departmental structures, processes, and ICT systems, unable to agree on a unified organisation.

12.6.2 Task

The task is to apply Enterprise Ontology to define the organisational essence. The management board agreed to use Enterprise Ontology (EO) to establish consensus on the essential construction of the future unified organisation, to be completed in six weeks. The assignment also included providing guidelines for ongoing debates on implementation solutions.

12.6.3 Approach

To perform this task, EO's Design and Engineering Methodology for Organisations (DEMO) method was applied as follows:

Step 1 As-Is analysis and model derivation

Both Agis and Zilveren Kruis were modelled in a separate Cooperation model (CM). EO's PSI theory, which states that all coordination is achieved through a universal transaction pattern, was used to identify transaction kinds and actor roles from existing procedures and operational data. The transaction kinds within a CM are abstracted from implementation and realisation, for example, an actor and its roles are separated from the person or team fulfilling it. This revealed that, while departments, job titles, and ICT differed at implementation level, core transaction kinds like "claim handling" and "healthcare provider procurement" had comparable social commitments for both organisations. An external advisor was retained to steer the task assignment. The advisor trained and coached managers and analysts in the EO approach, enabling them to address the reorganisation challenge.

Step 2 Designing a unified organisation

A unified CM was designed that preserved the uniqueness of all propositions. Key customer satisfaction factors, i.e. price, coverage, service, and trust of each proposition were mapped onto transaction kinds. For example, a "financial compensation within 3 days" promise was linked to the constraints of the claim transaction kind. This mapping showed that propositions affected how certain customer-facing transactions were performed, such as customer support. Most transaction kinds were proposition neutral; only the transaction outcome mattered, for example, not the procurement process itself but the contractual agreement with healthcare providers was influenced by a proposition.

Step 3 Using the unified CM to restructure the merger programme

The unified CM was used to re-scope the projects of the programme. Each project became accountable to deliver a coherent set of transaction kinds, including well-defined deliverables for actor role assignment, processes, and ICT. Instead of "integrate these processes and departments", a project had to "implement these proposition requirements in this set of transaction kinds".

12.6.4 Result

Through open discussion and willingness to solve organisational differences, the management board came to an agreement on how to preserve the propositions of each organisation. The created CMs supported the key finding: the core transactions of both organisations were comparable. The proposition mapping allowed joint verification of assumptions, strengthening management confidence in the validity of the proposed solution.

Project schedules could be accelerated, using the unified CM to ensure that every transition challenge had clear ownership, resulting in the transition programme to succeed before its deadline. Subsequently, in the following years, Agis propositions gradually merged with Zilveren Kruis propositions.

12.6.5 Reflection

This case confirms a core principle of EO: consensus on organisational essence is a prerequisite to free managers from debates on existing implementations. The CM supports this as a neutral, objective model, enabling constructive discussions.

Although the management board used the CM to establish consensus, EO did not prescribe a path to reduce the CM abstraction to the implementation level. Consequently, some sub-projects triggered implementation debates that occasionally required realignment at the management board level. The value of EO was that these debates no longer concerned the foundational construction of the future organisation.

In general one could say that it is astonishing that managers do not learn EE/EO during their education but only learn to deal with operational processes. This results in managers who are not equipped for the task of reorganising the current organisation and are only able to deal with implementation issues. This is not sufficient, however, as is very well pointed out in [24]. Why didn't they get this training? It is a good question.

References

1. De Lameilleure, M., Gielen, R., Mulder, H., & Verhaert, R. (2020). *Blockchain is van levensbelang—Uitdagingen voor overheid en onderwijs in de Lage Landen.* Vanden Broeke.
2. Ombudsman, N. (2017). *Geen powerplay maar fair play: Onevenredig harde aanpak van 232 gezinnen met kinderopvangtoeslag (Rapportnr. 2017/095).*
3. International, A. (2021). *Xenophobic machines: Discrimination through unregulated use of algorithms in the Dutch childcare benefits scandal.*
4. Persoonsgegevens, A. (2021). *Besluit tot boeteoplegging [wegens overtredingen bij de verwerking van nationaliteit in het risico-classificatiemodel en bij de opsporing van georganiseerde fraude].*
5. Toeslagen, D. (2025). *Feiten en cijfers.*
6. Kinderombudsman. (2023). *Waar ik bij ben.*
7. Donner, J. P. H. (2020). *Omzien in verwondering: Eindadvies Adviescommissie Uitvoering Toeslagen. Den Haag: AUT.*
8. POK, P. (2020). *Parlementaire Ondervragingscommissie Kinderopvangtoeslag. Ongekend onrecht. Den Haag: Tweede Kamer der Staten-Generaal.*
9. DUO, D. U. O. (2018). *Programma-eindrapportage: DUO-Programma Directe Financiering Kinderopvang (Versie 1.0).*
10. DUO, D. U. O. (2018). *Programma-eindrapportage DUO-Programma Directe Financiering Kinderopvang (Versie 1.0).*
11. Friesl, M., Inger, S., & Colman, H. (2024). Strategy implementation: taking stock and moving forward. *Long Range Planning, 54*(4).
12. Pavlov, A., & Micheli, P. (2023). Rethinking organisational performance management: A complexity theory perspective. *Journal of Operations and Production Management, 43*(6), 889–915.
13. Tawse, A., & Tabesh, P. (2021). Strategy implementation: A review and introductory framework. *European Management Journal, 39*(1), 22–33.
14. Twun, F. O. (2022). Why strategies fail? A review on strategy implementation. *International Journal of Business Management, 9*(8), 240–245.
15. MacLennan, A. (2011). *Strategy execution—Translating strategy into action in complex organisations.* Routledgde.
16. Janssen, T. (2016). *Enterprise engineering—Sustained improvement of organisations.* Springer.
17. Christie, A., & Tippman, E. (2024). Intended or unintended strategy: the activities of middle managers in strategy implementation. *Long Range Planning, 57*(1).
18. Dietz, J. L. G., & Mulder, H. B. F. (2024). *Enterprise ontology—A human-centric approach to understanding the essence of organisation* (2nd ed., p. 475). The Enterprise Engineering Series. Springer Nature.
19. Mudavanhu, T., & Emwanu, B. (2025). Rethinking strategy execution: An enterprise engineering appraoch. *Management Decision, 63*(13), 244–271.
20. Bobbert, Y. (2018). *On improving the maturity of business information security: On the design and engineering of a business information security artefact.* Radboud University.

21. Bobbert, Y. (2023). *On the empirical validation of a zero trust security framework via group support system research.* Springer Nature Swizerland AG.
22. Bobbert, Y., & Ozkanli, N. (2020). Lockchain technology as one source of truth for cyber, information security and privacy. In *SAI 2020*. AISC.
23. Bobbert, Y. (2020). Exploring research methods for the design and engineering of business information security artefact. In *EEWC*. Springer.
24. Dietz, J. L. G., & Mulder, H. B. F. (2025). *Enterprise design fundamentals—Settling an enterprise business and devising the enterprise organisation* (Vol. 1, p. 357). The Enterprise Engineering Series. Springer Nature.

Abbreviations[1]

ADT **Authorisation Delegation Table** [cross-model representation form of the *Ontological Model* and the *Implementation Model* of an SoI] (Chap. 9).
AM **Action Model** [*aspect model* of the *ontological model* of an *organisational layer*] (Chap. 9).
APT **Actor role Position Table** [cross-model representation form of the *Ontological Model* and the *Implementation Model* of an SoI] (Chap. 9).
ARS **Action Rule Specifications** [representation form of the *Action Model*] (Chap. 9).
BAT **Bank Access Table** [representation form of the *Cooperation Model*] (Chap. 9).
BCT **Bank Contents Table** [cross-model representation form of the *Cooperation Model* and the *Fact Model*] (Chap. 9).
CM **Cooperation Model** [*aspect model* of the *ontological model* of an *organisational layer*] (Chap. 9).
CSD **Coordination Structure Diagram** [representation form of the *Cooperation Model*] (Chap. 9).
CUT **Create Use Table** [cross-model representation form of the *Process Model* and the *Fact Model*] (Chap. 9).
DFS **Derived Fact Specifications** [representation form of *Fact Model*] (Chap. 9).
et event time (Chaps. 8, 11).
FM **Fact Model** [*aspect model* of the *ontological model* of an *organisational layer*] (Chap. 9).
GRAF **General Requirements and Architecture Framework** (Chap. 9).
GSDP **General System Development Process** (Chap. 9).

[1] Hereafter, the most common abbreviations of terms in Enterprise Design, as used in this book, are explained, in alphabetical order. The chapter(s) where the term is de-fined, is indicated between "("and")".

J. L.G. Dietz and H. B. F. Mulder, *Enterprise Governance and Management*, The Enterprise Engineering Series, https://doi.org/10.1007/978-3-032-24318-8

ICT **Information and Communication Technology**. It combines Information Technology (IT) for information processing and information storage, and Communication Technology (CT) for transmitting information.

OFD **Object Fact Diagram** [representation form of *Fact Model*] (Chap. 9).

PM **Process Model** [*aspect model* of the *ontological model* of an *organisational layer*] (Chap. 9).

PSD **Process Structure Diagram** [representation form of the *Process Model*] (Chap. 9).

TPD **Transaction Process Diagram** [representation form of the *Process Model*] (Chap. 9).

TPT **Transactor Product Table** [cross-model representation form of the *Cooperation Model* and the *Fact Model*] (Chap. 9).

WIS **Work Instruction Specifications** [cross-model representation form of the *Ontological Model* and the *Implementation Model* of an SoI] (Chap. 9).

Glossary[2]

Aspect model Partial ontological model of an organisational layer. Unlike a sub model, an aspect model takes a specific view on the organisational layer and is therefore in itself not a complete ontological model (Chap. 9).

Assess part The part of an action rule containing the propositions regarding the *state* of the coordination world and the production world to be evaluated (Chap. 9).

Attribute Instance of an *attribute type* (Chap. 9).

Attribute type A binary type. The extension of an attribute type is a mapping from a concrete (object) class or an abstract (object) class, called the domain of the attribute type, to an abstract (object) class, called its range, so that every object in the domain is mapped to exactly one object in the range, and that every object in the range is mapped to zero, one or more objects in the domain (Chap. 9).

Composite transactor role A collection of transactor roles, connected by initiator links, possibly also by access links and wait links (Chap. 9).

Conceptual schema A coherent collection of types. A conceptual schema works as a mental lens through which one perceives concrete complexes and subsequently creates corresponding conceptual complexes in the mind. If the concrete complex is the world of a system, the conceptual schema determines the state space and the transition space of the world (Chap. 9).

Enterprise The general term to refer to any kind of collaborative activity by human beings. An enterprise commonly is, but need not necessarily be, an economic and/or legal body. Examples of enterprises are: companies, governmental agencies, health care institutions, sports clubs, and building projects (Chap. 1).

Enterprise architecture A consistent and coherent set of requirements for an *enterprise*, both functional and constructional, holding for a class of systems.

Enterprise engineering (EE) The discipline that takes an engineering perspective on *enterprises* (Chap. 1)

[2] Hereafter, the definitions of the key terms in Enterprise Governance and Manage-ment, as used in this book, are summarised, in alphabetical order. At the end of every entry, the chapter(s) where the term is defined, is/are indicated between "("and")".

J. L.G. Dietz and H. B. F. Mulder, *Enterprise Governance and Management*, The Enterprise Engineering Series, https://doi.org/10.1007/978-3-032-24318-8

Enterprise ontology The understanding of an *enterprise*, abstracted from its implementation.

Event part The part of an action rule containing the agendum to be settled when executing the action rule (Chap. 9).

Focus When applying DEMO to an enterprise, one always chooses a *Scope of Interest (SoI)*. Within this SoI one chooses a focus. In the CSD, the focus is indicated by the white colour of the shapes. The shapes of the elements outside the focus but within the SoI are coloured light-grey. The AM is only made for the actor roles within the focus (Chap. 9).

Governance Every change in the ontological model of any of the organisational layers in an enterprise is an act of governance. As a metaphor, we have said that governance is about setting a route for the ship, while management is about keeping the ship on a set route (Chap. 8).

Initiator link A link between an actor role and a transaction kind, indicating that actors in the actor role play the role of initiator in transactions of the transaction kind (Chap. 9).

Intellectual manageability One of the three general goals of EE. Intellectual manageability means that one has insight into and overview over the *organisation* of an *enterprise*. It is achieved through appropriate and well-controlled reduction of complexity, notably the one that is offered by the *essential model* of an enterprise (Chap. 1).

Interaction structure One of the three coordination structures in an *organisation*. It consists of a number of *interaction trees* (Chap. 9).

Interaction tree Building block of the *interaction structure* in an *organisation*. It consists of a collection of *transactor roles* that are connected to each other by *initiator links* (Chap. 9).

Impediment The influencing between actors through *wait links* (Chap. 9).

Interimpediment structure One of the three coordination structures in an *organisation*. It consists of *wait links* between *transactor roles* in different interaction trees (Chap. 9).

Interstriction The mutual influencing of *actors* in an *organisational layer* that consists of taking into account the current state of the *coordination world* and/or the *production world* when being active, i.e. when settling *agenda* (Chap. 9).

Interstriction structure One of the three coordination structures in an *organisation*. It consists of *access links* between *transactor roles* (Chap. 9).

Management (Enterprise) management is concerned with controlling the operations of an enterprise's *organisation*, so with keeping the ship on a set route. As soon as management is not able to achieve this, *governance* has to take over (Chap. 8).

Multiple transaction kind A collection of *transaction kinds*. Multiple transaction kinds may be useful if one does not (need to) know exactly the constituent transaction kinds (e.g. because they are outside the *Scope of Interest*) (Chap. 9).

Organisational concinnity One of the three general goals of *EE*. Organisational concinnity means that the organisation of an enterprise is a harmoniously integrated whole. This can be achieved through coherent and consistent *enterprise* design (Chap. 1).

Point in time A particular value on a *time scale*, expressed in the corresponding *time unit*. Examples: week 36 (week), today (day), tomorrow at 11:25 h (minute) (Chap. 9).

Property Instance of a *property type* (Chap. 9).

Property type A binary *fact type*. The extension of a property type is a mapping from a concrete (object) class, called the domain of the property type, to a concrete class, called the range of the property type, in such a way that every object in the domain is mapped to exactly one object in the range, and that every object in the range is mapped to zero, one, or more objects in the domain (Chap. 9).

Response part The part of an *action rule* containing the *act(s)* to be performed in response to settling the *agendum* in the *event part* (Chap. 9).

Self-activating actor role An *actor role* is called self-activating if its fillers are *initiator* as well as *executor* of the same *transaction* (Chap. 9).

Scope of Interest (SoI) The delineation of the (part of the) *enterprise* or the collection of enterprises, that one has chosen to model with DEMO (Chap. 9).

Social devotion One of the three general goals of *EE*. *Enterprises* should be designed in such a way that its employees get all the opportunities and facilities they need to develop and exert their *competences*. Social devotion implies that the employees are empowered with proper *authorities* (Chap. 1).

Time scale A division of a (discrete and linear) time dimension in consecutive pieces of equal length (duration), called *time units* (Chap. 9).

Time unit The unit for indicating or measuring amounts of *time* on a *time scale*. The length of a time unit depends on the needed precision. Examples: day, hour, minute, second (Chap. 9). [See also point in time].

Value (1) A *typed abstract thing*. Values are commonly ordered in *value scales*. Examples of values are days, meters, and boolean values (Chap. 9).

Value (2) The intensity of the experience that is evoked in a *subject*'s mind by the recognition of an affordance. This notion of value is commonly expressed in economic or monetary terms ([1] Chap. 7).

Value scale An ordered class *values* (according to definition 1). A value scale has a dimension (like time, length, mass, temperature, or money) and a scale unit (like minute, meter, gram, degree Celsius, or euro) (Chap. 9).

Work instruction Guideline for performing (the implementation of) a *production act* (Chap. 9).

Reference

1. Dietz, J. L. G., & Mulder, H. B. F. (2024). *Enterprise ontology—A human-centric approach to understanding the essence of organisation* (2nd ed., p. 475). The Enterprise Engineering Series. Springer Nature.

J. L.G. Dietz and H. B. F. Mulder, *Enterprise Governance and Management*, The Enterprise Engineering Series, https://doi.org/10.1007/978-3-032-24318-8

MIX
Papier aus verantwortungsvollen Quellen
Paper from responsible sources
FSC® C105338

If you have any concerns about our products,
you can contact us on
ProductSafety@springernature.com

In case Publisher is established outside the EU,
the EU authorized representative is:
Springer Nature Customer Service Center GmbH
Europaplatz 3, 69115 Heidelberg, Germany

Printed by Libri Plureos GmbH
in Hamburg, Germany